The publisher and the University of California Press Foundation gratefully acknowledge the generous support of the Constance and William Withey Endowment Fund in History and Music.

Sophisticated Giant

Sophisticated Giant

The Life and Legacy of Dexter Gordon

Maxine Gordon

Foreword by Farah Jasmine Griffin
Afterword by Woody Louis Armstrong Shaw III

UNIVERSITY OF CALIFORNIA PRESS

University of California Press, one of the most
distinguished university presses in the United States,
enriches lives around the world by advancing scholarship
in the humanities, social sciences, and natural sciences. Its
activities are supported by the UC Press Foundation and
by philanthropic contributions from individuals and
institutions. For more information, visit www.ucpress.edu.

University of California Press
Oakland, California

Library of Congress Cataloging-in-Publication Data

Names: Gordon, Maxine, author. | Griffin, Farah
    Jasmine, writer of foreword. | Shaw, Woody Louis
    Armstrong, III, writer of afterword.
Title: Sophisticated giant : the life and legacy of Dexter
    Gordon / Maxine Gordon ; foreword by Farah
    Jasmine Griffin ; afterword by Woody Louis
    Armstrong Shaw III.
Description: Oakland, California : University of
    California Press, [2018] | Includes bibliographical
    references and index. |
Identifiers: LCCN 2018012012 (print) | LCCN 2018014103
    (ebook) | ISBN 9780520971622 | ISBN 9780520280649
    (cloth : alk. paper)
Subjects: LCSH: Gordon, Dexter, 1923–1990. |
    Saxophonists—United States—Biography. | Jazz
    musicians—United States—Biography.
Classification: LCC ML419.G665 (ebook) | LCC ML419.
    G665 G67 2018 (print) | DDC 788.7/165092 [B]—dc23
LC record available at https://lccn.loc.gov/2018012012

Manufactured in the United States of America

25   24   23   22   21   20   19   18
10   9   8   7   6   5   4   3   2   1

This book is dedicated to the spirits of

Dexter Keith Gordon
1923–1990

Woody Shaw
1944–1989

Shirley Scott
1934–2002

John L. Cooper
1936–2001

Shakmah Anna Branche
1931–2010

W. E. B. Du Bois
1868–1963

and to
my Godfather, Wilson Carrero
and my son, Woody Louis Armstrong Shaw III

Contents

Foreword

Sophisticated Giant is a creative telling of the life of Dexter Gordon, best known as one of the world's greatest jazz musicians, but who was also a talented composer, writer, storyteller, and actor. Through this series of lovingly rendered sketches, impressions, and scenes a portrait emerges of an artist in all of his beauty and complexity. This is not a conventional biography or autobiography, nor should it be. Contained herein we have a number of voices: Dexter's; that of his widow and the book's author, Maxine Gordon; the historical and journalistic record, including voices from the archive; and a community of fellow artists and friends. It is a creative, collective telling of a life too large to be contained by a straightforward, linear narrative.

This book will find its place within a larger body of life writing that includes Sidney Bechet's *Treat It Gentle,* Charles Mingus's *Beneath the Underdog,* Miles Davis's *Miles,* and others. *Sophisticated Giant* differs from these texts because Maxine Gordon's voice, like a carefully woven thread, crafts a coherent whole. She is a life partner who possessed a deep knowledge of and love for the music and the people who made it, long before her life-changing encounter with Dexter Gordon. And just as a musician acquires the necessary skills and discipline to shape an inspired performance, so too has she. She set high standards for herself as teller of this tale. It was not enough to have lived through much of the story or to have heard other parts of it narrated firsthand. It was not enough for her to know in depth and detail the technical innovations, record and performance dates, and band personnel, though she knows and shares all of this. For she also saw the necessity of placing the music and her beloved's life in historical, social, and political context. Who were his people? Where did he come from? What histories, migrations, and communities shaped him? All of this background provides the foundation to better tell a story of Dexter Gordon and others of his generation—artists who gave the world one of its greatest art forms but who were not always treated kindly or fairly by the nation into which they were born. These were people who accomplished and achieved what they did in the face of the harshest forms of anti-Black racism. And yet among them they exemplified the best that humanity has to offer.

I first met Maxine in the late 1990s. Since that time I have not only come to count her as one of my dearest friends and colleagues; I have also had the privilege of watching her become a first-rate scholar, archivist, and interviewer. These roles all inform her as the legacy-bearing widow of one of the world's great artists and as a significant scholar in her own right. Each role has contributed to the book she gives us now. I have long admired her tenacity and devotion; the esteem in which I hold her has only grown since reading the book. *Sophisticated Giant: The Life and Legacy of Dexter Gordon* is one aspect of Dexter Gordon's legacy that she tirelessly works to preserve; it is one element of her fierce advocacy for jazz and for jazz musicians. Both Maxine and Dexter bear witness to and uplift the names and contributions of many who did not survive to tell their own stories.

While Dexter's life and art are a testament to the majesty of the music we call jazz, neither he nor Maxine sugarcoat the reality of his life and times. He lived through periods of brutal racism, through the inhumane treatment suffered by those in the throes of drug addiction, and through the economic exploitation gifted artists too often experience at the hands of unscrupulous record label owners and producers. However, this is no victim's tale. The book honestly portrays a life as full, multidimensional, and indeed beautiful as Dexter's most eloquent solos. Throughout the vicissitudes of his life there is one constant: his devotion to and love for the music and its makers. Because all aspects of this story are told with such forthright clarity, we are especially appreciative when his fortunes turn. And turn they do, time and again, but especially in the last decade of his life when he receives the attention, accolades, and celebration he so deserves.

To read *Sophisticated Giant* is to behold and share the love and generosity of spirit that animated Dexter Gordon and that animates this telling of his life. Indeed, the world is a bit more beautiful for Dexter's having been here. It is even more so because we now have his story to listen to and learn from—an accompaniment to his musical body of work. For this we owe Maxine Gordon a debt of gratitude.

Farah Jasmine Griffin

CHAPTER I

The Saga of Society Red

He did everything wrong and it all turned out right.
—Dizzy Gillespie[1]

These days people will say to me, "Oh, gee, you're out here alone now. All these people are gone." Well, I don't really know what they're talking about. They're all still here.
—Sonny Rollins[2]

When Dexter played, everybody listened. He could really power you off the stage if you were up there with him. Long Tall Dexter. He will never be forgotten.
—Jimmy Heath[3]

Dexter Gordon was known as "Society Red." He got this name when he was with the Lionel Hampton band as a seventeen-year-old in 1940—just about the same time Malcolm X (then Malcolm Little) was being called Detroit Red. Dexter wrote a tune with that title and decades later, when he began working on his autobiography, he decided to name it *The Saga of Society Red*. The irony of that nickname has many levels and it became an "inside" jazz nod to an earlier time when young Black men konked their hair and wore zoot suits. Dexter began writing his life story in 1987 after the big fuss was made about his Academy Award nomination for the leading role in the film *Round Midnight*. When the noise had died down and we were living in Cuernavaca, Mexico, where he would play his saxophone in the garden, float his stretched-out body in the pool, and saunter to the *zócalo* (main square), Dexter would jot down his memories and thoughts on yellow legal-size pads.

He had originally hoped that James Baldwin would write the book with him, but sadly, Baldwin was ill and he died in December 1987.

James Baldwin was one among many of our shared passions. Dexter and I owned the same Baldwin books, loved talking about *Go Tell It on the Mountain,* and would laugh about the fact that we traveled with our individual copies. Dexter knew Baldwin well enough to call him Jimmy. I only got to meet him once, at a party in Harlem, and I was stunned and wordless. Being speechless is a very rare condition for me. Dexter joked that if I pulled myself together he would introduce me to the great author. As he said that, Baldwin yelled across the room, "Hey Dex, I read in the paper that we were expatriates. I thought we were just living in Europe." Dexter roared, then strolled over and bent down and hugged Baldwin, who seemed to disappear in his embrace. *I thought we were just living in Europe*—that remark has resonated with me for years.

The years Dexter lived in Europe—1962 to 1976—are treated as "lost" years by many fans, friends, and critics. Those Europe years were when he went missing from the scene in the United States, which many believed to be not only the center of jazz at that time but also the center of the world and anything interesting that was happening in it. But Dexter was aware of everything that was happening in the States and stayed connected to his home country in many ways. Like Baldwin, he found humor in the designations that suggested he was something of an outsider.

I tried to be cool when I was introduced to Baldwin. I tried not to look nonplussed. I was New York cool—nothing, and nobody, could impress me. Baldwin was just another partygoer. But Dexter said I had tears in my eyes and looked like I was going to faint. And his ability to see past my pretensions, and make me laugh about them, was something I especially treasured. Dexter did that—he made you see yourself a little clearer and always did so with wit (sometimes a biting wit; every now and then the humor was a knife turning).

Dexter knew he had an important story, and a very interesting one, to tell. It was his story but also the story of Black "expatriates," a story about the history and culture of remarkably creative jazz musicians, a story about people's love for Baldwin and other brilliant writers, a story about America and the way it embraces and also pushes away brilliant and creative Black people. He knew he had a story to tell about himself and this country. He recruited the very talented Wesley Brown, who wrote the novel *Tragic Magic,* to work with him on it. When Dexter learned that Wesley had spent a year in jail for refusing to serve in the military during the Vietnam War, he felt that he had found the right collaborator. Wesley came to our New York apartment several times and then came to visit in Cuernavaca, talking with and interviewing Dexter. He wrote about Dexter's first trip to New York City with the Hampton band and Dexter liked it, but soon afterward Dexter decided that he wanted to write his own book, in his own voice.

He thought about writing it in the third person about a character known as "Society Red" who moved in and out of trouble while loving his life as a jazz musician and most of the people who played the music. Dexter began by writing notes to himself and vignettes on those yellow legal-size pads. His idea for the book was greatly influenced by one of his favorite novels, *The Ginger Man,* by J. P. Donleavy. He always had a paperback copy of *The Ginger Man* with him on the road and on the nightstand at home and could quote from it at length. He liked it because of the improvisatory feel of its narrative voice with an unexpectedness to it. Some chapters ended in poetry, some sentences had no verbs, and the thoughts would sometimes rush at you—Dexter wanted his book to be the same. Most of all, he loved the comic element of the novel and wanted his book to carry a sense of humor, the aspect Dexter thought most important in our complicated, harried lives.

Dexter would fill a few pages with his writing; I would type up the notes on a small portable Olivetti typewriter; then he would read them over, make changes, and talk about how he wanted to tell the story. One time when we were sitting on the patio in Cuernavaca, I remarked that I thought he needed to make an outline to better organize the book. He thought that was a bad idea and said he did not want a book written along a linear timeline. He wanted to improvise and have the book play out like a long jazz set, letting the story unfold as he reflected on the life of "Society Red." I insisted that an outline was necessary and recall that I won that argument—which was a very rare occurrence. (He later said that he agreed to make the outline just to quiet me down. But, as so often happened with us, Dexter saw the "long game": he knew that over time I'd come to see the wisdom of his approach. This book is, in part, another posthumous win for Dexter in one of our many spirited debates.) The way Dexter wrote the book is the way he wrote his life—on his own terms, in his own voice, in his own inimitable way. As I watched him work, and helped and argued with him about it, I saw why his story was important, even essential: to know the story of Dexter Gordon is to know the story of his community, the story of how some of the most creative people in the twentieth century projected their unique voices.

FIGURE 1. Dexter at the Royal Roost in New York City in 1948.
This photo has become the iconic jazz image and is considered the
epitome of "cool." © Herman Leonard Photography LLC.
www.hermanleonard.com

As he worked through the outline, he got to 1948, when he was
twenty-five years old and working at the Royal Roost in New York,
where Herman Leonard took the photograph of him as he was rehears-
ing with Kenny Clarke and Fats Navarro. Years later, Herman thought
he would try to remove from the famous photo the cigarette smoke that
swirled above Dexter's head. He was concerned that the smoke might
encourage young people to equate being "cool" with smoking. But after
retouching the image on his computer, Herman killed the idea, saying,
"The photo is nothing without the smoke." The image still stands as the
epitome of what was considered hip and cool at the time, and it is to
this day widely accepted as *the* iconic jazz photo.

This Dexter Gordon—the icon—is the Dexter who is now known and beloved and celebrated, on albums and on film and in jazz lore, even in a street named for him in Copenhagen. But this image of the cool jazzman fails to come to terms with a three-dimensional figure full of humor and wisdom, a man who struggled to reconcile being both a creative outsider who broke the rules and a comforting insider who was a son, father, husband, and world citizen. This book is an attempt to fill in the gaps, the gaps created by our misperceptions, but also the gaps left by Dexter himself.

After finishing up the details of 1948 in his outline, Dexter skipped directly to 1960. I said, "You left out a decade. You can't leave out an entire decade."

"It's my life and I can leave it out if I want to," he replied. "I don't want to write about it and I definitely don't want to think about those years."

I argued—to no avail. Dexter had that look in his eyes that let me know that no matter how hard I pushed or how many logical arguments I might make, he had made up his mind. That was that. There were many times when there was no point in discussing something that he had already decided about, and the 1950s was something not open for discussion. Then he said, "If you want it in the book, you will have to write it yourself." This book is my unexpected acceptance of that challenge.

In 1988, for his sixty-fifth birthday, we threw a big party in Cuernavaca. It was one of the great parties, featuring two bands, copious quantities of food and drink, local women making blue tortillas on the patio, and an interlude during which Dexter played "Bésame Mucho" on the soprano saxophone for Gil Evans, who had come to Cuernavaca for health treatments. As the party wound down, Dexter thanked the guests for coming and said, "If you had told me that I would be at my own sixty-fifth birthday party, I would not have believed it. This is a jazz miracle. So many great friends and musicians died young. I salute them and pledge that they will not be forgotten."

Two years later, when Dexter began to have serious health problems, we had some conversations about how he wanted things to be handled should he die before me. His mother had lived into her nineties and I kept thinking he would live into old age as well. He said that living past thirty-five was old age for a jazz musician. Dexter wrote out a set of instructions to be followed upon his death, directing that his ashes be cast into the Harlem River and that there be no funeral nor church service. He insisted that if musicians played, it should not be in a commercial venue. We did our best to follow his wishes. He also insisted that I promise to finish college. He said that he thought I had regretted leaving college at nineteen, but the fact was that *he* was the one who regretted not going to college. Dexter was a passionate reader and admired people who valued academic skills and intellectual pursuits. I agreed to finish college. Then he asked me to make another promise. "If I don't finish the book," he said, "promise me you will finish it. I have talked to you more than anyone else about my life and you are here in this time when I am reflecting on the past. I never had time for that before. I was too busy running up and down the road." I promised to finish the book if he didn't, but I did not want to think about what that promise meant. But in April 1990 Dexter died, and I was forced to consider all the things I had been pushing out of my mind the previous few months.

Thanks to the urging of my good friend Shirley Scott, the legendary jazz organist who had gone back to school and was teaching at Cheyney University, I enrolled in college. When I began writing "the book," I realized that there was no way to write about Dexter without writing about so much more—the early history of African Americans in Los Angeles, the criminalization of drug users in the 1950s, the political economy of jazz, and more. The story of Dexter's life is nothing less than a cultural history of creative Black Americans in the interwar and postwar years. Dexter being Dexter, though, it would have to take the playful, circuitous, improvisatory route that he so adored in life and left as a legacy for us in death.

Now you have in your hands *Sophisticated Giant*, the story that began as one more creative and musical spark in Dexter Gordon's mind as *The Saga of Society Red*. It is my voice, yes, and also my story—my attempt to close and fill in gaps, even in some cases against Dexter's will—as well as, for many of his years, our story. But it's also an ensemble affair. This book is my nod in agreement with Sonny Rollins that all those jazz greats of days past, "They're all still here." Throughout *Sophisticated Giant* you will find original vignettes, notes, and thoughts, exactly as Dexter laid them down on those yellow legal-size pads as he relaxed and reflected in Cuernavaca, "City of Eternal Spring." When you arrive at those passages, always rendered in italics, think of Dexter (or "Society Red") stepping out to take a solo—sometimes eight or sixteen bars; sometimes a full chorus, or three. Those passages appear exactly as Dexter wrote them on his yellow pads. Other italic passages, including original letters and quotes from Dexter with noted attribution to previously published sources, indicate similar "solo" turns.

The 1950s was the decade that Dexter wanted to leave out of his book. He had his reasons—relationships he did not want to talk or think about, in which he preferred not to face his weaknesses or, perhaps more likely, his neglect. He said to me that he chose to go on the road to play the music he loved, and his family was lost in the course of his travels. "I messed up my family life," he said, not wanting to elaborate because to break the silence was to face heartbreaking facts. Of course, it wasn't only the 1950s that was problematic for Dexter. Decade after decade, I recognized, he wanted to leave out many pertinent details. Anything he found to be unhappy or negative was out of bounds. It was the personal that was the problem. But, of course, there were happy moments in the 1950s. He married his first wife, Josephin A. Notti, known as Jodi, and they had two daughters, Robin and Deidre, during that decade. They all lived with Dexter's mother in the family home on Los Angeles' Eastside. (Dexter and Josephin divorced in the mid-1960s.) His daughters surely have their own stories about their childhoods and we hope they will one day write them. This, we know, must have been a very difficult time for the family, people who heard too little of the voice that this book celebrates.

When digging to uncover a hidden past, one comes upon a life in the form of fragments. This book is a jazz composition that gratefully gives the bandstand over to different voices to play their tunes, and lovingly pushes against Dexter's inclination to turn away from the uncomfortable. But it does not lose sight of what is most crucial in this story—an individual voice and its determination to assert itself in a world too often arrayed against it. Arriving on the scene just as the new phenomenon of recorded sound was mixing with the cultural explosions that were jazz and then bebop, and the growing vibrancy and confidence of an emerging and demanding group of young Black radicals, Dexter and so many of his contemporaries made themselves heard like none that had been heard before, bringing joy, hope, and fulfillment through their voices—musical, political, racial, cultural. This is a book about voice—playful, poignant, funny, firm, querulous, confident.

My voice didn't enter the story until 1975, when I met Dexter in France, the year before he returned to the States. Mine is quite a loud voice (as I have often been told) that was formed by jazz from the late 1950s when we teenage jazz fans had a little listening club (mainly boys) that would get together at Joel O'Brien's house and listen to the latest LPs. Joel's father was a well-known morning radio host who received DJ copies of all the latest albums. We went to matinees in New York City's Village Vanguard and sat in the listening section at Birdland. I always wondered how I might find a way to spend as much time as I could around this great music and these fascinating people. I often say that hearing Art Blakey and the Jazz Messengers at the Village Vanguard with Lee Morgan, Wayne Shorter, Bobby Timmons, and Jymie Merritt was my moment when I entered the jazz life, or at least wished I could claim to be part of that world. This became a life that chose me as much as I chose it. I was a road manager for Gil Evans, worked with Shirley Scott and Harold Vick, and learned from them what it meant to keep things together while traveling, to handle the payroll and find places to eat after the gigs and go to meetings at record companies acting as if I knew what I was doing before I actually knew what I was doing.

By the time I met Dexter in France I acted as if there was nothing anyone could tell me about jazz. I had been on the road with Clifford Jordan, George Coleman, Cedar Walton, Billy Higgins, and Sam Jones. Sam, in particular, thought I could learn the job and might one day be helpful to the musicians. He is the person who suggested I keep studying the European train schedules printed in that one huge book and know how to exchange the various European currencies (long before the Euro, the internet, cell phones, and online train schedules). When I worked in Europe as a road manager, I learned that there was an enthusiastic and respectful audience for the music and that bands were paid *before* the concert, not after. Dexter would say that he could play the blues even better when he got paid before playing.

When he left for Europe, alone, in 1962, Dexter said that he had hoped his wife, Jodi, and his daughters would join him there. But after he began to create a new life in Europe, the marriage ended. What I learned as a road manager with jazz groups is that the life out there is not easy and the temptations are great—drugs, alcohol, women, financial neglect. One tends to live in the moment, not think about the future. Of course, not all musicians messed up. Many were good with their money and had stable home lives, but many of the musicians I have known over the years did not have a plan for the future. The joy of playing music and being in the company of each other and of loving fans makes for an exciting and fulfilling life on the bandstand, but as Dexter said later in his life, it is those times off the bandstand that can be very tough.

When Dexter moved to Copenhagen in the early 1960s, his letters to Alfred Lion and Frank Wolff, the cofounders of Blue Note Records, carried as a return address "c/o Nielsen." For my research on his years in Europe I turned to Dexter's very good friend, the journalist Leonard

"Skip" Malone. When I asked Skip about this person named Lotte Nielsen, he looked at me and said, "Walk away from that. Leave it alone." He had that same look that Dexter would have when I would ask about the 1950s or about his being in prison. Dexter never mentioned Lotte to me, nor did he mention being arrested in Paris in 1966 until he showed me a letter that he was required to carry in order to be allowed to enter France. When I asked him about a photograph of this short, happy girl named Lotte, taken behind the Montmartre Club in Copenhagen, he just looked wistful and did not reply. The story of Lotte has a tragic ending and, against Dexter's wishes, it is told in this book because I decided that it is an important part of his story.

While living in Copenhagen and traveling on the road in Europe in the mid-1960s, Dexter had two sons whom he did not raise—one of whom he never met. I've come to know both these men, who resemble Dexter physically and have become much like him in certain ways. They walk like him, and sometimes I notice that they think like him in the way that they tend to be optimistic when times are hard. Morten lives in Denmark and Mikael lives in Sweden. Neither ever lived with Dexter. These sons were born from relationships with women Dexter met on the road or when he was working in Copenhagen. Both are proud of their father, know and listen to his music, and understand many things about his life. I only learned about Mikael late in Dexter's life. He has grown into a remarkable man with a beautiful wife and family, has learned much about Dexter and his music, and is profoundly influenced by him. I met Morten when he came to visit me after Dexter's death. I know nothing about Dexter's relationships with their mothers.

When Dexter finally "got himself together" (as he put it) and bought a home in the Valby district of Copenhagen, he met and married Fenja Holberg. According to Dexter, Fenja was descended from Danish royal lineage. Their son, Benjamin Dexter Gordon, called Benjie, was born in 1975 and named after Ben Webster, the great tenor saxophonist. Dexter said that he wanted to try to live a "normal" life and put an end to his years of unrest and struggle. Life was going very well at this point for Dexter, and Benjie was his pride and joy. When Dexter returned to the States in 1976, Fenja and Benjie came with him. But being back in the States meant yet another new life, and Dexter, after signing with Columbia Records and having me as his manager, had his own band and was on the road continuously, renewing old friendships and hanging out until the early morning hours. When he was in New York City, he spent many hours with his old friend Charles Mingus and musicians he hadn't seen in years. He was able to get an apartment in the same building as Mingus and his wife, Sue. There were many welcome-back celebrations, often spilling into long stretches in the after-hours clubs of Harlem. Dexter carried a business card with our office number on it so that I could always be reached if there was ever a problem. One thing Dexter and I agreed upon was that if he was not working I didn't need to ask him where he was going or when he would be back. I abided by that rule.

Unfortunately, his marriage with Fenja did not survive his return to the States, and she returned to Copenhagen with Benjie. Dexter planned for Benjie to visit and grow up in New York for part of each year but, sadly, that never happened. The marriage ended with a very acrimonious divorce, and after that Dexter did not permit any mention of Fenja again. Both Jodi and Fenja are now deceased. Dexter has five grandchildren. He knew and loved Raina, Robin's daughter. The other grandchildren were born after Dexter's death—Benjie's son Dexter, Mikael's son Dexter Gordon-Marberger, and Robin's sons Jared and Matthew. Dexter had heard of other children who claimed that he was their father, but these are the facts as we know them and as he wrote them out.

The story of how I met Dexter and how we planned his return together, opened an office, and began a life together in 1983 is told in the chapter called "Homecoming." We were first of all friends, then business partners. We spoke more than once every day. Sometimes I had to catch a flight to a city where there was some problem that had to be solved. "Red, the band needs you here," he would say. Every year on New Year's Eve we agreed verbally to continue working together. We had no paper between us. He would say, "Let's give it another year. Okay, Little Red?" (Yes, it is a curious coincidence that "Society Red" would one day pair up with "Little Red." Woody Shaw had written a beautiful composition for me called "Little Red's Fantasy" because of the color of my hair, and that became my new nickname.) The producer Michael Cuscuna and I had an office on West Fifty-Third Street, and during those years I worked double shifts—probably sleeping four hours a night at most.

Earlier, when I was road manager for the Louis Hayes–Junior Cook Quintet, traveling to Europe for six weeks at a time, I met the phenomenal trumpeter Woody Shaw and we began a relationship. In 1978, by one of the greatest miracles in my life, our son, Woody Louis Armstrong Shaw III, was born. This baby grew up in the office, on the road, in the kitchen of the Village Vanguard, and on weekends in Newark with his grandparents. Woody Shaw and I lived together for a short time, but things didn't work out between us and we ended our relationship in 1983.

Things had changed for Dexter around his birthday that year when we had a big party at the Village Vanguard. We agreed to end the business relationship, live together, and as he again put it, try to have a "normal life." Clearly, that was something Dexter craved, but after all, what really is a "normal" life? We closed the office and Dexter became Woody's stepfather. This normal life, for my part, included cooking three meals a day, walking Woody to and from school and taking him to after-school activities, and finding time to rest and recover from our lives on the road and in the office. Once, when Dexter was adding my name and information to the apartment lease, the building agent said to me, "Oh, you don't work?" Dexter looked at her and said, "This is the hardest job she has ever had. She is staying at home to be a wife and mother." He was right about that. Sometimes Dexter would wake up and ask, "What time is the gig?" and it would take some time until he realized that he was actually at home and didn't have to go anywhere.

We agreed that we both lived jazz lives—a way of seeing the world and knowing that there was always a way out of any problem you might have to confront. Of course, having great friends and the best lawyer, doctor, and accountant helped. Woody has grown up in this environment and I see him viewing life in a very wide angle and finding solutions to monumental problems just as his father and stepfather did. Art Blakey once said to me, "We can always knock down that brick wall they build in front of us. We have power."

Dexter was determined to put some things right about being a father. Woody traveled with us on the road, went to the International School in Cuernavaca when we lived there, and went with us to Paris for the filming of *Round Midnight*. In Paris he hung out on the movie set when he wasn't in day camp in the park in Saint-Mandé. Dexter watched from the third floor of our house as Woody walked to the boulangerie in the morning to buy croissants and baguettes. He was very proud of who this seven-year-old child was becoming. He wanted to do what he hadn't done with his own children—he wanted to be a real father.

The result of my promise to finish his story is this book, which sets out to give a meaningful portrait of one of the world's most influential and beloved jazz icons, my husband and former partner in the so-called jazz business, tenor saxophonist, composer, and Academy Award-nominated actor Dexter Gordon. The Dexter Gordon story is the story of the phoenix rising. He was a towering figure at six feet five inches, the epitome of cool, the musician who translated the language of bebop to the tenor saxophone, the man who disappeared for a decade into drugs and jail terms and managed to emerge with a sound to be heard, the musician who left the States for a gig at Ronnie Scott's Club in London in 1962 and returned fourteen years later to standing ovations in New York City, the musician who made a movie with French director Bertrand Tavernier and got nominated for an Oscar for best leading actor. One could tell the story of his life in shortcut by perusing the titles of some of his most significant albums: *Resurgence, Go, Our Man in Paris, Homecoming*. Dexter Gordon believed in life and in music. He loved being a jazz musician, and although his life was complicated with some very dark, very low moments, he was not a man to burden himself with regrets. In fact, Dexter was not even sorry to run out of time before he could finish his book, probably because he knew I would. No, "Society Red" left this world a very contented man. When asked if he had any regrets, he replied, "Only one. I never got to play in the Count Basie band—in Lester Young's chair."

CHAPTER 2

An Uncommon Family

Said he was fighting on arrival
Fighting for survival
Said he was a Buffalo Soldier

—Bob Marley[1]

When Dexter walked into a room, he did not go unnoticed. It wasn't only his height, good looks, and wardrobe—people were drawn to his charm and flair. This flair began at an early age. It came from seeing Duke Ellington with his parents when he was seven years old and remembering how they looked and behaved and always wanting to be like those men up on the stage. But it also came from his family—his father, Dr. Frank Gordon, and his grandfathers, Edward Baker and Frank L. Gordon. These were fearless men who forged new lives in new places and were "fighting for survival."

When Dexter started work on his autobiography, in a section named "An Uncommon Family" he made a small drawing of a face with a beard and labeled it "Grand-père," French for grandfather. He had seen a few photos of his mother's father, one of five African Americans to be awarded the Medal of Honor for bravery in Cuba during the Spanish-American War. (Years later, in one of the many interesting twists in his life, Dexter would become the fifth African American man to be nominated for an Academy Award as leading actor for his role in the film *Round Midnight*.) Dexter knew that his mother's family name had originally been Boulanger, his great-grandparents were named Edouard and Eugenie, and that Boulanger was translated from French to the English "Baker" when they crossed the border from Canada into the Wyoming Territory in the nineteenth century. He knew that his father's family came from Fargo, North Dakota. He joked that they must have been the only Black family there, but of course that proved not to be the case. He had heard the family lore that his paternal grandfather had been a barber and a dentist.

Dexter knew that his father had studied medicine at Howard University Medical School and interned at Freedmen's Hospital in Washington, D.C., paying for his education by playing clarinet and working as a sleeping-car porter in the summers. But Dexter was fourteen years old when his father died; he left home at seventeen and never really returned to that family except at times for short visits. He created a new family—his jazz family. His elders became Louis Armstrong, Duke Ellington, Count Basie, Lester Young, and Coleman Hawkins. He considered Wayne Shorter, Joe Henderson, and John Coltrane his "children" when he proudly heard them play. When I was walking down a hallway with Dizzy Gillespie as he was about to receive his Kennedy Center Honor in 1990, he stopped, turned to me, and said, "The people who love this music and play this music are more like our family than many of the people we are related to by blood. Our people are everywhere in the world." I never forgot that, and even though the jazz family has rifts and drama like all families, in the end we are joined together by our love of the music and our love of the musicians who have sacrificed so much to play it night after night.

Dexter talked often about the fight for survival, climbing out of the holes he had fallen into, the fight to play music and be recognized as an artist, the fight to refuse to go into any place by the back door. In my search for the story of Dexter's "uncommon family," I found that these great people's lives mirrored Dexter's in many ways. Dexter's flair for turning an unexpected corner was definitely inherited from his forefathers. At first, when the search began, I assumed that Dexter's musical talent came from his father, who played clarinet and whose patients included Duke Ellington and Lionel Hampton. But when I discovered that his maternal grandfather, Edward Baker, was first trumpeter in the U.S. Army's Tenth Cavalry, I realized that the talent came from both sides of the family.

The search for everything I could learn about Dexter's family began when I went back to college after his death. As I was finishing my studies in 1995, doing research with my study partner Euphemia Strauchn-Adams at the Schomburg Center for Research in Black Culture in Harlem, I saw a large red volume on the librarian's shelf entitled *On the Trail of the Buffalo Soldier: Biographies of African Americans in the U.S. Army, 1866–1917* by Frank N. Schubert. I asked if I could look in the book because Dexter said that his grandfather had been a Buffalo

FIGURE 2. Captain Edward L. Baker Jr., Dexter's
maternal grandfather. Photograph from the National
Archives, Washington, D.C.

Soldier and I wondered if this man might be mentioned in the book. The
librarian said that the book had just arrived and was not yet catalogued,
but I could stand there and look for the reference. I opened the book
and was startled when the first thing I saw—on the frontispiece—was a
photograph of Captain Edward L. Baker Jr. The family resemblance
was unmistakable.

As I began to learn about Captain Baker, I tracked down the author
and sent him a letter requesting a copy of the photograph. Frank Schubert (who is called Mickey) sent me a print of the image and invited me
to his home near Washington, DC, for dinner and also to meet some
other people who studied Black military history. I took a train to Alexandria, Virginia, to meet the man who had graduated from Howard
University, who was a Vietnam veteran, and who now worked as a historian in the Joint History Office, Office of the Chairman, Joint Chiefs
of Staff, located in the Pentagon. Dr. Schubert is, without a doubt,

the foremost living authority on all matters relating to early Black military history and all matters relating to Dexter's grandfather, Captain Baker.[2]

Stepping off the train in Alexandria, I stood on the station platform looking for a man who I assumed would be the distinguished Black historian. Since Dr. Schubert had attended Howard and had spent his life studying and writing about Black military history, I had an idea of what he must look like. I began to approach a man who seemed to fit my imagined description of Dr. Schubert, but he did not respond to my nod and smile. When the commuter traffic had diminished to a trickle, I noticed another distinguished-looking man—this one was white—looking around at the far end of the platform. He approached me and asked if I was Maxine Gordon. After I replied yes and he introduced himself as Mickey Schubert, he said that he had been looking for a Black woman, assuming that someone who had been Dexter's wife and had majored in Black and Puerto Rican Studies in college must be Black. We had a good laugh while pondering the utility of the identities we had created for each other. We never tire of telling the story every chance we get. He and his wife, Irene, a former chief of the Preservation Reformatting Division of the Library of Congress, welcomed me into their home and their lives, and remain dear friends. There is nothing I can add to Frank Schubert's remarkable work on Captain Baker. (I will continue to refer to him as "Captain," although technically when he retired from the military his rank was Quartermaster Sergeant.)

What I discovered in my search for Dexter's family history was that both sides of the family are filled with enormously accomplished and impressive people. Both sides had roots in the western territories, still sparsely settled—especially by African Americans—in the mid nineteenth century. His maternal grandfather, Baker, was born in a part of the Dakota Territory that later (1868) became the Wyoming Territory, and his father was born in Fargo, North Dakota. On his mother's side he is descended from the family Boulanger from Normandy, France, and a great-grandmother who emigrated to France from the Indian Ocean island nation of Madagascar. Those great-grandparents moved from France to Canada and then crossed the border, where Edward Baker was born in 1865, thirty-five years before Wyoming became a state. These were people who were living in the still-wild West, and they would be among the very first Black families to make their way to Los Angeles in its early-modern history. My research uncovered information about Dexter's grandfathers, but much less is known about his grandmothers, which is not to say they were any less accomplished or vital to the ultimate development of Dexter's parents and Dexter himself.

In the photo of Edward Baker, wearing the uniform of the Forty-Ninth Volunteer Infantry in which he served from 1899 to 1901, we see the family resemblance to Dexter, and when I did my research on Baker's life, there were many pieces that are later reflected in Dexter's life. In a career that spanned twenty-eight years, Baker saw action on the western frontier as well as in the Spanish-American War in Cuba and then in the U.S. occupation of the Philippines. He was sergeant major of the Tenth Cavalry from 1892 to 1898, and a hero who received the Medal of Honor for gallantry in the Cuban campaign. Yes, Dexter's grandfather was a Buffalo Soldier.[3]

The Tenth Cavalry was formed at Fort Leavenworth, Kansas, with free men of color and formerly enslaved men, recruited from the northern states. The Tenth Cavalry was organized by Benjamin Henry Grierson (1826–1911), a white career officer in the U.S. Army who had been a music teacher. He led the Buffalo Soldiers of the Tenth Cavalry Regiment from 1866 to 1890. Well into the 1890s, the Black regiments served at remote locations west of the Mississippi River because prevailing racial attitudes following the Civil War precluded their stationing at posts near centers of population. The Buffalo Soldiers' primary mission mirrored that of other units at the time: to protect settlers as they moved west and to support the westward expansion by building the infrastructure needed for new settlements to flourish. A primary objective of this mission was to "compel" Native groups to move onto reservations and force them to stay there. The name "Buffalo Soldier" has long been thought by some to have been bestowed by Native peoples as a token of their respect for the soldiers. This is one possible scenario, as many Black soldiers remained in Indian territory and raised families there. The soldiers' mythic nature has been reinforced over time in film and literature as well as song, perhaps most popularly in Bob Marley's "Buffalo Soldier." In an essay about the naming of the units, Frank Schubert wrote:

> The alleged bestowal of this name "Buffalo Soldiers" as a sign of respect by Indian warriors has not gone unchallenged. The most serious objection has come from contemporary Native American leaders, who were angered over the publicity attending the issue of a Buffalo Soldier postage stamp in 1994 and resented the suggestion that there was some special bond between the soldiers and their warrior ancestors. The first salvo of dissent came from Vernon Bellecourt of the American Indian Movement. Writing in the weekly

Indian Country Today, Bellecourt denied that the name reflected any "endearment or respect." As far as he was concerned, Plains Indians only applied the term Buffalo Soldier to "these marauding murderous cavalry units" because of "their dark skin and the texture of their hair." The Buffalo Soldier remains a hero for many because of their stature in the military and because of their continued struggle for their rights and for their inclusion in history. The story remains complicated to say the least.[4]

Thanks to T. G. Steward, author of *The Colored Regulars in the United States Army,* we know that somewhere in some archive lies a manuscript that may actually have been a diary kept by Captain Baker during his twenty-eight years of military service. If the diary ever turns up (Frank Schubert doubts it will), it would surely provide vivid details of the history of this man, who was born on December 28, 1865, on the North Platte River, Laramie County, Dakota Territory, died in San Francisco on August 26, 1913, at the age of forty-eight, and was the maternal grandfather of Dexter Gordon.

Schubert wrote that "Baker grew up with a cowboy's toughness and skills in riding and roping . . . He also developed a fondness for education. As a youth he learned French from his father, studied Spanish, and dabbled in Russian and Chinese. Bright and ambitious, he left the northern plains and enlisted in the Ninth Cavalry in 1882, midway between his sixteenth and seventeenth birthdays."

Learning this, I couldn't help but be struck by the coincidence that fifty-eight years later, in 1940, Captain Baker's grandson Dexter would also leave home at the age of seventeen, to "enlist" in Lionel Hampton's band. Dexter learned French while in Chino Prison, considered *Les Misérables* an example for his life, and wore a beret. Once while he was working in Paris, the legendary drummer Kenny Clarke said to him, "Hey Dex, why do you wear that beret and try to speak in French? You are from Los Angeles, not Paris." Dexter replied, "But Klook, I *am* French, you know." Of course, he was joking about being French, but it was not far from the truth since his grandfather's father came from Normandy.

The list of Edward Baker's military highlights reads like a screenplay waiting to be written: Enlisted in D Company/Ninth Cavalry, 1882 (age seventeen); kicked by a horse, 1882; scouting in Utah Territory, 1883; engaged in arresting Oklahoma intruders at Ft. Reno, Wyoming; chief trumpeter, Tenth Cavalry, 1890; fell ill with dysentery, 1890; prepared map and itinerary of march to Big Horn Mountain, Montana; "Drove [Spanish troops] from their entrenchment with the loss of one man killed and 10 wounded," Spanish-American War, Cuba, 1898; fought at Las Guasimas and San Juan Hill, wounded slightly by shrapnel, left side and arm; awarded Medal of Honor for bravery at Santiago, Cuba, "for leaving cover and, under fire, rescuing a wounded comrade from drowning," 1898; appointed Captain, Forty-Ninth Infantry, 1899; served on the islands of Luzon and Samar, Philippines, 1902–9; retired, 1910.[5]

As I studied Edward Baker's military career, I saw many events that seemed very much like the life Dexter lived on the road. Over the course of his career, Baker served in Utah, Arizona, New Mexico, Texas, Colorado, Kansas, Nebraska, Wyoming, Montana, Cuba, and the Philippines. Dexter traveled to most of those places and more in his career. How does it change a person to travel the world? What do travelers learn from those they meet and from new environments they wake up in? As a road manager, traveling with bands, I know that waking up in a different place almost every day makes you think in a different way. You learn that the world is not just your neighborhood, and you learn to be yourself wherever you find yourself. When Dexter stopped traveling, he would often wake up in the morning and ask, "Where am I?" and "What time is the gig?"

Edward Baker married Mary Elizabeth Hawley (born Mary E. Prince in 1866 in Canada). The Bakers had five children: Edward Lee III (born 1889, New Mexico), Myrtle Mary (1892, Wyoming), Eugenia Sheridan (1893, Montana), Gwendolyn James (Dexter's mother, 1895, Michigan), and finally the uncle for whom Dexter was named, Dexter Murat (1899, Montana). Two of the children were given names suggesting their father's reverence for military heroes. Eugenia had the middle name of Sheridan, presumably after Civil War Union general Philip Sheridan, and Dexter Baker had the middle name of Murat, presumably after Joachim Murat, marshal and admiral of France under the reign of Napoleon. During Edward Baker's seven years of service in the Philippines, Mary Baker traveled to Paris and lived with her husband's relatives for a while. Then she moved to Los Angeles where the family reunited and settled.

Dexter's paternal grandfather, Frank L. Gordon, also lived in the sparsely settled northern Great Plains. Like Edward Baker, Frank L. Gordon would become very well known in the region, not as a military man but as an important businessman and leader in social circles. He was born in 1857 in Tennessee, and Dexter's grandmother, Fanny L. Gordon, was born in Kentucky in 1861. More research is needed to know about their lives in Tennessee and Kentucky and about their families there. In 1885 they traveled northwest from Kentucky some 1,300 miles to North Dakota, most probably in a mule-drawn covered wagon, along with their son, John D., born in Kentucky in 1881. They settled in Fargo and had four more sons: Richard J. (1886), Frank A. (1888), Osceola (1890), and Clifford M. (1900).

Judging from many mentions in the local press, Frank Gordon was a colorful and popular character. He operated his own barber shop and ran for city alderman in Fargo. He was referred to as "Professor" Gordon, probably because of his scholarly bearing and the refined manner with which he presented himself in public: "Professor Gordon, the popular Hotel Webster tonsorial artist, is announced as a candidate for alderman at the coming municipal election—if he can run as well as he can shave—it's easy." As part of the election preliminaries, the paper published this letter to the editor:

> Colored Man's Plea to the Forum: I wish to say a word to the voters of the First Ward in behalf of the colored citizens. There is an opportunity now for you to show your appreciation of the colored people of Fargo, who have never before asked for anything. F. L. Gordon is a popular colored man. He is now running for the office of alderman in the First Ward. He is a man of irreproachable character and integrity and if you elect him, he will fulfill his duties in behalf of the First Ward and the city in a fearless and creditable manner. We beg of you to give him your support. We, as citizens, ask our white brothers to support him at the ballot Monday. He will work for the best interest of the city in an intelligent manner. The colored republicans of the ward have worked faithfully for the candidates in the past, always content with the white men being the candidates. This time they ask recognition and put up a candidate against whom nothing can be said. When you come to vote Monday remember F. L. Gordon and give him a vote for alderman.
>
> (Signed) W. S. Harris.[6]

When the votes for the alderman's race in the First Ward were counted, A. J. Craig received 164 votes while F. L. Gordon received 88. The newspaper reported that "Professor Gordon's total was really quite respectable. Such a sizable vote indicates that Gordon's candidacy was no joke. It was a genuine candidacy for a serious political office."

When Frank Gordon moved his family to Williston, nearly four hundred miles west of Fargo, a local publicity magazine heralded his arrival with an article entitled "The Virtues of a Certain Black Williston Barber":

> Visitors in Williston from the eastern part of the state as well as the residents here will be pleased to know that Prof. F. L. Gordon, the well-known tonsorial artist of Fargo, has located in Williston and opened in the new Union block the finest barber shop in the western part of the state, with an equip-

ment in the way of fixtures, etc. surpassed by no tonsorial establishment west of Chicago. Prof. Gordon is one of the pioneers of the state, having been a resident of Fargo for twenty years, and there are very few men indeed who have a wider acquaintance in the state. He has for years been a recognized leader among his people. He is a knight of the razor with few equals, and makes a specialty of massage and hair dressing. He employs only skilled assistants. The members of the traveling fraternity who appreciate the luxury of a good shave, should make a note of it and remember Prof. Gordon. He is fitting up also a complete equipment of baths, hot, cold, vapor, etc.[7]

Frank and Fanny soon became homesteaders in the area. By that time, probably 1904 or 1905, all the best land close to Williston had been claimed. The Gordon family's claim was in the community of Gladys in what would later be named Good Luck township, about twenty miles north of Williston. Fanny and the children made their home there to complete the community's residence requirements, while the "Professor" earned the family living in his Williston shop. According to the local newspaper, the Gordons were well liked, as Fanny was experienced in nursing and helped care for the ill, and also volunteered to do the cooking for many dances and other community gatherings. Author Bill Shemorry provides some colorful, if probably apocryphal, details of Frank's life:

> The Gladys community had many unique things about it, but having a black homesteader was one which was shared by few others. Frank L. Gordon in his youth had been with a circus several years. During that time the "big tent" show had gone to Norway and remained there for quite a stint. The better to get along, Gordon learned to speak Norwegian fluently . . . Now Frank was known as "Professor" Gordon. He had learned the barbering business and was about to begin a career in Williston that would last nearly two decades.[8]

The bit about Frank Gordon having been a circus performer and going to Norway seems to appear nowhere but in Shemorry's book. But there is evidence from other writings that Frank did learn some Norwegian from immigrants in Fargo, and also that he had a gift for humor.

> Gordon . . . may have been unofficially entitled to his sobriquet of "Professor" because of his business psychology. With the coming of Scandinavian immigrant settlers he cultivated a Norwegian accent which he lapsed into readily. In time, he learned the language. That class of customer relaxed happily in the chair while Gordon chatted away into his ear. To the Scandinavians, a black man was an oddity. When they asked him why he was so dark he replied evasively that by the time they had been in the country as long as he had, they would be dark too. That statement never failed to draw suspicious, hooded glances.[9]

One local account went on to conclude: "Gordon's halo faded away some time later, though, when he was arrested for holding gambling games in his shop." Dexter would surely have his share of "faded halo" experiences as well.

Barbers played an important role in frontier life. In the book *African Americans in North Dakota,* many Black barbers are listed. A "tonsorial establishment" in the first decade of North Dakota's history was not a simple operation. It was a gathering place which offered a variety of social amenities. It would seem that barbering had special advantages, such as requiring the ownership or rental of a fixed piece of property and the equipment needed to run the business. It was also a highly visible profession, and as clientele would gradually develop, advertisers would pay to display their goods there, and the proprietor became a public figure. And of course the time spent waiting for a shave and actually sitting in the chair allowed the patrons and the proprietor to engage in no small amount of conversation and debate. In short, being a barber allowed a turn-of-the-century Dakota workingman a chance to achieve both economic and social advantages. The barber shop is also central to the story of bebop in the 1940s, as the latest records were discussed, sold, exchanged, and played there—many had turntables—and the barber shop has always served as a meeting place for Black men and a reliable locale for political discussion and strategy sessions.

Frank and Fanny Gordon's sons all have stories to be told. The oldest, John, homesteaded on Section 17 of Twelve Mile Township, Williams County, east of Williston. Clifford Gordon was Williston High School's star quarterback in 1917; he sustained a wound during World War I and recovered to become the first nonwhite athlete to participate in intercollegiate athletics at the University of Southern California, starring as an end on USC's undefeated football championship team of 1920. Osceola F. Gordon served in the 163rd Depot Brigade and the 809th Pioneer Infantry in 1918–19 and may have seen action in the Battle of Argonne Forest in France. Both Frank A. and Clifford studied medicine, graduated as physicians, and were among the first Black doctors to practice in Los Angeles.

Dr. Frank, as Dexter's father was cordially known in Los Angeles, attended college at the University of Minnesota and Fisk University in Nashville. He received his medical degree in 1914 from Howard University School of Medicine in Washington, D.C. To support his studies, he worked as a railroad porter and also played clarinet part-time at the

Howard Theatre. He interned at Freedmen's Hospital in Washington and in 1916 moved to Los Angeles at the invitation of a doctor there who needed assistance. There he met and married Gwendolyn L. Baker in 1919, when he was thirty-one and she was twenty-four. Dexter was their only child.

Dexter talked quite often about his father and his love of music, and believed that Frank would have been very pleased to know that his son had become a musician. He recalled going on house calls with his father in his Model A Ford and waiting for him as he attended patients in the fancy homes in the Hollywood Hills. Dexter said his father made house calls to some famous white patients, including movie stars (or so the story goes), while most of the patients who came to his office on Jefferson, off Central Avenue, were from the neighborhood, which was known as the Eastside. On many evenings Frank would go to the bar at the Dunbar Hotel to meet with friends, many of whom were musicians as well as patients, including Duke Ellington and Lionel Hampton.

Dexter told the story of Ellington visiting the Gordon home for dinner and his mother preparing her specialty, spaghetti and meatballs, specifically at Mr. Ellington's request. There would be a big fuss in the neighborhood whenever Ellington arrived, and Dexter's friends would come by to peek through the windows for a glimpse of the great man. Dexter was allowed to sit at the table for dinner but he had to promise to remain quiet and use his best manners.

Tragedy struck on Christmas Eve 1937 when Dexter was just fourteen years old. Ellington recalled the moment in his book *Music Is My Mistress*: "I had made a date to meet my Los Angeles doctor . . . Dexter Gordon's father, in the bar of the Dunbar Hotel on Forty-first and Central at four o'clock Christmas morning. A friend came in right on the nose and told me the doctor couldn't make it, because he had just died of a heart attack. That completely ruined my chances of a happy Christmas celebration."[10] Dr. Gordon was forty-nine years old. Dexter often referred to this Christmas Eve when his father died and wondered how his life might have been different had his father lived longer. Many years later he spoke about his father when he went to Howard University to perform a concert with Lionel Hampton in Dr. Frank's honor. Dexter's mother lived another fifty years, remarried, and worked for the U.S. Government. In 1987 she was able to attend the Los Angeles premiere of *Round Midnight*, in which her son starred. Clifford Gordon took over Dr. Frank's medical practice and kept the office at 1069 East Jefferson Street on the corner of Central Avenue.

In 2014 I was invited to Madagascar to participate in a tribute to Dexter at the International Festival called Madajazzcar. The invitation came after I had met the festival director, Désiré Razafindrazaka, on a trip to Paris. I had told him that Dexter's maternal great-grandmother had come from Madagascar, moved to France, married a man named Boulanger, emigrated to Canada, and crossed the border into the Wyoming Territory, where Dexter's maternal grandfather was born. Désiré was delighted to hear this and said that I must come to Madagascar and find out more about this woman. For several years we exchanged e-mails and finally, in 2014, I arranged to go. There would be a big-band tribute to Dexter with arrangements of his compositions, a screening of *Round Midnight,* and a program during which I would talk—in French—with journalists and fans about Dexter's life.

My hope was to learn more about Dexter's great-grandmother. In U.S. Census files, she is identified only as "Negro woman." I could not find her name. With the help of Malagasy scholars, we were able to speculate on the circumstances of her emigration from Madagascar to France. She was probably expelled near the end of the reign of Queen Ranavalona I (1828–61), when European traders, mainly from France and Britain, were encroaching on Malagasy culture and the Queen issued a royal edict prohibiting the practice of Christianity on the island. Assuming that Dexter's great-grandmother did consider herself Christian, she would have gone to France (which would claim Madagascar as a colony in 1896), where we do know she met and married Monsieur Boulanger. Unfortunately my Malagasy researchers could find no hard evidence to confirm this emigration theory—nor could they determine her name.

The rest of my trip was sublime. The people greeted me warmly and were especially proud that Dexter was descended from the people of Madagascar. I traveled with two young Malagasy men, who shared their time treating me to the beautiful countryside and delicious meals and a ride on a *pousse-pousse* (a bicycle taxi); when the car broke down (which did not seem uncommon), they put Bob Marley on the iPod and we waited for help. Yes, they played "Buffalo Soldier" and we sang along. At my discussion of Dexter's life and work, a woman studied a photo of him and remarked that she could definitely see Malagasy roots in his face. Many people in the audience nodded in agreement. For now, all we know is that Dexter did in fact have a great-grandmother from Madagascar, and I was honored to be invited there to pay homage to her memory.

The search for Dexter's "uncommon family" took me into many archives, and with the help of experts I was able to uncover some of his family history, but not all of it. The story could have gone on and on had I been able to trace Dexter's family history further back than the nineteenth century. Because Dexter's father had a brother named Osceola, is that a clue that they were somehow related to the famous Osceola, born Billy Powell (1804–38), of Creek, Scots-Irish, Black, and English background, who became the leader of the Seminole resistance? Maybe it was just in his honor that the Gordons so named their fourth son. There are so many unanswered questions about these remarkable people, just as there are unanswered questions about the jazz family. Often in jazz histories, the stories begin with the first gig and the first recording. Dexter often laughed about the way his biography was usually presented in jazz publications: "*He was born in Los Angeles, his father was the first Black doctor there* (not true, he was the second), *he went on the road with Lionel Hampton, recorded on Dial and Savoy, had a drug problem, went to jail, went to Europe, came back, made a movie, got nominated for an Oscar.*" Life is far more complicated than a career sketch would have us believe. What does it take to be a jazz musician? How did they manage to survive the road, the indignities of racism, and the struggle to create beauty as what Sonny Rollins refers to as "artists in an artist-hostile society"?

Dexter's story weaves its way through Madagascar and France, through Canada, Tennessee, Kentucky, the Dakota and Wyoming Territories, and to the city of Los Angeles at the turn of the twentieth century. The family includes doctors, musicians, a famous military hero, and a locally legendary barber. It's no wonder Dexter loved to describe himself with the line once uttered by his friend the great tenor saxophonist Junior Cook: "*I'm not just your ordinary B-flat.*"

CHAPTER 3

Education of an Eastside Altar Boy

You can learn something new every day of your life, from
anybody, if you pay attention . . . This was the university
of the streets! Where Black people would imitate and then
figure things out for themselves.

—Jimmy Heath[1]

When Dexter was born, on February 27, 1923, African Americans in
the city of Los Angeles made up only 2 percent of the total population
of about 940,000 people. Dexter's father, Dr. Frank A. Gordon, was
just the second Black physician to practice medicine there. Frank,
Gwendolyn, and their only child, Dexter, lived at 238 East Forty-Fifth
Street in the neighborhood known as the Eastside. I learned a great deal
about what coming of age there was like for Dexter and his friends from
a group of those friends who gathered for a "roundtable social" in February 1998 at the venerable Dunbar Hotel on Central Avenue. The
group, assembled at my request by Dexter's good friend Clint Rosemond, called themselves the "Eastside Elders," and the first thing they
stressed to me was the proper usage of the neighborhood's name. It had
to be "Eastside," one word, and never "East Side" as it is in what must
be hundreds of other American cities and towns.

The Dunbar Hotel (originally named the Hotel Somerville) was chosen for the site of the social because it was the focal point of the African
American community on Central Avenue during the 1930s and 1940s.
Built in 1928 by John and Vada Somerville, it hosted the first national
convention of the National Association for the Advancement of Colored
People (NAACP) to be held in the western United States. In 1930 the
hotel was renamed the Dunbar in honor of the poet Paul Laurence

Dunbar. Soon thereafter a nightclub opened at the Dunbar, and it became the center of the Central Avenue jazz scene. The club hosted Duke Ellington, Cab Calloway, Billie Holiday, Louis Armstrong, Lionel Hampton, Count Basie, Lena Horne, Ray Charles, and many other legendary performers. Among the famous clientele at the hotel were W. E. B. Du Bois, Joe Louis, and Thurgood Marshall. Former heavyweight boxing champion Jack Johnson also ran a nightclub at the Dunbar in the 1930s.[2]

The Eastside Elders, whom I met almost eight years after Dexter's death (April 25, 1990), proved to be an extremely impressive and accomplished group. It included Edward "Abie" Robinson, a former newspaper reporter with the *Los Angeles Sentinel;* Halvor Thomas Miller, an attorney and nephew of Judge Loren Miller, who along with his law partner Thurgood Marshall successfully argued the case before the U.S. Supreme Court in 1948 that struck down racially restrictive real estate covenants; Wallace M. DeCuir, one of the first Black firemen and paramedics in Los Angeles; Alvis W. Parrish, who was younger than Dexter but remembered the neighborhood well; Andrew Wallace, a former probation officer; Walter Gordon Jr. Esq., one of the first Black lawyers in Los Angeles (unrelated to Dexter, he died in 2012 at the age of 103); Arnett L. Hartsfield Jr., a firefighter, lawyer, and educator who helped lead the battle to integrate the Los Angeles Fire Department and who became a historian of the struggle; Lloyd Thomas, a quiet gentleman who was a schoolteacher; and Celes King III, a civil rights leader and founding state chairman of CORE (the Congress of Racial Equality), whose father once owned the Dunbar.

Jack Kelson, the saxophonist known professionally as Jackie Kelso, did not attend the Elders social, but he had been a high school classmate of Dexter's and also an alter boy at St. Philip's Episcopal Church along with Dexter. In an oral history, Kelso recalled the sidewalk in front of the Dunbar as the most desirable spot to hang out on the city's coolest street. "That's my favorite spot on Central Avenue . . . because that to me was the hippest, most intimate, key spot of all the activity," he said.[3] "That's where all the night people hung out: the sportsmen, the businessmen, the dancers, everybody in show business . . . People who were somebody stayed at the hotel . . . By far that block, that Dunbar Hotel, for me was it . . . Sooner or later you walked in front of that hotel, and that's where everybody congregated."

The day after the Eastside Elders social, I went to St. Philip's Episcopal Church to examine its records and see if Dexter really was an altar boy as he had said he was. In fact, it was true. Dexter, Kelso, and also James Truitte (the renowned dancer with the Alvin Ailey Company) had all been altar boys in the church. As I was leaving, a very elegant Black woman pulled up in a Cadillac. She got out, walked over to me, and said, "You must be Mrs. Gordon."

"Yes, how did you know?" I said.

"The word is out," she replied. "Everyone knows you are in town."

We laughed. Then she said that she heard I had invited the Eastside Elders to a social to discuss Dexter and his family, and thought that was very nice. "You should have invited the women for tea instead," she said. Her name was Anne Cunningham. "We know the real story."

Dexter's parents attended St. Philip's, which was an easy walk from their home. Dexter was baptized there on May 8, 1923, and his name is in the church records as being confirmed in 1934. When he started working at night with bands in 1938, he stopped getting up for church and, not incidentally, started developing a habit of being late for school.

Halvor Thomas Miller, one of the Elders at the roundtable, remembered some relatives who lived on Dexter's street

> constantly complaining about him practicing his instrument because of the noise he was making. You know, it's so obvious. Dexter is a product of this community. Every man sitting around this table is from Los Angeles, and had the same experience that he had. Every one of these stories is the same as his. Each one. It didn't make a difference what porch you were standing on, the mother in that house was going to tell you the same thing that the lady down the street was going tell her kids: it was all the same. Everybody was treated the same.

Robinson, the newspaper reporter, chimed in: "But the issue I want to present is the fact there was no room in the neighborhood. Things [outside the neighborhood] were under a very strict covenant, a very restrictive covenant. And Blacks couldn't buy, sell, or rent. Chicanos couldn't buy, sell, or rent. Orientals couldn't buy, sell, or rent." The restrictive racial covenants effectively forced the minorities into living on the Eastside, which caused very crowded conditions. These enforced restrictions were finally struck down by the Supreme Court in *Shelley v. Kraemer* in 1948.[4]

Dexter's memories of his childhood are mostly blissful and largely centered on music:

> *I started listening at a very early age, before I even started playing . . . When I was nine and 10 years old I was listening to the bands on the radio on my own. Prior to that my father used to take me to the theaters in town to dig*

the bands and the artists. He was a doctor and knew a lot of them: Duke, Lionel Hampton, Marshal Royal, Ethel Waters. They'd come by for dinner. And I'd go see them backstage, things like that. It was just part of my cultural upbringing. On the radio I was picking up the late-night shots, air shots from the East: Chicago's Grand Terrace, Roseland Ballroom, you know, and people like "Fatha" Hines, Fletcher Henderson and Roy Eldridge. So when my father gave me a clarinet when I was 13, I had done a lot of listening.[5]

For his first jobs Dexter had a paper route and mowed lawns. He used his earnings plus his allowance and lunch money to buy secondhand jukebox records for fifteen cents apiece from dealers in the neighborhood. Having already sat at the dinner table with Duke Ellington and Lionel Hampton, Dexter listened to all of their records and radio broadcasts, and many others' as well. As a novice clarinetist, he listened carefully to Benny Goodman, Buster Bailey, and Barney Bigard. He took lessons from John Sturdevant, a clarinet player from New Orleans. Dexter:

John was a very nice cat who had that big fat clarinet sound like Bigard's. I remember asking him about that, which knocked him out. I said, "How ya get that sound, man?" Almost all of those New Orleans clarinet players—Irving Fazola, Albert Nicholas, Bigard—have that.

When I started playing I had some kind of idea about music, about jazz, because I was into everybody . . . people like Benny Carter, Roy Eldridge, who is one of my all-time favorites, and Scoops Carry, who played alto with Roy's little band. I also liked Pete Brown. Of course I heard Chu Berry, and Dick Wilson, who played tenor with Andy Kirk, and Ben Webster. I first heard Ben on a record he made with Duke called "Truckin'." He was shoutin' on that. But then I got my first Basie record and that was it. I fell in love with that band—Lester, Herschel Evans, the whole band. Duke was just fantastic, but the Basie band really hit me.[6]

Dexter's best friend, Lamar Wright Jr., lived directly across the street from Lionel Hampton. Walter Gordon Jr. remembered that "there was a single house on the corner of Wadsworth and Forty-Third Street. The Philips Temple Church is on the northeast corner. The northwest corner is where Lamar lived, and on the southwest corner is where Lionel Hampton lived. We called Lamar and Dexter 'Mutt and Jeff'—Dexter was so tall and Lamar was very short. Dexter used the excuse of coming over to our house, because we were acceptable, but really, he went around and spent the time with Lamar." All the better to get a chance to spot Hampton, or maybe hear him practicing.

Walter Gordon also remembered when the Count Basie Orchestra came out to play the Paramount Theater in 1939: "They had green gabardine suits, and green suede shoes. We all tried to get them. We went down to Black & Sons and bought material. Everybody had some kind of gabardine suit, and at that time we wore white buck shoes when Easter came. Everybody switched over from brown and black shoes to white buck shoes."

Wallace DeCuir remembered Dexter from their elementary school days:

> On Saturdays, Dexter would go for his music lesson at Grace Conservatory, then he would come over. We lived down the street, on what was Forty-First Street and Wadsworth. Norman Houston lived on the corner, I lived three doors down, and Dexter would come and play with us until his dad closed the office around two o'clock and picked him up. And my uncle lived across the street from the gardens, and so this was like a family kind of thing. In fact, the first time we ever went on the rollercoaster at Ocean Park, my uncle Doc Clark took us. Our different dads would take us places. My dad would take us down to Wrigley Field when the All-American Stars would come play football. And that was the kind of thing that, whatever dad was off, he just happened to be your parent at that time. And, you know, we also grew up at the Y. Donald Derrickson was the one who gave Dexter the nickname "Joe Louis." I have a lady looking for the picture they took at the Y camp with Dexter—he looked just like Joe Louis.

Dexter attended Main Street Elementary School from the first through sixth grades. From seventh through ninth grades he went to McKinley Junior High School. His classmates there included Melba Liston, Bill Douglass, and Lawrence Marable, all of whom became accomplished musicians and lifelong friends. Liston became the legendary jazz trombonist and arranger, and Marable and Douglass were accomplished drummers. (Douglass also was a union officer in Local 767, known as "the colored musicians' union," and later in the integrated Local 47.)

Dexter's first performing ensemble was a jug band (the others played on washtubs for drums, pie plates for cymbals, and kazoos) that played in amateur shows in the neighborhood. Dexter started playing alto saxophone when he was fourteen, and at fifteen switched to tenor when his mother bought him the larger horn to fit his larger body. The 1937 McKinley yearbook shows a very tall fourteen-year-old Dexter as an auditorium usher and in the swing band, the orchestra, and the marching band. He studied privately with Lloyd Reese, a multi-instrumentalist who played lead trumpet with the Les Hite orchestra. Reese had a rehearsal band that met on Sundays at Local 767. Both Charles Mingus and Buddy Collette studied with Lloyd Reese and played in his rehearsal band. About Lloyd Reese, Dexter said:

He was a very fine trumpet player. He was very special. He knew all the instruments: piano, bass, trumpet, trombone, saxophone, clarinet—and he was also a patient of my father. When I got the alto saxophone, I started studying with him, along with all the guys. Reese's approach was to treat us like we were going to be professional musicians. It wasn't just a matter of playing a lesson. Sometimes we would play a tune together so he could see how advanced I was. He helped me to know about Art Tatum and to be aware of film scores and he opened up the spectrum of this prolific jazz.[7]

When it was time for high school in 1938, Dexter first attended Manual Arts for a year and then transferred to Jefferson High primarily because of the band director, Sam Browne. Dexter's classmates at Jefferson included Chico Hamilton, Jackie Kelso, Vernon Slater, Lamar Wright Jr., Vi Redd, and Ernie Royal. There were a few disciplinary incidents, such as lateness and unexcused absences, that led to transfers, first to Polytechnic High School and then back to Manual Arts, but Dexter continued to study music at Jefferson.

Of the many music teachers in Los Angeles, undoubtedly the most influential were Lloyd Reese and Sam Browne. While both men received classical training, they nevertheless left their mark on the Los Angeles jazz world. Browne, a former student at the Wilkins School of Music, earned degrees in music and education from the University of Southern California and headed the music department at Jefferson High School. He had graduated from Jefferson but had a long and hard fight to get the position as band director at the school. All the other teachers were white and some transferred out when he was hired in 1936. In addition to Dexter and his contemporaries, Browne helped develop such jazz notables as Horace Tapscott, Sonny Criss, Frank Morgan, Big Jay McNeely, Marshal Royal, Art Farmer, and Don Cherry.

Before Browne arrived at Jefferson High, the school had already achieved a reputation as a junior conservatory thanks to the community's strong promotion of music education and support from the city. According to Marshal Royal, the school's music curriculum began with a keyboard class, then followed with Harmony One, Two, Three, and Four—one semester for each. The students all learned to write scores and compose. Early in his musical training Royal concentrated on the violin, leading the orchestra as concertmaster, but he received no formal jazz education there. With Browne at the helm, the school continued its devotion to classical music training and also added instruction in jazz. Browne's approach ultimately defined music education at Jefferson High and the music of his students. In his interviews over the years,

Dexter always mentioned Lloyd Reese and Sam Browne for teaching him music and encouraging him to be a musician.

While still in school, Dexter played in a dance band that worked in bars on weekends for a dollar and a half a night plus the kitty. He then joined a Pasadena band called the Harlem Collegians playing stock arrangements from Glenn Miller, Count Basie, and others. Because of his height—he was a full-grown six feet five inches at fifteen—he easily gained entrance into clubs and bars as both a patron and a musician. Dexter:

> *When I was about sixteen years old I was starting to gig around town, get-ting my hair konked and being late to school because of working nights. The authorities got tired of it and sent me to truant's school for a few weeks. One of my classmates was a Mexican-Irish kid, Jimmy Doyle. The school was located in old town L.A. and we rode the old B trolley car line back to the neighborhood. He went to Jeff also. He told me he was into boxing and was starting to box amateur like a lot of guys around the neighborhood. I would hear about him in the Golden Gloves, AAU, and later he turned pro, fighting at the old Hollywood Legion, home of the Golden Boy, Art Aragon, and also Lauro Salas and Milo Savage. A few years later Jimmy became a con-tender and unfortunately he was booked to fight in the annual Christmas Benefit in Cleveland—his opponent Sugar Ray Robinson, welterweight champ at that time. Later, Ray moved up to middleweight when he fought Jake LaMotta five times, Rocky Graziano, Carmen Basilio, Gene Fullmer, etc. It was a non-title bout, 10 rounds. In the middle rounds, Ray caught Doyle in a corner and went to work. The referee should have stopped the fight before Doyle slumped to the floor unconscious. They rushed him to the hospital but he was DOA. They asked Ray why he did it, which was a stupid question. Ray said that he couldn't help it. "Besides, that's what they pay me for."*

Speaking of Dexter at the Eastside Elders roundtable in 1998, Halvor Miller said, "I remember how imposing he was. I'm six five and a half; Dexter was as tall as I am, but much larger. And ganglier. And walked with knock knees. And always smiling. He had a very rich baritone voice, and his instrument was a very rich tenor voice. He spoke with two voices, in my opinion. He was a person, he had things to say, with his speaking voice, and a lot to say with his instrumental voice."

Wallace DeCuir shared all the good childhood memories but recalled a few others, when the guys were a bit older, that were less than posi-tive: "When I came back from college, I worked for the probation department, and Dexter was aware of this. Every time Dexter got in trouble, I got a phone call. And there were a couple of times when I was able to intercede for him. Dexter was not a bad guy, but Dexter loved his drugs, let's face it. Back then, marijuana was a felony. Dexter was always getting caught with drugs of some kind."

He had been able to meet many of his musical idols through his father. But the chance to meet his number one tenor saxophone hero, Lester Young, came about not through Dexter's father, but through the father of one of his friends. Dexter:

The first time I met Pres was in May, 1939, backstage at the old Paramount Theatre in Los Angeles. My buddy Lamar Wright Jr. and I were both sixteen years old and we ditched school that morning to go see Count Basie's band. Fortunately, we caught an eleven a.m. show that featured Mr. Five by Five— Jimmy Rushing—along with girl vocalist Helen Humes, Lester and Buddy Tate (tenor sax), Earl "Butter" Warren (lead alto), Jack Washington (baritone sax), Buck Clayton, Harry Sweets Edison (trumpets), Dicky Wells, Benny Morton (trombones), and Jo Jones, Freddie Green, Walter Page, and (Plink) Count Basie—the fabulous Basie rhythm section. You could set your watch to them. The band had come roarin' out from K.C. with Lester floating in from some astral planet to steal our hearts and revolutionize our daily lives.

Lamar says, "Come on and I'll introduce you to the cats."

I say, "How? You don't know these cats?"

"Yeah, but my father does."

With that we trek into the alleyway, leading to the stage door. We stand around waiting for the members to trickle out and in a few moments they do, and Lamar sees Harry Sweets and says "Hi, Sweets, I think you know my dad and he told me to say hello."

"Yeah, who's that?"

"Lamar Wright."

"Sure, we all know 'Slop.'" (They called him that because he was so clean.)

Lamar's father played trumpet in Cab Calloway's band from the thirties and for many years after that. Right away I was introduced as "my friend Dexter, the tenor player. He likes Lester." And suddenly we had taken our first step into the magic circle. It became obvious that being introduced as a "jazz musician" to other jazz musicians was some kind of "Open Sesame" to this society of gifted individuals. I said, "Oh, Yeah."

This has been going all my life, as it is today.

"Hey, Man, where're you from?"

"I'm from L.A. You?"

"K.C. Hey, you know Fat Arnold?"

"Sure, last time I heard him was with McShann. Likes to play those lip trills like Louis."

"Right, that's the cat, big fat tone. I see you got your axe with you, feel like blowin'?"

(Nod yes.)

"I know a joint we can drop by."

"Solid . . ."

We can only imagine how Dexter's heart must have raced and his mind soared when he was invited to go blow his horn with the cats. It was not very long after that night when Dexter, still in his senior year at Jefferson High School, got the phone call that changed his life and sent him on his way to realizing his dream.

CHAPTER 4

Leaving Home

New York was where it was at, and I had heard the story
that when Dexter came to New York, he got down and
kissed the ground at the train station. New York!

—Jimmy Heath[1]

Dexter loved to tell the story about the phone call that afternoon in
1940:

> The voice on the phone said, "This is Marshal Royal."
>
> I said, "Yeah, who is this really?" and hung up. I thought it was one of
> my school friends playing a joke on me. I was seventeen years old. The
> phone rang again and the man said, "This is Marshal Royal. Would you like
> to come over to Lionel Hampton's house and audition for him?"
>
> So we went down to Hamp's house for a little session, we blew a while
> and that was it. Three days later we were on the bus, without any rehearsal,
> cold. I was expecting to be sent home every night.

Marshal Royal was a music legend in Los Angeles. He was born in 1912
in Oklahoma and came to Los Angeles when he was five years old. Dexter
always said that he owed his entire career as a saxophone player to Marshal and thanked him many times for not sending him home when he first
joined the band. Dexter's high school friend Ernie Royal was Marshal's
younger brother, and it was he who recommended Dexter to Marshal for
the Hampton gig. As Marshal wrote in his autobiography, *Marshal Royal:
Jazz Survivor*, Dexter got the gig at the last minute because one of the
original tenor players, Bob Barfield, "had a couple of problems." He had
moved to L.A. from San Francisco and had only been with the band a
short time. And "when the band came back through San Francisco, his
wife gave him a hard time and he left . . . We decided to try Dexter Gordon
as his replacement on tenor. Dexter's father was my doctor and a personal

FIGURE 3. The Lionel Hampton saxophone section, 1940 (left to right): Dexter, Ray Perry, Marshal Royal, Illinois Jacquet. Publicity photo from the office of Joe Glaser. Photo from the personal collection of Dexter Gordon.

friend of the family. Besides that, my brother and Dexter had gone to Jefferson High School at the same time and they knew each other . . . So I recommended Dexter to Lionel and he joined us."[2]

Once when Dexter was on a European tour, in 1980, and Marshal was on tour there with a Count Basie reunion band, I had a chance to sit up late at night with him in a hotel lobby in Italy. I asked him about Dexter's father, Dr. Frank. Marshal told me that he always remembered Dr. Frank because if a person didn't have the money to pay him, he would still give whatever care was necessary. The person would pay him with a cake or a chicken—sometimes a live one. Marshal also said that he regretted being the one to take Dexter on the road at such a young age. He thought Dexter should have stayed in Los Angeles a little longer and matured a bit more, and perhaps he would have had a better chance to resist some of the temptations of the jazz life.

The Hampton band reed section had five saxophones. Marshal played lead alto and Ray Perry played second alto. Marshal explained that the lead player "is the one who carries the melody, one of its many inversions or part of the chord." Jack McVea played baritone. The other tenor player was Illinois Jacquet. The trumpet section featured Jack Trainer, who played lead; Ernie Royal, who also played lead and took solos; and Joe Newman, a student at Alabama State College who was hired during the band's first southern tour after he came to audition in Atlanta. Joe and Dexter became close friends and remained so the rest of their lives.

Lionel Hampton liked to tell the story of Dexter's first trip with the band, how he got on the bus with his horn in a paper bag while his mother and aunties waved goodbye, wearing white gloves, hats, and pearls. Dexter always let Lionel tell his story, but the facts didn't quite line up with the way he told it. Dexter's tenor was in a case, but it wasn't a very professional horn, and when the band got to Chicago, Dexter bought himself a new one. His mother and aunt *were* there at the bus to send him off, and they did bring food for him to take on the trip (he remembered deviled eggs). And they did always wear hats, gloves, and pearls. The band gave him a very hard time about those ladies waving goodbye. Nobody else in the band had his mother waving, with tears streaming down her face, when he went on the road.

The band left Los Angeles in December 1940 headed for Texas, with gigs in Dallas, Galveston, Houston, El Paso, San Antonio, Fort Worth, and other cities. This was Dexter's first trip to the South, as it was for both Royal brothers. According to Hampton,

> It took us about three days to get to Fort Worth and from there we went to Arizona, and from there to New Mexico. It was winter, and it was cold, and the bus didn't have any insulation or any heat. And about that time the guys staged a mutiny. A guy named Jack Lee was our road manger, and the fellows told him "Get a real bus. We can't ride in our overcoats." So we switched to a Greyhound bus, which was bigger and insulated and had heat. Gladys [Lionel's wife, the business manager] worried about the cost, but we had to keep the guys comfortable.[3]

The band went on to New Orleans, a city too segregated for the musicians from the relatively more tolerant Los Angeles to feel comfortable visiting. Florida was no better. Marshal Royal recalled, "If a black person wanted to go out on Miami Beach, he had to have a [driver's] license with his picture on it! That was a new experience for me." Next the band went up through the Carolinas and finally made it to New York City to play at the Savoy Ballroom. From there they went to Chicago where they played the Grand Terrace Ballroom. Dexter recalled that they were paid ten dollars a night when they worked, and if they didn't work they didn't get paid. It took about a year before Gladys agreed to raise the pay to eleven dollars a night. For their Chicago gig, each member of the band got thirty-eight dollars a week.

In an interview with the journalist Pete Hamill, Dexter recalled the discoveries he made when he first joined the Hampton band:

> Everything was about music for me then. The band that really turned me on was Basie, but I listened to all the bands. And I was starting to buy used 78's from the garage of a jukebox dealer: Lunceford, Royal, Teddy Wilson, Billie, Pee Wee Russell. And I used to listen to all these radio stations out of New York: bands coming from Roseland and the hotels. Earl Hines. Coleman Hawkins had a big band. Roy Eldridge, Les Hite, Freddy Martin even. Plus all that reading in the Black newspapers. So after a while, I more or less knew them. So when I finally came to New York I said, hmmm, no problem.
>
> I got there and looked around and I knew that I was home. I was seventeen years old, standing on the corner of 126th Street, down the street from the stage door at the Apollo Theater, and almost everybody stayed there. Musicians, entertainers. Of course, we were staying at the Harlem YMCA, but I didn't care. There was a whole scene around the Braddock Grill. The pimps, the hustlers, the whores, the dancers and musicians. It was like the cartoons of E. Simms Campbell, who I'd read in the Courier since I was nine. Those cartoonists did such a great job of depicting Harlem that when I got there, I knew everybody. But to be there added another element. I identified. It was heaven on earth. It was everything I'd dreamed and visualized. And there I was, seventeen years old, standing on the corner with the cats. All these cats walking around: Ben, Lester, Billie, Charlie Shavers, Roy, Milt Hinton, Catlett—you name 'em. All right there. I couldn't believe it. Aaaand . . . the brown-skinned beauties too. Ha.[4]

On that first visit to New York, Dexter stayed only five days. But he did get to hear two alto players who would have a big influence on him, Rudy Williams and Charlie Parker. Dexter:

> I first met Bird in '41, when he was still with Jay McShann. I was with Lionel Hampton's band. McShann's band was the house band at the Savoy Ballroom and we worked in there opposite them. They had a wild, swinging band, too—very groovy. That was Bird's initial exposure there, I guess. I liked him and everything, but I didn't hear him enough to realize at the time

that this was "the" cat. But he sounded real great and I dug him. I dug the whole band, in fact.

Lionel Hampton's band opened at the Grand Terrace Ballroom in Chicago in late January 1941 for a two-week engagement that lasted six months. Dexter:

> It was really my school. I learned so much. Marshal stayed on my ass all the time. He forced me to learn about crescendo, decrescendo, piano, forte, all those things I didn't know anything about when I was in high school. He taught me so much.

On February 11, 1941, the band made a live radio broadcast from the Grand Terrace, including "Flying Home," which was a big hit for the band and for Illinois Jacquet. The story was that it developed around a tune Hampton whistled as he nervously waited for his first flight on an airplane with the Benny Goodman band. Lionel Hampton:

> We were in Los Angeles, and we had to fly to Atlantic City. It was the first time I'd ever been on a plane. We had always traveled by train or bus. I wasn't the only one who wasn't used to flying. Benny had to explain to the whole band that the only way we could make the gig was to fly . . . So we got on the plane, and I started amusing myself. I started singing, and Benny said, "What is that you're humming?" I said, "I don't know. We can call it 'Flying Home,' I guess."[5]

The song was first recorded by the Benny Goodman Sextet on November 6, 1939, featuring solos by Hampton and guitarist Charlie Christian. Several other groups subsequently recorded the tune. However, the most famous version would be the 1942 recording by Lionel Hampton and His Orchestra, featuring Illinois Jacquet's tenor solo. Marshal Royal:

> The Hampton Band was a fiery young group of fellows with a lot of vinegar. To show you how young they were, my brother was not quite twenty at the time the band formed and Irving Ashby and Illinois Jacquet were about the same age. Ray Perry and Vernon Alley were maybe twenty-one or twenty-two. When Dexter Gordon joined us, he was the baby. I don't think he was even eighteen years old yet.
>
> I remember an unusual occurrence when we were playing the Regal Theater in Chicago. We were offstage ready to start the performance, just waiting for the curtain to be raised when all of a sudden we heard an argument in the wings. Gladys and Lionel were having heated words! This was a rarity between the two because usually Gladys did all of the talking and Lionel did all of the listening. But this particular time Lionel was refusing to go on stage and perform unless Gladys allowed him five dollars a day for

spending money. And he stayed off-stage until Gladys agreed that she would give him the five dollars a day. That's how tight she was with him.[6]

The *Amsterdam News* of November 29, 1941, carried a photo of Billie Holiday with a caption that read:

Chanteuse with the style unique. Billie Holiday is one of the choice attractions on a super-bill which starts at the Apollo Theatre this Friday. Lionel Hampton, master of the vibes and ace hide-beater and one-time mainstay of Benny Goodman's ork, leads his own hot aggregation into the Apollo for its first Eastern appearance to headline the proceedings. And as if that isn't enough, the Three Peters Sisters, those merry mountains of melody, Big Time Crip, the amazing lad who dances on one leg better than most do on two and the team of Joyner and Foster are also billed. Thanksgiving is past but for such a bill local fans can but be grateful.

The show at the Apollo also included a "talking picture program." Think about the bill, and the thrill, that Dexter must have felt at the age of eighteen to be a part of these moments. The band played as many shows as tickets could be sold for, and this is what he referred to as his college education, musically and in all ways possible. Whenever he had some difficult tours in Europe or when he was making the film *Round Midnight* and getting up at 5 a.m. to prepare, he would say, "*I was on the road with Lionel Hampton. Nothing is difficult after that experience.*"

In December 1941 the band played the Apollo Theater in Harlem on the bill with Billie Holiday. Dexter always considered this *the* moment when he could call himself a real jazz musician. He never forgot it. The band had sixteen musicians and the audience went wild for them. On December 24 the band recorded four sides for Decca in New York: "Just for You," "Southern Echoes," "My Wish," and "Nola." This was Dexter's very first studio recording. He said he felt like he was on his way to fulfilling his dream when those sides were released and he could hear himself on the radio. Lionel Hampton:

We went over so big at the Apollo Theater that every time we appeared there, the crowds lined up around the block for tickets. Gladys saw this and made a deal with Jack Schiffman, who owned the Apollo. Instead of a straight salary, we would play for a percentage of the gross. We would also play as many shows a day as we could fit in. There were times when we played nine or ten shows a day, and still people were turned away at the ticket booth.[7]

By 1941 Dexter had started to gain a name for himself. Coleman Hawkins recognized him as one of his twelve favorite tenor players in

Music and Rhythm magazine: "Dexter Gordon is another young new-comer, and like [Don] Byas he's doing very well by himself. In drawing comparison, I would say that he is most closely allied to Charlie Barnet. Dexter has the same drive and push, a terrific rhythmic attack. Of course, Dexter hasn't developed as far as Charlie, but I think he will." George Simon said in *Metronome* magazine that "young Dexter, a handsome six foot four eighteen-year-old comes across with some fine melodic ideas as well as a mighty pretty tone."

The band made another southern tour in early 1942. There were two tours a year, sometimes three. On one tour, things heated up in Mississippi. Normally, the musicians would have to get their food from the back doors of restaurants, but when the bus pulled into a filling station for repairs, Dexter and Joe Newman decided to eat in the nearby diner. They walked right in the front door. Dexter would always say, "I'm from Los Angeles and we don't do that segregation thing there." (That might have been an exaggeration, but it was a line he liked to repeat.) When the waitress said, "Where would you like to sit?" they were surprised, but they took up her offer and sat down and started eating. Lionel Hampton:

> When the band saw Dexter and Joe sitting down, their eyes popped out. Then they started going in and sitting down, too. Pretty soon, this Mississippi diner is filled with black guys ordering and eating.

The way Dexter recalled the moment, when the filling station attendant finished repairing the bus and realized that the band had gone into the diner, he rushed in and shouted, "Where's my gun?" The musicians moved fast and the band manager tried to calm the situation by explaining that they were from New York and Hollywood and didn't know the local customs. Dexter and Joe Newman told the story over and over for many years and would burst out laughing, remembering how fast that bus left Mississippi.

On May 26, 1942, the band recorded "Flying Home" on Decca with an arrangement by Milt Buckner. Illinois Jacquet's solo on the recording made the tune a hit. From then on, crowds would demand to hear it at length at every performance, and went crazy every time. It could go on for twenty minutes and there was always applause and stomping and yelling for more. This was quite an experience for a young man who left home at seventeen, but after a while Dexter began thinking about playing something else and became restless. Lionel Hampton:

> Dexter Gordon was a real showman, and I was sorry when he left. He was always late, just barely made it onto the bandstand when we started to play.

One time at the Paradise in Detroit, he still wasn't there when we started, and we were doing a number that he was supposed to solo on. Just as we go to his solo, he walked out of the wings blowing his horn. The crowd went wild. So did the guys and I. I couldn't even be angry with him, because I couldn't believe the effect he had on that audience.[8]

Thinking about this makes me laugh, because people were always asking about Dexter being late and worrying about him showing up on time. I hadn't realized until working on the book that this tendency started so young. Somehow, he always managed to make a dramatic entrance and all was forgotten when he began to play.

A 1942 mention of Dexter in a jazz publication reads: "Dexter Keith Gordon, tenor, the Superman of jazz, only 19, he's 6 ft. 4 in. and a dead ringer for Joe Louis. Gigged on clarinet at 13, later got an alto and only took up tenor less than two years ago. Lionel knew his pa and got him to let the lad go right from school into the Hampton band. Likes Lester Young, Don Byas, Ben Webster. Boys call him 'Stoop.'"

Here is another excellent example of how a jazz myth begins. Dexter's father had died in 1937, so he did not get to know that his son was going on the road with Lionel in 1940. Dexter was hardly a dead ringer for the boxer Joe Louis, although some of his Eastside friends thought so and this observation would be repeated in the press often. Even so, to be mentioned at all at that early age must have been quite thrilling to young Dexter.

One of Dexter's favorite stories was about a night in 1943 during a stop in New York with the Hampton band to play an engagement at the Apollo. That night at Minton's Playhouse was his second encounter with his idol, Lester Young, and a first with Ben Webster. His path would cross with Ben's years later when they got to perform and record together and live in Copenhagen at the same time. Dexter:

> After the gig at the Apollo with the Lionel Hampton Band, some of the cats decided to go over to Minton's, on West 118th Street in Harlem. We took a couple of cabs over to the club. Lester Young and Ben Webster were sitting in with a rhythm section of Thelonious Monk, Kenny Clarke and Oscar Pettiford, the house band. Lester and Ben were sitting down playing. Lester was wearing his pork-pie hat and Ben was wearing a slim-jim snap-brim Knox, with a jaunty feather sticking up on the side, Tyrolean style.
>
> Lamar Wright, Joe Newman, Joe Wilder, Ernie Royal and L. D. Jackson, Carnell Lyons and Jesse Franklin (bebop tap dancers who were working the Apollo with us) had gotten the word that "The Tenor Players" were in attendance at Minton's at that very moment.

There was a whole lot of shoving, shakin' and nudging going on as we made our way down the aisle to the bandstand. Centered in front of the bandstand was a tiny dance floor with several couples one-stepping, and grinding away. The rhythm section was watching my approach, digging the tug of war, understood what was going down and grinning and pointing to the action. This long tall kid being pushed up on the stand to challenge Ben and Lester, the masters! In this era musicians played sitting down, the swing era. Later in the bebop era, the horn players stood up and played, except of course for the pianist and drummer who get seats with their instruments.

I tiptoed on the stand and found a chair behind "the Masters." Monk laughing and mouthing, "What you doing up here, boy?" I gave him my chicken-shit grin and pointed to my boys, grinning in the corner. Fortunately, the band was playing a known standard tune, "Sweet Georgia Brown." Monk gave me the OK and I began to play. My boys were hollering and in a little way I was sounding good. After eight bars, Ben says, "Who the hell is this?" In order for him to turn around he had to use his whole body because his neck was naturally and permanently stiff. There I was staring into these bulging Frog eyes. I almost swallowed my mouthpiece. On the other hand, after a half chorus, Lester stretches and casually, coolly, looks back and gives me the once over.

I played a couple of choruses, not to overdo it, and while the band finished up I packed up and was a hero to our gang—they're shouting "Alright, alright, Dex, my man Dex, yeah Dex." I was glad to get out of there in one piece. But, of course, a minor incident like this added to my rep and legend. "Yeah man, Dex played at Minton's last night with Ben and Lester . . ." "Aw shit, man, you lyin' . . . " "Naw, man, I was there." It was like I had put the gloves on for three rounds with Kid Gavilán or somebody. I think there is an affinity between boxers and musicians. Both professions take plenty of heart and only a few become legends. Both take study, practice, dedication, and courage.

By the end of 1943, Dexter had left the Hampton band and gone back to Los Angeles. He played locally with Lester Young's brother, Lee Young, and Jesse Price and spent a few weeks with Fletcher Henderson's big band. It was during this period that he made his first recordings: "Found a New Baby," "Rosetta," "Sweet Lorraine," and "I Blowed and Gone" with Nat King Cole on piano and Harry "Sweets" Edison on trumpet.

Dexter didn't know it yet, but a dream encounter with another trumpeter—the legendary grand master of the instrument—would be coming up next.

CHAPTER 5

Pops

I had then and still have a very large band—made up of
youngsters I'm sure you haven't heard of . . . But they are
all first class musicians . . . They have to be in order to be
in Satchmo's orchestra . . . Cute?

—Louis Armstrong[1]

Dexter:

*He was a born ambassador and he really was a beautiful, warm human
being, just the way you hear him and see him on stage and on film. That was
Louis. He was always the same, always a beautiful man.*[2]

*I was working at the Club Alabam, which was a nightclub on Central
Avenue with Lee Young [Lester's younger brother] who was the leader of
the band. Art Pepper was in the band. We had about six, seven men . . .
Mingus was in the band too. This was a gig that was from eight to midnight.
This is when they started having a curfew and everything closed at midnight.
The after-hours joints would open up after the clubs closed. They were
something like speakeasies. I was working out at a joint called Honey
Murphy's which was in deep Watts. We had Jesse Price, drummer out of
Kansas City, with us. He had come up with Basie and the piano player
was called Jack LaRue because he looked like the movie star with the same
name.*

*One night Louis' manager came out and he heard me and then the next
night Louis came out. I didn't know he was there. After the set someone
came over to me and said, "Son, say son, I really liked that sound you get."
I looked up and it was Louis. I said, "Thank you, thank you very much." It
was a great honor. So that was the first night and then the next night, the
manager came out and asked me if I'd like to join the band. By this time I
felt that I had built on my foundation and I wanted to get back to New York
so I joined the band and we did a couple of flicks in Hollywood.* Atlantic
City *and* Pillow to Post *with Dorothy Dandridge and Ida Lupino. In those
movies, they shot the scenes with Louis and the band and then when they
showed the movies in the South, they would cut those scenes out.*

Oh, that was a thrill. Every night. He had such a big, beautiful, fat, blaring sound, just ran right through you. And that was really the reason I joined the band, to play with him. To play with him every night. The band was a mediocre type band. He was playing the swing type arrangements from the '30's . . . especially "Ain't Misbehavin" and "I'm Confessin'." The arrangements were just a showcase for him. But, he liked me and he always gave me a chance to blow. He featured me a lot.

All the memories and feeling—he was gorgeous, he really was. I knew he liked reefer and I brought several cans of some real Mexican moto down, tastes like the good earth, and took three drags, you know, that's all you need. So we left Hollywood, and went up the Coast to visit Frisco and Portland—we were doing theaters and we hadn't got into the one-nighters, but this is on the West Coast so it's a little different, but anyway whether it was the club date or the ballroom on every night, intermissions, I'd come out with my Mexican moto and he had a big paper bag full of, what do you call it, New Orleans Golden Leaf . . . So we'd trade off rounds of smoke and then after about a week or so I noticed that he didn't bring out the Golden Leaf anymore. Another week or so goes by, so one night I said, "Pops, whatever happened to all that New Orleans Golden Leaf ?" He said, "Shit, son, that's like bringing a hamburger to a banquet." So I mean, it was a great time in my life, with him.

Working with Louis was love, love, love . . . That was what it was all about. All love. He was just beautiful—always beautiful. It was just a gas being with him. He let me play all the time. He really dug me.[3]

Dexter joined the Louis Armstrong Orchestra in May 1944 and stayed for six months, until November 1944, when he got an offer to join the Billy Eckstine band. This experience shaped Dexter's life in many ways. He was forever grateful to Louis Armstrong for liking his sound and giving him the chance to play. But mainly he was grateful for the time he got to spend with the great man, observing how he treated people and how he brought so much beauty to the music. Dexter always paid tribute to Pops, and if he had won the Oscar in 1987 for his role in *Round Midnight,* he was going to say, "I would like to dedicate this award to Louis Armstrong for devoting his life to the music we love." Then he was going to sing "What a Wonderful World." If anyone ever said anything disparaging about Louis, which was fashionable at a certain time, Dexter would get out of his seat and stand up and remind the person that there would be no possibility of making a living as a jazz musician without the sacrifices made by Louis Armstrong. He would also remind people that it was Louis who in 1957 was quoted in the newspapers saying, "The way they are treating my people in the South, the government can go to hell. It's getting so bad a colored man hasn't got any country." He also reminded people that Louis said President

FIGURE 4. The Louis Armstrong Orchestra performing at the Seattle Civic Auditorium, July 17, 1944. That's Dexter in the front row, far left. Photograph by Al Smith. © Museum of History and Industry, MOHAI, Seattle, Al Smith Collection. 2014.49.002–027–0096

Eisenhower had "no guts" to let Arkansas governor Orval Faubus call in the National Guard to prevent black children from integrating Little Rock's Central High School.

When Dexter joined the orchestra, the first gigs were in California, beginning with a performance on May 26, 1944, at the Trianon Ballroom in South Gate, about seven miles southeast of downtown Los Angeles. Thanks to the excellent research on Louis Armstrong done by numerous historians and especially the work of Ricky Riccardi, who can ferret out the most obscure detail about Louis and his bands, we are able to follow Dexter for the six months he spent with Armstrong. These months are especially significant because they include many appearances at army bases during wartime. Dexter, twenty-one at the time, had refused to serve in the army when he was called by the draft just before he joined the Armstrong band. As an avid reader of newspapers, Dexter was very aware of what was happening in the world and the war. We can wonder if he and Louis (who was then in his mid forties) discussed these news dispatches.

During this world-changing period when Dexter was with Louis Armstrong, the war was coming to an end. Germany surrendered in May 1945, Japan surrendered in September, and World War II was officially ended. There was hope, at least on the Allied side, that the world had changed for the better, especially among people of color and particularly for Black men who had served in the military.

When we study jazz history we must consider how the musicians who were working on the road were affected during this wartime period. As Dexter said many times later in his life, "It seems as if bebop was created by musicians who refused to fight in World War II." Refusing military service was an unpopular stand, and each person made the decision for his own reason. Some musicians, like Connie Kay and Sun Ra, were conscientious objectors. Some went to dramatic lengths to be given 4-F status, which meant that they were deemed not qualified for service in the Armed Forces by a Military Entrance Processing Station under "established physical, mental, or moral standards." Dizzy Gillespie avoided service by telling his local draft board he would not serve: "In this stage of my life here in the United States, whose foot has been in my ass?"

The Louis Armstrong Orchestra was extremely popular at the many military bases at which it performed. Photos of those performances show us that the soldiers were in segregated units. When Dexter was called up for the draft and was told to move into the section for "colored," he told the sergeant that they didn't have segregation in Los Angeles and he refused to move. After a psychiatric evaluation, he was given 4-F status. This doesn't mean that those who refused to serve didn't support the cause and weren't sympathetic to the great loss and suffering that the war invoked. Dexter read the African American press as often as he could and was very aware of what was known as the "Double V Campaign." In 1942, the *Philadelphia Courier* published a letter from James Thompson, a young Black cafeteria worker from Wichita, Kansas, who questioned whether he could defend a nation that treated him as a second-class citizen. Thompson called for a "Double V" approach to fighting—for victory over the fascism of "enemies from without" and also over the continued prejudice of "enemies from within." By that he meant the injustices of Jim Crow-style racial segregation in the Armed Forces and in the states. This public criticism led to the banning of Black newspapers from military libraries and to FBI director J. Edgar Hoover seeking to charge Black publishers with treason. The publishers met with the U.S. attorney general and struck a deal that allowed them to print the truth so long as they didn't escalate opposition to the war.

Dexter always said that some of the best musicians didn't get big names or record deals and were overlooked, but it didn't mean they weren't as good as anyone who stayed on the road and sacrificed a home life and stable living for life as a jazz musician. With that thought in mind, here are the personnel of the Louis Armstrong Orchestra when Dexter joined the band in May 1944: (trumpets) Jesse Brown, Lester Currant, Andrew "Fats" Ford, Thomas Grider; (trombones) Larry Anderson, Joe Taswell Baird, Adam Martin; (alto saxophones) John Brown, Willard Brown; (tenor saxophones) Dexter Gordon, Teddy McRae; (baritone saxophone) Ernest Thompson; (piano) Ed Swanston; (guitar) Emmett Slay; (bass) Alfred Moore; (drums) James Harris; (vocals) Velma Middleton, Jimmy Ross; (trumpet, vocals) Louis Armstrong. Sixteen musicians, one stupendous girl singer, one male singer, and one Louis Armstrong, all traveling and playing music in a time of war.

The recordings of this band came mainly from radio broadcasts for the Armed Forces Radio Service and the Jubilee Programs that were produced mainly for African American troops. On June 7, 1944, the band played in Stockton Fields, California, and in the version of "Ain't Misbehavin'," the broadcast announcer says, "Louis Armstrong singing 'Ain't Mis*believing.*'" Just before the tenor solo, Louis can be heard beckoning "Brother Dexter!" Then twenty-one-year-old Dexter comes on with a signature solo that reminds us of what was to come. The entire composition runs only two minutes fifty-five seconds, which is how long musicians had to tell a story in those 78 rpm days.

What also makes this performance extraordinary is that it came one day after the Normandy invasion, also called Operation Overlord, which was the largest amphibious military assault in history. Some 156,000 American, British, and Canadian forces landed on five beaches along a fifty-mile stretch of the heavily fortified coast of France. By late August 1944, all of northern France had been liberated, and in the following spring Germany surrendered.

On July 2 the band played in Twin Falls, Idaho. On July 17 they were in Seattle, Washington. On August 18 they played at Fort Huachuca, Arizona. That was the training headquarters of the Ninety-Second and Ninety-Third Infantry Divisions, composed of African American troops. These were "colored," segregated units that fought in both World War I and World War II. On September 12 the band played at Camp Reynolds, Pennsylvania, the army base where ten months earlier (July 11, 1943) simmering racial tensions had exploded into violence and an exchange of gunfire that left one African American soldier dead and seven others wounded.

When they toured California, the band filmed scenes in two movies, *Pillow to Post* and *Atlantic City*. The wartime romantic comedy *Pillow to Post* follows a tired traveling saleswoman, played by Ida Lupino, who goes to great lengths to find a room for the night by pretending to be married to a soldier, played by Vincent Sherman. In the film, the Armstrong band performs "Whatcha Say," with Dorothy Dandridge and Louis singing together. Dexter is not visible on camera in the scene. We may wonder what Dexter was thinking when he went to the Warner Bros. lot in Burbank to film and record the scene. He had grown up in Los Angeles as a big film fan, and later in life he would tell stories about his boyhood friends being taken to the studio to play "natives" in Tarzan films while he was left behind because he wasn't dark enough. In *Atlantic City*, the whole band is shown and Dexter makes the most of his time on screen. Since the musicians in the scene were actually pantomiming with their instruments to music already recorded, Dexter seems to have taken the moment to be certain he'd be noticed on camera. Dorothy Dandridge[4] performs "Harlem on Parade" in front of the band, and then Louis appears singing "Ain't Misbehavin'." He sounds so relaxed and so Louis as always, while Dexter can be seen right over his left shoulder. Dexter appears to be holding his horn in a very Lester Young tilt. In the next scene, with the legendary piano and tap dance team Buck and Bubbles,[5] the band also appears and Dexter is obviously enjoying the dancing.

On December 21, 1946, Louis Armstrong wrote a letter on his Satchmo stationery from Anderson, Indiana, to *Melody Maker* magazine in London:

> On tour—U.S.A.
> We usually travel by bus most of the times . . . P.S. THAT'S "Charabank" to you . . . Tee Hee . . . During the War—we traveled to every Army Camp and Naval Base in America—laying out the Jive (hot music) sending those Sailors and Soldiers like nobody's business . . . And boys believe me they really did eat it up—yum yum . . . Honest—I played so many Army Camps until I'd begun to feel like I was a Lt. General, or, etc. . . . We would give them an hour or more concert—playing lot of my recordings and popular tunes also—whatever their hearts desired . . . I had then and still have a very large band—made up of youngsters I'm sure you haven't heard of . . . But they are all first class musicians . . . They have to be in order to be in Satchmo's orchestra . . . Cute?[6]

Dexter's time with Louis ended after he got a call in September 1944 with an invitation to join the Billy Eckstine band. Dexter went to Louis to let him know:

> *Pops asked me if I wanted more money. I told him that wasn't the problem. It was that we young guys wanted to play some new music. He wished me the best and said I always had a place in his band if I wanted to come back.*

Anytime he was asked about Louis Armstrong, Dexter would smile and nod his head and say,

> *Oh Pops. He was the best.*

CHAPTER 6

Blowin' the Blues Away

I play it cool
And dig all jive.
That's the reason
I stay alive.
My motto,
As I live and learn,
is:
Dig And Be Dug
In Return.

—"Motto," by Langston Hughes[1]

The first time I heard Dexter would probably be with the
Billy Eckstine band. "Blow Mr. Gene, Blow Mr. Dexter,
too!" and "I Love the Rhythm in a Riff." Dexter was a
continuum of the bebop style that started with Lester.
Charlie Parker also played some of Lester's solos when he
was learning, and then he carried it further, and he became
the genius of bebop. What was so interesting about Dexter
is the way he played swing. He could really swing. He was
a hard-swinging musician. From the musical standpoint,
Dexter played
kind of behind the beat, and this is a comfortable way to
swing. He's not real nervous. He played in the pocket,
right in the pocket, and groove, and that's what was so
good about him.

—Jimmy Heath[2]

As soon as Dexter got that call to join the Billy Eckstine band while he was still working with Louis Armstrong in September 1944, he knew right away that he had to say yes. He explained to Louis that the young musicians with Billy were trying to do something new and that he would have to leave the Armstrong band. Louis said he understood and that Dexter could come back if things didn't work out.

That something new was the early days of bebop. At the same time that the war was coming to an end, Black culture exploded with unprecedented exuberance and innovation. For musicians like Dexter, that meant breaking out from the constraints of the traditional dance bands and allowing improvisation to extend into unknown places. Dexter said that the "young turks" wanted to express a social statement through their music. They were developing their own lifestyles around the new music at a time when things were moving very fast for them and for the world. Many of these young beboppers had stayed out of the army. Dexter said that they were committed to making a change. "It was a revolution," he said. Instead of endless repetitions of swing standards, the young beboppers—Dizzy Gillespie, Charlie Parker, Thelonious Monk, Bud Powell, and others—evolved into masters of a dazzling new improvisational poetry, every night reinventing their music with new harmonies, tempos, rhythms, and complexities. Exuberant audiences started leaving the dance floors to fill a growing number of intimate jazz clubs and larger concert halls across the country.

Dexter joined up with the Eckstine band at the Howard Theatre in Washington, D.C., on September 21, 1944, the last night of the band's engagement there. Dexter:

> I hadn't heard the band before. I really didn't know what to expect. I joined them at the Howard Theatre in Washington, D.C. taking the chair of Lucky Thompson, who had just left the band. And man, I didn't have any rehearsal, just sat in with the band cold and I didn't know what was going on. The whole conception was new. Art Blakey was on drums, Tommy Potter on bass, John Malachi was on piano, Connie Wainwright on guitar. The reed section was Gene Ammons, myself, John Jackson, Leo Parker and a third alto player named Billy Frazier. A few months later Sonny Stitt took his place. But gee, man, that first night there was so much going on that I couldn't believe it. It was such a difference, coming out of Louis' band to a band like this. It was a whole new world for me because here was the exact opposite—crazy arrangements, wild young musicians, the esprit de corps—I was just thrilled. This was the kind of band that I think every musician dreams of playing in.
>
> It was the last show on the last night of the engagement at the theatre. They opened up with a number called "Blitz"—an up-tempo Jerry Valentine

FIGURE 5. The Billy Eckstine Band sax section (left to right): Gene Ammons, Leo Parker, John Jackson, Bill Frazier, Dexter. Photograph by Teenie Harris. © Carnegie Museum of Art, Charles "Teenie" Harris Archive, Pittsburgh, PA.

arrangement. They were off to the races—everything was flying. Every time Art Blakey would roll and kick I'd just come up out of the chair! Yeah, Billy's band was the band—the first modern jazz big band. It's just too bad that it started during the war at a time when big bands were on the way out. It stayed together a couple of years until things really started getting tight. The cost of living was rising every day, so the handwriting was on the wall regarding the big bands. I was with the band about a year, leaving before it broke up. Bird was in there originally when the band was formed in [early] 1944. When I joined in September 1944, he had already left and John Jackson had taken over on first alto. Diz was still in the band and, of course, that was a gas.[3]

"There was no band that sounded like Billy Eckstine's," wrote Dizzy Gillespie in his autobiography, *TO BE, or not . . . TO BOP.* "Our attack was strong, and we were playing bebop, the modern style. No other band like this one existed in the world."

On September 22 the band opened at the Apollo Theater in Harlem in an "all-headline revue" featuring Sarah Vaughan; the team of Leroy,

Leroy, and Juanita; and tap dancer Doris Smart. Reviews of the show mentioned the trumpet player Shorty McConnell on "Second Balcony Jump," the instrumental whose title became a joke, with at least three different stories about the derivation of its title. One version has it that during the Lionel Hampton band's 1941 concert at the Apollo, a man in the second balcony got so excited when they were playing "Flying Home" that he climbed up on the rail and started shouting, "I'm flying, I'm flying!" And then he jumped. Lionel suggested that Jerry Valentine wrote "Second Balcony Jump" for Earl Hines on the inspiration of that incident. Another version has the title referring to a fan who fell out of a balcony during an Eckstine performance of "Jelly, Jelly."[4] In any event, "Second Balcony Jump" became the Eckstine band's theme song and Dexter usually played lead on it.

The gig at the Apollo drew raves and Dexter was thrilled to see the theater packed with bebop fans who wanted to hear the new sound. They played seven shows a day. Eckstine, movie-star handsome as he was, became a huge star and was sought out for product endorsements. One was for Snow White hair dressing: "For radiant, sporty looking hair, use the hair dressing Billy Eckstine endorses." After a gig at the Brooklyn Palace on October 7, the band went to Pittsburgh where Eckstine was the hometown hero. They performed at the Hill City Auditorium to a cheering crowd.

The band went on to play weeklong engagements at the Royal Theatre in Baltimore, Club Bali in Washington, D.C., the Metropolitan in Cleveland, the Paradise in Detroit, and the Savoy Ballroom in Chicago. After a return engagement at the Brooklyn Palace in New York on December 2, the band gathered for a recording session for De Luxe. Among the songs they recorded were "If That's the Way You Feel," "I Want to Talk about You," "Opus X," "I'll Wait and Pray," and "The Real Thing Happened to Me." Another was "Blowin' the Blues Away," a rousing bebop blues classic composed by Jerry Valentine that starts with a twenty-four-bar piano and bass intro (by John Malachi and Tommy Potter, respectively) followed by a brief vocal by Eckstine that sets up an escalating series of tenor saxophone chase choruses between "Mister Gene" (Ammons) and "Mister Dexter":

> I got the blues 'cause my baby put me down . . .
> I'm gonna grab a train and leave this lonesome town
> So blow Mister Gene and blow Mister Dexter too . . .
> Maybe you can help me and blow away the blues

Two takes were issued of the song, with Dizzy's trumpet soaring high above the rest of the ensemble on the closing chorus.

The band ended the year with a Christmas week engagement at the Apollo. When Dizzy left the band to go out on his own in 1945, he got Fats Navarro to fill his chair in the Eckstine band. Dexter loved Fats and said he was one of the best trumpet players he had ever known. His early death in 1950 at the age of twenty-six was one of the losses that Dexter often lamented. While traveling on the bus with the Eckstine band, Dexter became one of a group of saxophone players that the others dubbed "The Unholy Four"—along with Sonny Stitt, Leo Parker, and John Jackson. They would sit in the back of the bus, smoking reefer and practicing their parts. According to Dexter, this made them ready for anything once they arrived at the gig, and no other band's reed section could come close to matching their level of precision and swing. Of course, they also got their name because of their unruly and raucous behavior at times.

In the front of the bus sat Bob Redcross, Eckstine's road manager. He would read out loud to the band from the daily newspapers, mostly news about World War II, which looked to be finally approaching its end. The Japanese were increasing their use of kamikaze tactics against the American navy, which was attacking Japanese strongholds on the island of Formosa. Hitler was now firmly ensconced in his Berlin bunker with his companion Eva Braun while Allied forces pressed ever closer. Franklin D. Roosevelt was sworn in for his fourth term as U.S. president. The German concentration camp at Auschwitz was liberated by Soviet troops.

Dexter always remembered Redcross reading the news as they rolled along the highways, practicing, napping, talking. He said that the band bus became a world unto itself where so many things that were happening outside seemed impossible to fathom. In February 1945, the band traveled west to play at the Club Plantation in Los Angeles but Dexter didn't go with them. After he began showing up late for rehearsals, or showed signs of being high, Eckstine warned him to get himself together, *or else*. When Dexter failed to reform, Eckstine fired him. When the band got to Los Angeles, Budd Johnson, who was also the musical director, sat in Dexter's tenor sax chair. This caused Dexter great embarrassment since Los Angeles was his hometown and people were waiting to see and hear him with the Eckstine band. When I had my "Eastside Elders Social" in Los Angeles in 1998, there were people there who swore they saw Dexter with the band when they came to town, but memory has a way of playing tricks on people. Dexter never made that trip to the West. He did return to the band in late 1945 to record for National on "Lonesome Lover Blues," "A Cottage for Sale," "I Love a Rhythm in a Riff," and "Last Night." Dexter:

> *What happened was that the Unholy Four left the band. Ammons stayed, Gene was a loner. He's got a thing going now where he's an Unholy 'One.' . . . We had been fuckin' up really—specially me—and wanted more bread. And he [Eckstine] didn't want to come up . . . I don't know whether he didn't want or couldn't. I don't know what it was, but anyway he didn't. In fact, for a couple of months before I left the band, he had been bringing tenor players up on the stand to try the book. It was a very together reed section, so all the cats split. Of course, since that time—since I've mellowed a little bit—I feel kind of bad about that. Because actually B was and is a great guy, and it was nothing he had done to me. It was just me, just youth.*[5]

Dexter and Gene Ammons remained friends from those early days, played together whenever possible, and even recorded together at the Montreux Jazz Festival in 1973, a year before Gene's death. Dexter said that with one note, often a low B-flat, Gene could get a crowd to go wild. Dexter liked to tell a story about an ongoing argument he had with Gene. Dexter would tell Gene to stop coming up behind his solos and playing exactly what Dexter had just played. News of this conflict must have made the rounds because once, when Dexter ran into Lester Young, Lester said, "Well, Son, I hear you and Brother Gene had a spat." Dexter told Lester that he was tired of Gene stepping up and copying his solos. Pres looked back at him and said, "Well . . . is that so?" Dexter immediately realized that, of course, *he* had been playing many of Lester's solos note for note, and he had just made a total fool of himself. Whenever he told this story, he would cover his face with his large hands and sigh.

In 1987, when we were living in Cuernavaca and Dexter was making notes for his autobiography, he made it clear how much he loved his life in the 1940s, touring the country with the three great bands led by Lionel Hampton, Louis Armstrong, and Billy Eckstine. He found everything about the life enthralling, even the long bus rides to new places, the musicians and other colorful characters he met, the gigs, the food, the beautiful women, and especially the after-hours sessions in sultry, mysterious, dark, and exciting places, none more so than the infamous Mae's Place in Harlem. From Dexter's notepads:

MAE'S PLACE

Mae's Place, located in Harlem on West 114th Street, was a meeting place for dark and white in a very exclusive atmosphere. Actually, it was a den of iniquity for those who really liked it hot. It catered to the top entertainers of Harlem and Broadway, like Tallulah Bankhead and her crowd, John Barrymore, etc. Also, the big-time playboys and pimps and, of course, their ladies. Society people from Park Avenue and invariably members of the mob, the numbers barons and others of that stature. The main attraction at Mae's was the drugs. The very best quality cocaine, heroin, smoking opium (Hop Sing) and Crescent marijuana cigarettes with the filter and trademark of the Crescent Moon. Authentic goods.

Society Red paid his first social call to Mae's Place in the hip company of Lady Day, Clark Monroe and his lady. It was after closing time on the Street late in forty-five. Billie said to me, "Come on, baby, I'm going to show you something special this morning."

Everybody laughed and Clark said, "Yeah, come on with us Dex."

"OK."

We piled into his Lincoln Continental and went Uptown. We pulled up in front of a light-colored building with a fancy awning out front. We were greeted by the doorman, in uniform. (There was one man on the door and another one at the desk.) "Clark Monroe and guests to see Madame Mae." The doorman relayed the information upstairs and motioned us to the elevator. Arriving upstairs to the top floor, the sixth, we were greeted by a Black dude wearing some kind of Indian suit and discreetly ushered into the apartment. We gave up our hats and coats and proceeded into a large, lush living room filled with pillows and cushions.

There was a white baby grand piano situated in a corner and the sound of another tinkling piano coming from the apartment next door. Settees, sofas, easy chairs and lush purple drapes filled out the room. The grande dame herself entered from stage right and immediately dominated the room. Mae was a well-preserved brown-skinned woman of indeterminate age, wearing a shimmering hostess gown and multiple jewels. She greeted Clark ("You pretty thing!") and Lady ("Miss Brown to you, but baby to me!") and winked. I said: "Hello and nice to meet you too." She replied: "My pleasure indeed," then she said, "Arthur, show Clark and his friends to the Hop Sing room."

Clark patted her on the buns and we were shown the way.

On another notepad, Dexter sketched out a screenplay for a movie that would show what life was really like for the twenty or so Black men who lived a portion of their lives traveling nonstop on the Billy Eckstine band bus, crisscrossing the country in 1944. He said that he would probably have to cast rappers to play these young musicians since they had the same wild look in their eyes as his band did in those early days on the road.

ON THE ECKSTINE BAND BUS
NOTES FOR A SCREENPLAY
BY DEXTER GORDON AND MAXINE GORDON, 1987

Setting:

> *It is 1944, somewhere in America.*
> *A large bus, perhaps an old Greyhound "Silversides."*
> *Rack in the back for band jackets.*
> *No bathroom.*
>
> *Each person always takes the same seat. Habits begin to appear as people settle into life on the road. Some sleep, some play cards, some talk, some keep an eye on the passing scene and comment to others who either listen or seem to be in their own world.*

Introduction:

These relationships, made over a period of six months to a year, are like schoolboy bonds that last a lifetime. The difference is that these boys become men at 17 or 18. They have a mission. They were born with a common goal and have dedicated themselves to learning to play jazz and to spread the word in order to enrich people's lives.

They all have common experiences even though their physical backgrounds vary.

They are united through an unspoken bond of being jazz musicians. It is a family, clan, tribe.

What makes them unique and what draws people to the music and to them?

How do you live a life that is one and the same with your art?

A life that improvises music cannot run by another's rules. This may bring problems if based on an ordinary observer's rules for behavior in a society that does not always understand what art is, or what an artist is, or why there is nothing without music.

How has this music survived?

The artist is not self-destructive.

The jazz artist survives and the music thrives despite the exploitation and attempt at destruction by ill-meaning usurpers and well-meaning elitists.

This story attempts to eliminate the incorrect information, often accepted as fact, that depicts jazz musicians as suffering from excesses that make them appear to be victims.

It is a story of the strength and bravery of these young revolutionaries who went out into a world of enemies to share their insight.

The musicians who came together in Billy Eckstine's band became leaders of groups who taught younger sidemen to be leaders, to stand tall, about the dullness of the worlds of greed and cruelty to those who are fearless enough to stand apart. They have always had each other.

Even after a death of one of the members, they continue to speak of him in the present tense. They depend on what they learned from this time together.

It is an unmatched era in the development of modern music, and an influence on the lives of all those fortunate enough to be touched without being limited by language, birthplace, size, shape or hairstyle.

These young men thought they were among the first to refuse to go in the back door through the kitchen. They didn't think that rule made any sense.

They didn't do stupid things. No discussion was necessary.

There are recurring incidents and identical moments in all their lives.

Show the energy produced by these musicians traveling, working, sleeping, eating and growing up together with the same purpose in life and having each other to reinforce their goals.

Why does nothing else matter when they reach the bandstand and the music comes through them from a higher force?

When you limit a story about what is jazz to one person, you make it difficult for people to understand that it is something developed and innovated by a very small group of people who are readily recognizable to each other.

In this story you see the music develop by the interaction of a group of remarkable characters.

Personnel:

Alto 1: John Jackson (Eggs Foo Young)
Feature: "Opus X"

Alto 2: Sonny Stitt (Stringbean)
Feature: "Jeepers Creepers" (Harry Warren, Johnny Mercer)

Tenor 1: Gene Ammons (Jug) (Son of Albert Ammons)
Feature: "Second Balcony Jump"

Tenor 2: Dexter Gordon (Vice Prez)
Feature: "Air Mail Special," "Blowin' the Blues Away" (Mr. B vocal)

Baritone Sax: Leo Parker (The Kid)
Feature: "Mad Lad"

Trumpet 1: Gayle Brockman (beautiful lead player)

Trumpet 2: John Birks Gillespie (Dizzy)
Feature: "Night in Tunisia"

Trumpet 3: Marion Hazel (Boonie)
Spot Solos

Trumpet 4: Maurice McConnell (Shorty)
Feature: "Stormy Monday Blues" (by Jerry Valentine)

Trumpet 2: Fats Navarro (Dizzy replacement, 1945) (Fats, Fat Girl)

Drums: Art Blakey (Boston Blackie)

Trombone 1: Chippy Alcott (arranger) (Chips)
Feature: "Mr. Chips"

Trombone 2: Jerry Valentine (Arranger)

Trombone 3: Taswell Baird (Taz) (with Bird in Jay McShann's band)

Bass trombone: Howard Johnson (Bags)

Guitar: Connie Wainwright (plays like Freddie Green) (Race Riot)
Feature: "Nurses"

Piano: John Malachi (later Sarah's accompanist)

Bass: Tommy Potter

Girl vocalist: Sarah Vaughan (Sassy)
Feature: "I'll Wait and Pray"

Band leader, vocalist: Billy Eckstine (Mr. B)

Mr. B's Confidante: Bob Redcross (Red Cross) Road Manager

Notes:

Each character has moments identical with others that were pivotal in their lives as jazz musicians.
   When was the first time you heard Duke Ellington's band?
   When was the first time you heard Dizzy and Bird?
   What did you think? How did it change things?
   Do you think the war is changing things? Does it affect the music?
   What do you think will be happening to jazz in 30 years?
   When did you leave home to go on the road?
   Do you ever think about a life outside of jazz?
   "The phone calls": How did you get your first gig on the road?
   How did you get the gig with Eckstine?
   Whatever happened to Lucky or why did Lucky leave the band?[6]
   It seems to be impossible to portray Dizzy or Bird by using actors. Their personalities are too difficult to capture. Better to talk about them and have actors portray characters who are not as well-known but who are very colorful.
   For instance, Fats Navarro was of Cuban descent from Key West, and brought a Latin influence to the band and fired a gun out the window of the bus as they traveled. A big man with a small high voice who lived fast and short in years but left a tremendous legacy.
   The Unholy Four: They hung out together, practiced together, got high together and were bad boys together until they got on the bandstand and then they were the best saxophone section out there. The Unholy Four: Dexter, John Jackson, Leo Parker, Sonny Stitt.
   Why was Dizzy always kicking Dexter's chair? He thought Dex was nodding when he was actually listening to the music with his eyes closed.
   We see most of the scenes on the bus going to the gig. Each character has his feature and everything leads up to the concert or dance they are going to play. There are scenes at the gig that would seem to make playing music almost impossible but still they do not let anything stop their mission.

In Boston:

Men's room in a club where they are playing for dancing. Dexter and Art Blakey doing their business. Two sailors from the South enter and make comments because they have never seen Black men in a men's room used for all men before. One says, "It's getting dark in here." One says, "We must be in the wrong room, or someone is making a big mistake." Dexter and Art ignore them, wash their hands and start to leave when Mr. B comes in. The sailors continue to make remarks. The musicians don't say a word. As Art and Dexter start to leave, they hear a short commotion and look back. The sailors are lying on the floor and Mr. B is brushing himself off. He knocked them both out cold. He says, "Now let's go play some music for the people."
    Lesson #1: Beboppers will take no shit.
    Review of the Billy Eckstine Band at the Apollo in Metronome, *November 1944, Leonard Feather: "Dizzy's musicomic effects with the other three trumpets added wit to good music in 'Jelly Jelly,' and Eckstine adding his own horn to make it a five-trumpet climax. The fine drumming of Art Blakey; Johnny Malachi's intelligent piano; the Lester Youthful tenor of Dexter Gordon."*

Whenever Dexter reflected on his time working in New York and hanging out with Lady Day, he would get a rather wistful expression and talk about what might have been had she lived longer and not been treated so badly by the police and the world around her. He loved that story about going to Mae's Place with her and Clark Monroe. He said he was so young and naïve about life, and he had come from such a sheltered place. He did seem to grow up very quickly and learned to be as hip as possible in no time at all.

The notes for the screenplay were his reflections on one of the most inspiring and important times of his life. He often said that the Billy Eckstine band was the hippest band ever and that all the musicians took the message of bebop with them when they moved on from "the band." Of all the bands they would join or know, Eckstine's was the one that was always referred to as simply "the band." Dexter wanted to let the world know what it was like to be with those great young musicians and to show how dedicated they were to the music and to each other. The screenplay was the beginning of a project he was serious about but that he never got to complete, and it reminds me of all the ideas he had when he sat in that garden in Cuernavaca reflecting on his life.

CHAPTER 7

Business Lessons

Coltrane and I would listen to Dexter on his Savoy discs.
"Dexter's Deck" is one we really listened to, and "Dexter's Minor Mad," "Dexter's Cutting Out," "Long Tall
Dexter," "Dexter Rides Again," and "Dexterity." He was
letting you know that "this is me, and this is my style, and
this is what I do. I'm playing the saxophone with power."
He was a very powerful saxophonist—a big man—and he
was a very charming, handsome man, as the ladies would
know.

We listened to those sides at Coltrane's house or my
house. John lived in North Philly and I lived in South
Philly, but he would come down to my house, because I
had the band, and we'd rehearse in my living room. And
we'd put on earphones and listen to records for hours.

What was interesting when we listened to Dexter was
that Dexter set the pace. "The Chase," that's what we
played. "The Chase," with Wardell Gray, was a very big
jazz record, and a lot of Dexter's stuff—the bridge of
"Dexter's Deck" had it—was the rhythm. And also,
Dexter was in the bottom of his horn doing fingerings that
would make it sound like it was muted. He would do
certain fingerings that would make it sound like trumpets
and trombones with a mute. The clever musicians, like
Ben Webster and certain others, would find ways to make
the tone sound different. Ben could play a certain D and
make it sound different. He would blow and hum; it's a
way of expressing yourself. Dexter knew all those ways,
and Coltrane and myself, we all learned from hearing
them. You could play a D with the six fingers like you do
and it sounds a little muffled. Then you push a side key
open, which is in no books!

—Jimmy Heath[1]

A search for Dexter's first recording contract with Savoy Records begins with a flight to Atlanta and a sixty-mile drive to the Madison, Georgia, headquarters of Denon Digital Industries, which was a subsidiary of the Japanese electronics giant that owned the record label Nippon Columbia. Nippon had bought the Savoy label and catalog from Joe Fields of Muse Records, who had bought it from Arista Records, which had acquired it after the death of Herman Lubinsky, who had founded Savoy in 1942.[2] In a storage room, I pored through dusty and moldy cardboard boxes marked "Dexter Gordon" filled with old files, letters, and contracts. It was well worth the effort because I found some treasures that I didn't know still existed.

The other invaluable source of information on Savoy Records comes from Teddy Reig, the A&R (artists and repertoire) man for Savoy who tells his life story in *Reminiscing in Tempo: The Life and Times of a Jazz Hustler,* written with Ed Berger. Reig is the best source for details on Savoy's business practices. The preserved letters and contracts are invaluable in helping us trace the steps through these early years of jazz recording. Whenever I begin a discussion of what I call "the political economy of bebop"—that is, the role of public policy in influencing the economic and social welfare of the musicians—most people sigh and their eyelids grow heavy. But this information helps us understand the lives of the musicians we admire and the music from which we continue to find inspiration.

Jazz history is full of debates about who was first, or who should wear the crown for presiding over some important moment. When the great tenor saxophonist Teddy Edwards died in 2003, a small debate erupted over which tenor player was the first to actually record a bebop solo. Ira Gitler, the historian and journalist who has always been a leader of the Dexter Gordon crusade, pointed to Dexter's recorded solos with the Billy Eckstine band on "Blowin' the Blues Away" (December 5, 1944), "Lonesome Lover Blues" (May 2, 1945), and particularly "Blue 'n Boogie" with Dizzy Gillespie (February 9, 1945), which strongly display Dexter's bebop phraseology. Teddy Edwards didn't record his legendary bebop solo on "Up in Dodo's Room" until October 18, 1946. What we do know is that bebop did not just pop out of nowhere one day. It started to develop as early as the late 1930s, but we can all probably agree that Dexter Gordon was the first musician to translate the language of bebop to the tenor saxophone. He liked that distinction and said he would keep it and try to live up to it.

Dexter referred to himself as a bebopper. He liked being called a jazz musician and was proud to list that as his profession on his passport and other documents. (This did not particularly help whenever he opened a bank account or applied to rent an apartment, but he persisted.) He understood the debate about the word "jazz," but he stood proud of the word and considered himself very lucky to be in the company of all those great musicians he admired. Langston Hughes, in his wonderful 1951 poem *Montage of a Dream Deferred*, referred to those musicians as "Be-Bop Boys":

BE-BOP BOYS

Imploring Mecca
to achieve
six discs
with Decca.[3]

"Imploring Mecca" refers to the embrace of Islam by jazz musicians in the 1930s and 1940s. There were quite a few young musicians "imploring Mecca" who are part of the discussion of bebop, including Sadik Hakim (Argonne Thornton), Abdullah ibn Buhaina (Art Blakey), and Liaquat Ali Salaam (Kenny Clarke). "Six discs with Decca" refers to the record company that was the first to sign an agreement with the musicians' union after its strike, from August 1942 through September 1943, over the demand for royalty payments. Because of this strike (also known as the first "recording ban"), when people first started hearing bebop on recordings as World War II was coming to an end, it seemed as if the new style of music just appeared out of nowhere. Of course, the musicians had been developing bebop during the recording blackout period, which also happened to coincide with the escalation of the war. Only select radio broadcasts and Armed Forces recordings, which were not subject to the ban, enabled some of the new sounds to be heard. In a way, the end of the recording ban made the music seem even more revolutionary, creating more opportunities for people to hear the new sounds. It did leave a void in the recorded history of the beboppers' development, however. We are reminded that it is not always the recordings that are central to jazz history. There were live performances and radio broadcasts everywhere during the period of the strike.[4]

By 1945 Savoy Records began to fill the void left from the ban by recording the young bebop musicians who were working on New York's Fifty-Second Street. Musicians who recorded on Savoy included Sadik Hakim, Gene Ramey, Eddie Nicholson, Leonard Hawkins, Bud Powell, Max Roach, Curley Russell, Leo Parker, Tadd Dameron, Nelson Boyd, Art Blakey, Fats Navarro, and Art Mardigan. Although he is considered the father of bebop drummers, Kenny Clarke was not on these recordings, because he served in the army from 1943 to 1946. Charlie Parker and Dizzy Gillespie are "there" in all ways, having set the standard for bebop as the founding fathers of the form. As Dexter said, "The rest of us were just trying to live up to their example of the possibilities of this music." Dexter often observed that bebop was created by the musicians who did not go into the army or were rejected as unfit for military service. Dexter would say, "We may be unfit for the army, but we are just right for the band."

Shortly before he signed with Savoy Records, Dexter recorded a session for Apollo Records on September 4, 1945, with pianist Sir Charles Thompson. Charlie Parker and Buck Clayton were in the group as well. This session puts a complication into the notion that there was a clear break between swing and bebop, since we have musicians of both styles comfortably playing together here.

Dexter signed his first contract with Savoy on October 15, 1945. He was paid sixty dollars for the session with an option for Savoy to extend the contract for four more recordings. The sidemen were paid forty dollars each per session. For the future recordings, Dexter would receive seventy-five dollars. The contract also called for "all original tunes to be given to Savoy Music Co. as publisher and 1 cent royalty to composer." This meant that Savoy Records had its own publishing company, which would be the legal owner of any original composition recorded on its label. Savoy agreed to pay one cent from each sale of the recording to the composer. You can be sure that no royalty was ever received by Dexter. This contract was exclusive, meaning that at the age of twenty-two Dexter was locked into a binding contract that gave away ownership of his compositions to the label for a very small amount of money, and forbade him from recording anything else for any other company. The contract term was "in perpetuity," meaning that the label would own the recordings forever and could sell them to other companies. There was never a provision for the rights to return to the musicians. We know now that this was standard practice in the recording industry and was supported by the American Federation of Musicians. But it gives us pause to think how it affected the economic situation in the lives of jazz musicians.

The Savoy contract was a standard union contract that was the result of the agreement between the union and the record labels to end the 1942–43 recording ban. The union and the record companies came up with and agreed on all of the wording. Yes, the union blessed a contract that forbade a musician from recording for anyone else, paid him a very small wage, and assigned publishing rights to the label as well as owner-ship in perpetuity. The rights of the labels to control the power of the musician to earn a living are all on the page. In return for approving these favors to the labels, the agreement to end the recording ban also included the establishment of a musician's "relief fund" in the form of millions of dollars deposited by the labels into a union pension fund. And yet there are absolutely no benefits to the musician included in any of the contract documents. The union was an organization meant to protect and support artists and their work. Instead, it became an adjunct to an industry that felt entitled to own all products and publishing rights, as if the people who created the work were casual employees brought in as hired hands on a part-time, one-off basis.

Over the years relations did improve between the musicians and the union. Minimum-wage scales were set and pension, welfare, and life insurance policies were added. Dexter was a lifetime member of Local 47 in Los Angeles. He had joined the union as a teenager when there was a separate black union, Local 767, which in 1953 was amalga-mated with Local 47.

Dexter made his first recordings for Savoy on October 30, 1945, while he was working for several months at the Spotlite Club on Fifty-Second Street with Charlie Parker, Miles Davis, Sir Charles Thompson, Leonard Gaskin, and Stan Levey. The Spotlite, opened around Novem-ber 1944 by Clark Monroe, was the second black-owned club on the famed jazz street after Tondelayo's, which was named for the dancer Wilhelmina Gray, who used that stage name. Monroe also owned Mon-roe's Uptown House, which was one of the important Harlem spots where young musicians gathered and performed. According to Miles Davis, the gig with Dexter and Bird at the Spotlite Club didn't last long: "The police shut down the Spotlite and some of the other clubs on 52nd for some bullshit about drugs and phony liquor licenses. But the real reason I think they shut it down for a couple of weeks was because they didn't like all them niggers coming downtown. They didn't like all them black men being with all them rich, fine white women."[5]

On his first recording date for Savoy, Dexter was joined by Sadik Hakim on piano, Gene Ramey on bass, and Eddie Nicholson on drums, and they recorded "Blow Mr. Dexter," "Dexter's Deck," "Dexter's Cut-ting Out," and "Dexter's Minor Mad." These tunes were given their names not by Dexter but by Savoy's A&R man, Teddy Reig.

On November 26, Charlie Parker recorded his first session as a leader for Savoy. The group was called Charlie Parker's Reboppers and

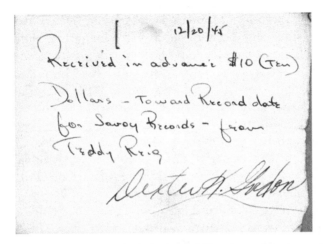

FIGURE 6. The receipt for Dexter's ten dollar advance from
Teddy Reig, December 20, 1945. Savoy Records. From the
personal collection of Dexter Gordon.

included Dizzy Gillespie, Miles Davis, Sadik Hakim, Curley Russell,
and Max Roach. It is an understatement to say that this was a landmark
day in jazz history.

On December 20, Dexter received an advance from Reig for his next
record date. The sum was ten dollars. Dexter signed a second contract
with Savoy on January 7, 1946, and had a recording session on January
29 with Leonard Hawkins (trumpet), Bud Powell (piano), Curley Russell (bass), and Max Roach (drums). Because the labels' publicity
focused so much on individuals, particularly Charlie Parker and Dizzy
Gillespie, many people got the impression that bebop developed as a
solo pursuit, with a leader out front under the spotlight. But in fact
these young musicians were working together, practicing together, writing together, even in some cases living together. The music was a collective effort, and the musicians spent many hundreds of hours practicing
and working on their compositions and their ideas together.

For a time during this period, Dexter shared living quarters with
Miles Davis and the drummer Stan Levey. I had always assumed that
their place was an apartment. But when I asked Levey about those days,
he laughed raucously and explained that it was a single room—in the
Dewey Square Hotel, around the corner from Minton's Playhouse on
116th Street and St. Nicholas Avenue—and that they took turns sleeping in the only bed. He said that they were so happy to be playing on
Fifty-Second Street and that every night was a thrill. They heard the best

players in the world, and Stan said that Dexter would walk up and down the street with his horn out and sit in at various clubs between sets at the Spotlite. Dizzy Gillespie had brought Stan to New York from Philadelphia, where he was also a part-time boxer.[6]

The second Savoy date produced recordings of "Long Tall Dexter," "Dexter Rides Again" (written with Bud Powell), "I Can't Escape from You," and "Dexter Digs In." The terms of the second contract were only slightly better than the first. Dexter got one hundred dollars as leader, and there was a one-year option with notice in writing (by January 8, 1947) for an additional four tunes as part of the deal. The next session would also pay Dexter one hundred dollars.

From the release of the first Savoy 78s in late 1942 until his death in 1974, the sole owner of Savoy was Herman Lubinsky. He was born in 1896 and operated the United Radio Company of Newark, New Jersey, a business that involved retail and mail-order sales of electronic parts and tubes. Phonograph records were added to the retail business in the late 1920s. In 1924, Lubinsky founded New Jersey's first commercial radio station, WNJ. In her book *Newark Nightlife, 1925–1950*, Barbara Kukla describes Lubinsky as "a short, stubby cigar smoker, endowed with a shrewd business sense . . . Clearly, he was obsessed by money and went to extraordinary lengths to get and save it . . . From the artists' perspective, Lubinsky was a wily, unethical shark out for bucks, a man who could locate a vulnerable point, then go for the jugular." Fred Mendelsohn, a close associate of Lubinsky's, disputed the musicians' contentions of being cheated. Kukla quotes Mendelsohn as saying: "Herman was a tough, hard individual, difficult to work for and often an intolerable man. But he was honest. None of the musicians really were robbed. They all signed contracts and got five percent royalties."[7] That all of them got five percent royalties is apocryphal, to say the least.

The idea that a contract can never be amended, revised, or negated is absurd. Any contract is open for renegotiation if the parties can come to an agreement. None of the contracts that musicians signed—under duress, in my opinion—were ever updated or rewritten as times changed. Lubinsky's heirs profited from the sale of his companies, and the musicians did not. Lubinsky established his own publishing company, Savoy Music, and placed all of the copyrights there. This is crucial to understanding the history of jazz musicians and their struggle to live a life that allowed them to create. The confiscation of the music, the devaluation of their creativity, the notion that "spontaneous composition" in jazz—improvisation—is inferior to the kind of composition that is done over long hours with pen on paper, and the canard that players are not composers: all of this has plagued jazz history and caused economic hardship for musicians to this day. These are musicians and composers, after all, who have operated at the very highest levels of creativity.

Copyright ownership is an important part of the story of the political economy of bebop. Starting with the recordings for Savoy and Dial Records in the 1940s and continuing all the way to the present day, the record companies (with some notable exceptions) owned the compositions recorded on their labels. Simply put, copyright ownership gives a publisher the exclusive right to market a composition on records, radio, sheet music, and even in movies, television, and theatrical performances. The publisher collects money from all those uses and then distributes payments, in the form of royalties, to the record label and to the composer. Typically, the record label would receive most of the money, ostensibly because it shouldered the costs of production, manufacturing, distribution, and marketing. Very often the publisher and the record label were essentially one and the same, as with Savoy Publishing and Savoy Records. This is what made the record business so very lucrative—for them. What made it even more lucrative was a copyright law that so heavily advantaged a wealthy company staffed with highly paid lawyers against mostly young, inexperienced musicians usually without any significant legal or financial guidance. In almost every case, for a little bit of money and vague promises of future wealth, these young musicians would willingly sign away their work, often forever.

According to the Copyright Act of 1909, the term of a copyright was twenty-eight years with a renewal term of an additional twenty-eight. In other words, Savoy Music owned all rights to Dexter's compositions for fifty-six years from the first recordings of his compositions in 1945. That gave them the rights until 2001, eleven years after Dexter's death. There was nothing that Dexter, or his estate, could have done to get those copyrights back before they expired. Many composers also lost out even when their publishers chose not to renew a copyright after twenty-eight years, if they were not aware that they could reclaim their copyrights at that point. Or, if the composer was deceased, the family or estate lost out if for any reason it failed to claim copyright ownership at the end of the first term. There are stories about publishers arriving at the copyright office in Washington, D.C., just as valuable copyrights came up for renewal, and renewing them under their own names.

Dexter formed his own publishing company, Dex Music, in the 1960s. After his death in 1990, most of his catalog was placed in his publishing company, which is administered by Warner-Chappell Music for worldwide collection of royalties. Besides the income from publishing rights, composers receive income from their performing rights organization. Dexter was a member of BMI, which is an organization that collects income for public performances and issues licenses for use of compositions in all media. Although the Copyright Act has been amended several times over the years and things have improved for composers, it is still very difficult for them to earn a decent living.

By 1945 the hangout spot for musicians was the White Rose Bar on Seventh Avenue near Fifty-Second Street. As Timme Rosenkrantz wrote in his book *Harlem Jazz Adventures: A European Baron's Memoir, 1934–1969*, "The prices were better here—thirty cents for a whiskey and 10 cents for a beer. With a free lunch that wasn't half bad. The White Rose Bar, one of a chain all around the city, was an oasis for musicians on their breaks."[8]

According to Teddy Reig, Herman Lubinsky had a table at the White Rose:

> After a while, this little mental patient by the name of Herman Lubinsky started coming around. Herman would take up a table, spread out all his contracts, and use it like an office. He wouldn't buy a glass of water and never tipped anybody. Then he tried the same thing in the clubs. One night I was sitting on a car bumper in front of the Three Deuces, surveying the scene, and suddenly here comes Herman flying through the air. "Get the fuck out and stay out," they were yelling. "This is a club, not an office." The record dates were for union scale, which was $60, and the four guys were each $30. So for $180 you had four sides. If [Lubinsky] could sell 400 from the store, he was in good shape. Two thousand was like a national hit. He would get a dollar a record. The whole cost, including the quartet or quintet, mastering, processing and pressing was about 30 or 35 cents. I'm including royalties which were never paid. I never heard of Herman paying a royalty.[9]

In Reig's book, the record producer Bob Porter suggests that the musicians were "strange," and that Teddy had to pay plenty of dues to get the sessions done. By "strange," Porter meant that jazz musicians were not easy people to work with and that Reig had lots of problems getting them to the sessions. "What he had to put up with was incredible," Porter said. That may have been one way of looking at the situation. But if we consider the scene from another angle, perhaps Teddy Reig and Herman Lubinsky were a lot stranger than the musicians. At least that's the way it looks to me.

In April 1946 Lubinsky was searching for Dexter only to learn that he had left New York and gone back to Los Angeles. Dexter had said that he was ill and needed to be home in California, where his mother could care for him. But the truth was that Gwendolyn just wanted her son away from the temptations of New York. Only years later did Dexter learn that his friend Illinois Jacquet had called her to say that her son was hanging out with a "fast crowd" and was in trouble. She immediately got on a train and showed up in New York with Dexter's return ticket in hand. Dexter agreed to leave with her, but when the train got close to the Mexican border, he jumped off and went to buy drugs in Mexico. Charlie Parker had done the same thing when he went to Los Angeles with Dizzy Gillespie in December 1945.

On August 15, 1946, Lubinsky wrote to Dexter at his mother's house. These letters are from the personal archive of Dexter Gordon:

Dear Dexter: I am very sorry to hear that you are ill, but I think that there is no place like home in your mother's arms. I intend to be in Los Angeles very soon and will record you there so line up some boys union scale and get some original material—all on the same kick, fast, two bar piano intro, and three choruses for yourself, one piano chorus in the middle . . . Please confirm this letter so that I may know where you are and if you have any intentions of coming east, I won't make the trip.

Dexter replied on September 25:

Dear Mr. Lubinsky, I have been lining up some material and had expected you in Los Angeles before now. I have had several opportunities to record here but cannot do so because of my contract with your company. Since I am planning on staying in Los Angeles for some time [I] would appreciate it very much if you could advise when you are coming West, date of expiration of my contract and amount of indebtedness. My general health has improved a great deal since I left New York, and am enjoying this fine California climate. Hope you are ok. Sincerely yours, Dexter K. Gordon.

Not only did Dexter exaggerate his reason for leaving New York; he also told Lubinsky that he was not recording when in fact he was recording with Benny Carter, and with Russell Jacquet and His Yellow Jackets, which featured Numa Lee Davis on vocals—in violation of his contract with Savoy.

Dexter was still in Los Angeles on June 12, 1947, when he recorded "The Chase" for Dial Records, and on July 6 he played in the famous concert at the Elks Auditorium with Hampton Hawes, Sonny Criss, Trummy Young, and Howard McGhee. That concert was recorded by Ralph Bass, who tried to sell the recording to Savoy, which was ironic indeed given that Dexter's Savoy Records saga was still ongoing. On June 16, Lubinsky had written to Dexter in Los Angeles reminding him that he was under contract to Savoy and that it was too costly to record in California. Dexter replied to Teddy Reig on July 1:

> *A few weeks ago Mr. Lubinsky wrote me a letter which stated that I was still under contract to the company, but I fail to understand that. I guess there must be a mistake because our contract was scheduled to run from '45 to '46 and it is now '47. I hope you will look into it and advise me because I do not wish to be caused any financial embarrassment or otherwise. I am receiving no royalties from any of my tunes and after all I have to live until I get back to that jurisdiction. I am having some pictures made this week and will be very happy to send you one as soon as I receive them.*

The photo session he mentions was with photographer Ray Whitten on July 12, 1947. Dexter seems to have been planning to compete with Billy Eckstine on the suaveness scale.

On July 16, Dexter received a special delivery letter from Lubinsky asking him to call Reig. Apparently Dexter did not make the call, because on July 21 he received an extraordinary letter from Reig:

> I am very much depressed over your actions and attitude. I have meant you nothing but good . . . I have spent money in conversations with you over the phone totaling $10.00 and attempted to get things straight. Charlie Parker and myself are prepared to have you open at the Three Deuces with Miles and Mack [Max Roach]. I have always considered you a friend of a personal nature and have given you many, many chances which really taxed my patience. I am sure you are aware of that. I will not do anything which I consider detrimental to your welfare unless you force me to play my hand. By that I mean the following: You are under contract to Savoy Records. You have commitments to Savoy Records to do recordings.

I cannot be the only person who reads "unless you force me to play my hand" as more than a veiled threat. Reig's letter goes on:

> I asked you to phone me last Friday and still you did not . . . As for your playings on tune royalties, you have made an outright sale which was your own will, as you know, at the time, the position you were in and your requirements for money. We don't have to say any more about that. Savoy owes you nothing along those lines I am sure.

Reig's between-the-lines meaning: Dexter had a drug habit and signed away the royalty rights to his tunes ("your playings") for cash. To say that Savoy took advantage of "the position you were in" is an understatement, and to suggest that he signed the contract freely is questionable. Reig's letter continues: "If you would want to come to New York, I am in position to

FIGURE 7. Dexter Gordon's Dial Records publicity photo, July 1947. Photograph by Ray Whitten. Photo courtesy of the Harry Ransom Collection, University of Texas, Austin.

make arrangements for you immediately. Charlie wants you at the Deuces. I can make many other things happen; that is, if you will cooperate."

This letter tells us so much about the record business at that time. Dexter, at the age of twenty-four, was trying to figure out how to have a career and survive in a world that was new to him. He said that he felt as if he was inside a life he had no way of preparing for, and was just trying to keep up with the scene around him.

Apparently Dexter spoke with Reig on the telephone after he received the July 21 letter, because on July 25 Reig wrote in another letter:

Sometime within the next week or ten days I am going to send you two Union Contracts dated with two dates for some time in September which will be the time that you arrive in New York . . . The Money advanced to you for transportation will be deducted from the tune royalties which I feel is very fair as it will give you an opportunity to come to New York and laying your hands on some ready cash and keep you going . . . I hope that this is satisfactory, but I feel it is a real fair thing.

In October 1947, Dexter made a trip to Hawaii with Cee Pee Johnson's band, which included Trummy Young and Red Callender. In his book *Unfinished Dream: The Musical World of Red Callender,* Callender wrote, "A day or so before we left, Cee Pee got busted for marijuana. The headline that greeted us in Honolulu was: 'Famous Bandleader Jailed for Marijuana' . . . Arriving in Honolulu was like stepping into a dream. Already dazed from the twelve-hour flight, the air literally shimmered before my eyes. Orchids were placed around my neck . . . The following evening the Cee Pee Johnson Band played the Honolulu Civic Auditorium. The audience went wild for us. The Hawaiians had never heard the likes of Dexter Gordon or Arthur Dennis play saxophone in person before."[10] Callender reminds us of the many good musicians who have not received their due recognition in jazz history. Arthur Dennis is an example. The baritone (as well as alto and tenor) saxophonist recorded with vocalist Numa Lee Davis and Russell Jacquet (trumpet-playing brother of Illinois Jacquet), Charles Mingus, and Louis Armstrong.

On October 29, 1947, Dexter wrote to Reig from Honolulu:

I haven't heard from you recently and thought I had better write and see what was happening, especially with the record ban coming on. I'm still very much in favor of doing the rest of my sides. At present, however, I'm doing a travelogue with C. P. Johnson's band, which includes Trummy Young and Red Callender among others. I don't know how long we're supposed to be here but I am ready to come there if I have or had the ticket (plane) from Los Angeles to N.Y.C. [Dexter's reference is to a second recording ban that was expected to begin at the end of 1947.]

On November 4, Lubinsky wrote to Dexter in Honolulu:

Teddy and I have conferred over your letter and we feel that we would like to go along with you before December 31st. We will send you an airplane ticket from Los Angeles to New York provided you will sign the enclosed contract and stipulation. Don't forget that you did sign an exclusive contract with us—that you borrowed money and of course it was no fault of yours that you became sick and went to California, but then you should have contacted us but instead you made a number of records, especially for one of our competitors. However, what's done is done and we are not holding it against you. This is your chance to cooperate and don't worry about money, we will see that you are well repaid and will be glad to pay you any price within reason provided you will show some effort to be reliable.

It is clear that Lubinsky and Reig were anxious to stockpile as many recordings as they could before the onset of the second recording ban. After the strike and first ban of 1942–43 was settled and the unions began to grow too rich and powerful to suit Congress, a law was enacted that denied them the right to control their own unemployment funds. The record companies felt vindicated and let it be known that they did not intend to renew the first ban's settlement agreements when they expired on December 31, 1947. The union prepared for a second ban.

On November 10, Dexter returned the Savoy contract, unsigned, to Lubinsky. This is my favorite piece from all the Savoy Records correspondence. Dexter's letter from the Alexander Young Hotel in Honolulu reminds us why Dexter was one of the top students in English class (along with the drummer Chico Hamilton) at Jefferson High School:

> However, the terms of which you speak are not quite satisfactory. I am very much against selling, in any shape or form, any more of my compositions . . . The price stipulation in this contract is like the terms in our last contract, am I right? However, I really don't think the price is enough to warrant the exclusive contract. I consider $250.00 for the first session with $50.00 raise (fifty dollars) for each additional session, a fair price, what do you think?
>
> As you say it was you who gave me my start in recordings and I do appreciate it to the fullest extent. But I do think it's time that I have a chance to make a little money also. So am sending contracts back unsigned for you to make necessary alteration. Hoping this meets with your approval, I remain with deepest regards, Sincerely yours, Dexter Gordon.

Dexter seems to have learned a lot about the record business in a short time. He said that the young guys would listen when musicians talked at the union hall, especially the older ones who advised against signing contracts too soon. He may have also discussed his situation with his fellow musicians in Hawaii. Red Callender was quite up to date on recording contracts, as he had been very active in the union. (Callender would go on to be one of the musicians instrumental in amalgamating the two Los Angeles unions—Local 767, the "colored union," and Local 47, the white union—into one, in 1953.)

Lubinsky relented and sent a new contract countering Dexter's request of $250 with an offer of $200. He wrote: "We have great plans in store for you. We plan an Album of you exclusively. We also plan posters, streamers, newspaper and trade magazine publicity coast to coast, also blow up pictures of you. Please bring pictures East without any cracks in them so that they may be reproduced. The opportunity of a lifetime awaits you, and please, Dexter don't fail us as we have been on the level with you and expect you to be the same. We have found you to be a fine, upright, and honest young man." To me this sounds like Herman had become desperate to have some recordings on hand during the forthcoming ban. In the contract, Lubinsky made an error in indicating that funds would be sent to Local 47 of the musicians union. Dexter corrected him in a following note: *"Please send the money to Local 767, not #47, as that is a white local."*

Dexter returned to New York on December 11, 1947, and went into the Harry Smith Studio on Fifty-Seventh Street to record for Savoy with Leo Parker (baritone sax), Tadd Dameron (piano), Curley Russell (bass), and Art Blakey (drums). They recorded "Settin' the Pace" (parts one and two), "So Easy," and "Dexter's Riff." On December 19 he recorded with the Leo Parker All-Stars. On December 22 he went back into the studio with Fats Navarro (trumpet), Dameron, Nelson Boyd (bass), and Art Mardigan (drums) to record "Dexter's Mood" (written by Dameron), "Dextrose," "In-Dex," and "Dextivity." When the ball dropped on New Year's Eve, the recording ban went into effect and lasted for one year.

In total, Savoy owned seventeen copyrights on sixteen compositions written by Dexter ("Settin' the Pace" has two copyrights). Each of the compositions was written to fit on a three-minute side of a 78-rpm disc, except "The Chase" and "Settin' the Pace," which take up two sides. It is impossible to calculate how much money these compositions earned over the course of seventy years in all their various formats, from vinyl discs to digital streams. Perhaps in the millions. How much found its way to Dexter and his estate? A pittance.

Studying these documents from a brief period in Dexter's early career gives us an idea of what a struggle it must have been for a jazz musician trying to create music and make a living. So much of that struggle can be analyzed in terms of the racialized society of the 1940s: collusion between the union and the record companies, devaluation and ownership of compositions, formation of community and mutual support, and much more.

CHAPTER 8

Mischievous Lady

I think they were callin' me Mama already back then, 'cause
I used to fuss with them about smokin' their cigarettes or
drinkin' their wine—and they'd come and get me when
something was goin' on, and I would play little gigs with
them.

—Melba Liston[1]

On the afternoon of Thursday, June 5, 1947, at the C.P. MacGregor Studios in Hollywood, California, Dexter had a record date for Dial Records and wanted Melba Liston there. Not only did he want her to play, but he also wrote a tune for her, the aptly titled "Mischievous Lady." Dexter on tenor saxophone and Melba on trombone were joined by Charles Fox on piano, Chuck Thompson on drums, and Red Callender on bass for two three-minute recordings. Melba was twenty-one years old, Dexter was twenty-four, and the oldest member of the band was Callender, at thirty-one. Here was a recording with five musicians who were young in years but who had plenty of musical experience and were ready to do the job at hand, with Melba as both peer and "Mama." As Melba remembered:

> When he got his record date he said, "Come on, Mama"—I think they were callin' me Mama already back then, 'cause I used to fuss with them about smokin' their cigarettes or drinkin' their wine—and they'd come and get me when something was goin' on, and I would play little gigs with them. I was scared to go in the studio, though, because I didn't really hang out with them when they were jamming and stuff. I was home trying to write, so I didn't have that spirit on my instrument as an improvisational person. I was really very shy. I really didn't want to make that record session. I don't know which was worse—makin' it or trying to persuade them to leave me out of it.[2]

But she made it, and the recording became a part of the body of fertile music that young jazz musicians produced in the middle of the twentieth century, music that was the product of years of working

FIGURE 8. Dexter and Melba Liston, friends from childhood, in the studio in 1947. Photograph courtesy of the Ross Russell Collection, Harry Ransom Collection, University of Texas, Austin.

together in close community—studying together, eating together, laughing together, and yes, playing together. The recording also showed Melba as "Mama" in a different sense: she was the "boss" of an improvisational sound that made her, at the very least, first among equals and that won her a legendary status among jazz musicians. The recording date pays homage to an accomplished musician seemingly too modest to acknowledge her musical influence or dominance.

Melba was just sixteen in 1942 when she joined Local 767, the Colored Musicians Union in Los Angeles, so that she could take her first professional job as a member of the Lincoln Theater pit band. We tend to think of the postwar generation of innovative musicians as fully grown artists who made the world anew and blew the culture open with their revolutionary sound, but it is important to remember how young they were at these key moments in their own creative lives and in the changing cultural times. The environment around Los Angeles, and Central Avenue in particular, allowed for a community of young musicians to grow musically and socially. These relationships were formative and in the case of Dexter and Melba led to a friendship that lasted throughout their lives. The musicians lived near each other, many in the Central Avenue area or, simply, the Eastside, and they spent hours practicing together in living rooms and garages before and after school.

Dexter and Melba first started playing music together when he was seventeen and she was fourteen. Melba had come to Los Angeles from Kansas City three years prior, a shy eleven-year-old who had already decided that she would be a musician. She and Dexter went to McKinley Junior High School together before Dexter went on to Jefferson High. He always said that Melba knew much more about music than the guys in their group, and it was common for them to go to her for explanations of chord changes, transposition, and songwriting.[3]

During and after World War II, Black Los Angeles, and Central Avenue in particular, was crowded with musicians who came to town to work in the many defense plants. Indeed, Musicians Union Local 767 advertised in the *Pittsburgh Courier,* "urging musicians to get themselves post-haste to Central Avenue, the pot at the end of the rainbow."[4] By the end of the war, hundreds of musicians had arrived from all over. Many would stay initially for a string of dates or a season, hoping to get a call for a more permanent gig either in Los Angeles or in a touring band. Central Avenue became the training and proving ground for musicians playing all styles of music, including blues, boogie-woogie, swing, and bebop. There was money to be spent because there was ample work in the defense plants. As a result, clubs and after-hours places flourished, many holding jam sessions that went well into the early morning hours.

In a 1996 interview for the NEA Jazz Masters Smithsonian oral history program, Melba said of Dexter: "He and I were in school together. He was a bad, bad tenor player. Played all the time." She then thought ahead to the "Mischievous Lady" session in June 1947: "He was breaking this record. I said, 'I'm not—no, no.' He said, 'come on.' That was the first time I had played without any music. Oh, Lordy. That was terrible."

Melba had briefly joined Dexter at Jefferson High before transferring to Polytechnic High School, though they played together throughout their high school years. Of the band director at Jefferson, Sam Browne, she said: "He had all these wild young dudes. We used to call him Count Browne. We had a school marching band, an orchestra that used to play light classics, plus a swing band that played stock arrangements of Benny Goodman and Basie hits."⁵ While in Mr. Browne's band, Dexter learned "Lullaby in Rhythm," the song he would eventually record on the B side of "Mischievous Lady." Dexter was probably fifteen when he first heard the version of that Benny Goodman tune on a 1938 Victor recording. Dexter's own version of "Lullaby in Rhythm," recorded nearly ten years later, shows the influence of Goodman's version, but more important it reflects his formative high school musical experiences. And also Melba's: she was already writing and arranging at the same time that Dexter and the other young musicians were playing in the school band and jamming after school.

In the summer of 1946, after his stints with the Armstrong and Eckstine bands and his brief working visit to Hawaii, Dexter returned to Los Angeles where he frequented the Central Avenue clubs and participated in jam sessions that ran night and day. It was there that Ross Russell, the founder of Dial Records, heard Dexter and offered him the recording sessions on Dial. Russell obviously had heard all of the recordings Dexter had made for Savoy.

Ross Russell was born in Los Angeles in 1909 and grew up in Glendale, California. He served in the Merchant Marine during World War II, and after receiving a medical discharge in early 1945 he worked at Lockheed Aircraft until the end of the war. In July 1945 he opened the Tempo Music Shop in Hollywood where the latest jazz records were available, and by the end of the year the store had gained a reputation for featuring the new style of music known as bebop coming out of New York City. In a letter to his mother, Russell described the record shop as being located in a "new block of six stores, modern and attractive and different . . . 16 by 60 feet floor space . . . built-in counter with plastic top and rattan facing, two built-in booths, and attractive lounge where records can be played and friends meet."⁶ Record stores, like barbershops, became meeting places for jazz fans during this period. Groups of friends would come to play the latest releases, then one person would buy the 78 and the friends would gather at that person's home to listen over and over again. If the record was played too often, its grooves would wear out and someone would have to go back to the record store to buy another copy.

By January 1946 Russell knew all about Milt Gabler and his company, Commodore Records, which he had built upon the interest generated by the Commodore Record Shop in New York City. Russell seems to have patterned his record company after Commodore. His partner was Marvin Freeman, a Los Angeles lawyer he had met when they were students at UCLA. Among Freeman's contributions was the name "Dial," which he took from the twentieth-century literary review *The Dial,* which he had read as a student.[7] In the fall of 1946, Russell sold the Tempo Music Shop and bought Freeman's share of Dial Records, becoming the sole owner. Dexter recalled that Russell did not allow guests at the rehearsals or at recording sessions—he was fearful of drug dealers—and always wanted to be sure to have a photo taken of himself with the musicians. Dexter also recalled that practically all Russell talked about was Charlie Parker. Russell liked to brag that he "discovered" Parker and tell stories about the difficulties he had to overcome in getting Bird to the studio to make those now-famous Dial recordings.

By most accounts, including Dexter's, Russell was a "problematic" figure who was preoccupied with Parker. When Parker left Los Angeles to return to New York in March 1947, Russell made plans to follow him there. But before he left town, Russell recorded his eighth session for the still-new Dial: the Dexter Gordon "Mischievous Lady" date. Russell's ninth session, recorded a week later, was "The Chase" with Dexter and Wardell Gray. "Dexter and Wardell were playing around Los Angeles, conducting this musical chase almost every evening and it was creating a great deal of comment," Russell said. "It seemed like a good idea to get them into the studio and record it."[8] In a letter to his mother dated February 3, 1948, Russell wrote: "Dial sales have far exceeded our most optimistic expectations during the fall . . . Dial records are in strong demand. 'The Chase,' the two-sided sax battle record I made as an experiment and released late November, is proving a jazz best seller. It has already hit 12,000 and outsold anything, new or old, we have released."

The 1947 Dial recordings were pressed onto ten-inch 78s, which meant of course that the maximum time for each recording was three minutes per side. When originally released, a 78-rpm disc sold for $1.05. We have no information on the initial sales of "Mischievous Lady," but the recording continues to appear to this day on CDs, along with all the other Dial recordings. What we do know, however, is that Dexter signed over the rights to the compositions "Mischievous Lady" and "The Chase" to Dial Records for the sum of one cent per side for all records sold by the company. From sales of the twelve thousand 78s of "The Chase" that Russell enthused about to his mother, Dexter would have received $120 of the $12,600 that the record grossed.

In a report written by Russell entitled "The Progressive Record Store Center" found in his collection at the Harry Ransom Center at the University of Texas, he wrote: "Public buying did not enter the picture until 1947. Then it was the young urban Negro male who was not a musician who began listening and collecting. This particular buying trend came about through the rapid stages of sophistication and began with rhythm and blues . . . One of the biggest sellers on Dial was 'The Chase,' a two-sided saxophone duel between Dexter Gordon and Wardell Gray, which whipped up a lot of steam, offered a certain novelty in that it was the first of such instrumental duels on record and was a performance of some quality."

On October 22, 1947, in another letter to his mother, this time from New York, Russell wrote: "All in all we should be in a very solid position by January 1 . . . There is every prospect however that the resultant Dial catalog is going to be a property of permanent value. We won't ever make any large money out of it but we may be able to make a moderately comfortable living out of Dial for some years to come." Russell realized early on that this new music had a lasting value. The musicians also knew this, but of course the economic arrangements did not allow them, for the most part, a "moderately comfortable living"—surely not from the income their recordings earned them. Importantly, all of these recordings are still available and have been leased and sold so many times that it would take a detective with jazz skills to find the current owners of the masters and to know who is responsible for the royalties due.

The payment sheet for the Dial Session VIII, June 5, 1947, shows the wages, withholding, and net pay for the musicians. Melba Liston was paid $41.25 for the three-hour session. This would have been union scale at the time. Dexter received $100 as leader. This sheds light on the economic component of being a jazz artist at the time and illuminates much about the political economy of bebop. These important historic recordings did not make for a comfortable way of life for the artists who created the work and who influenced generations to follow.

In many of his writings about Dial and Charlie Parker, Ross Russell presented himself as something of an authority on drug use at the time. Dexter did not talk about Russell very often, usually saying that "the guy was complicated" and leaving it at that. Dexter usually took the high road and did not like to pass judgment on those with whom he disagreed. But his reservations about Russell lay with Russell's readiness to associate drug use with jazz musicians. Evidence of this can be found in the rather acrimonious comments written, probably by Russell, on the backs of photos taken by photographer Ray Whitten at

Dexter's recording sessions. One reads, "Dexter Gordon on horse. The Blue Bikini and Mischievous Lady session." The word "horse" suggests Russell's observation that Dexter was high on heroin during the session. "Blue Bikini" is a tune Dexter wrote about the 1946 atomic bomb tests on Bikini Atoll in the Pacific. It was recorded on June 12, 1947 (with Jimmy Bunn on piano, Red Callender on bass, and Chuck Thompson on drums), while "Mischievous Lady" was recorded on June 5. Hence, Russell's comment is inaccurate on two counts. Another print of the same photo has this comment on the back: "A lame effort at Cheesecake (or something!). Dexter Gordon recording (Mischievous Lady) session, C. P. MacGregor Studio, LA Calif, 1947. L to R. Melba Liston, trombone. Charlie Fox, piano, ——, drums, Russell, Dexter Gordon, tenor sax. This happens to be a rare and interesting picture of a man just going into a state of morphine narcosis (Gordon, not Russell!!)." This comment must have been written years later since Dexter's "Cheese Cake" was not written and recorded until 1962 on Blue Note Records. The comments about Dexter's "state" are the sort of so-called insider remarks that followed him around and colored his role in jazz history, sometimes vying with his musicianship for dominance. Perhaps it was the photographer Whitten who wrote the comments, since it would seem that Russell would have known the name of Thompson, the drummer, as his name was on the payment roster. We do know that Dexter wanted Melba on this session and it was his decision to have her there. Sadly, we have no comment by Ross Russell on her performance.

Look closely at the photo from the "Mischievous Lady" session and notice Melba's foot holding the slide and the way she is posed sitting up on the grand piano with her skirt above the knee and plenty of leg showing. Russell is the one putting the cymbal on Chuck Thompson's head, obviously thinking it was very funny. Years later, the humor does not stand up, if it ever did at all. There is something about this photo that makes us think about what Russell had in mind for his new venture. We can only speculate that he wanted to portray the music as "sexy" and "funny." The presence of Melba made it easier for him to present this image. In the publications used to promote the recording of "Mischievous Lady," the photo of Dexter and Melba alone (see the photo at the beginning of this chapter) was often used, and in one publication the photo of Melba on the piano was used with Dexter and Russell cropped out of the photo. What we do know, according to Dexter, is that these were some serious young musicians spending many hours practicing and playing together. We can be extremely glad to have

FIGURE 9. The June 5, 1947, Dial Records session (left to right): Melba Liston, Charles Fox, Chuck Thompson, Ross Russell, Dexter. Photograph at the C. P. MacGregor Studio, Hollywood, CA. Courtesy of the Ross Russell Collection, Harry Ransom Collection, University of Texas, Austin.

these photos of the sessions, but when we deconstruct the moment, there is much here to suggest that the atmosphere was uneasy in the studio. The recording session lasted just three hours, and somewhere during or after the recording the musicians were posed for photos. Red Callender is not in the photo; perhaps he left the session as soon as it was over and missed the photo portion.

Melba is positioned almost as a prop in the photo. In no way do the body positions of the men suggest that she is seen as their equal, even as she's elevated above them and presented as an object of beauty. This is obviously a posed shot that was probably the photographer's idea of something "cute." Russell seems out of place in the photo, particularly with his choice of the Hawaiian shirt. Since it is his record company, he may have wanted a group photo for publicity purposes. And then there's Melba—she's clearly in on the gag with that coy, coquettish look in her eyes. She has playfully positioned the slide of her trombone with her shoe, and she looks neither uncomfortable with the attention nor uneasy with the idea that she seems to be holding court with the other musicians. A feminist reading of this photo might blast a one-dimensional, beautified version of girlish Black womanhood that strips Melba of any command of her instrument or craft by way of her body position. Here the feminist viewer might interpret the lusty gaze of Melba's male colleagues as overtly demeaning or masculinist. More likely than not, however, the exchange was playful and ended with bursts of laughter over the ridiculous moment. It might be a stretch to say she looks "mischievous," but she does give a clue as to why Dexter named the tune "Mischievous Lady" for her.

These recordings, though brief in length, give us a chance to hear these two artists when they were still developing their craft, but it also gives us a glimpse into a friendship that lasted a lifetime. Dexter always said that Melba was so far ahead of the cats at Jefferson and she was always trying to push them to learn the changes, to think about the arrangements and learn to write music for each other. When Dexter left high school in December 1940 at the age of seventeen to join the Lionel Hampton band, he was the "baby" of the group. When we consider these musicians, their international reputations, and the impact they have had on the music, it gives us pause to think about how young they were when they began their journey into the jazz life. And we are reminded that the "Mama" of them was Melba, who was much more significant than a pretty figure sitting atop a grand piano.

In less than three minutes, we learn that Dexter Gordon can play and compose in the bebop idiom but already shows his individual style. The arrangement of the tune is also very rich, a quality that all compositions by Dexter share. We can speculate that Melba helped with the arrangement in much the same way she had done since she and Dexter were in high school. Melba plays a very swinging sixteen-bar solo that foreshadows her as one of the most prominent jazz musicians in the history of this music. Perhaps—almost certainly—it was Melba's influence on Dexter that helped him develop his composition style.

When Melba was living and teaching at the Jamaica Institute in Kingston in 1978, Dexter and I went there on a vacation and he played a gig with her at the Sheraton Hotel, where he met some of her students. They had a very happy reunion, laughing for hours and talking about Los Angeles when they were young. There did not seem to have been a span of thirty years since that recording session at Dial, or longer since their time hanging out in Los Angeles and playing those jam sessions after school. They just picked up the conversation where they had left off. Unfortunately, I never thought to ask Dexter why he named the tune that he wrote for Melba "Mischievous Lady." But he did say, "Melba seems so quiet and ladylike, but has that twinkle in her eye that tells us that she can get into just as much trouble as the rest of us."

In 2012 I did ask Melba's longtime collaborator and friend, pianist and composer Randy Weston, if he thought Melba was mischievous and why Dexter would choose "Mischievous Lady" as the name of his song for her. "Well, she definitely was," said Weston. "Because she was like Monk: very few words spoken. The only time she was speaking was when she got angry. And when somebody messed up her notes in the band"—he laughed—"you might hear a few expletives. But she was a very quiet person . . . And she has that aura about her . . . She had that kind of—Dexter was right—kind of a mystic quality. Some people have some kind of a magic that you can't explain. And you know we were together for many years, but there are some things I couldn't explain."

What we can explain, though, is how crucial she was to the community of musicians who rightly called her "Mama," first among equals and a mischievous lady in all the right ways. In Melba Liston's life, there were many times when the relationship with fellow musicians was not as harmonious as hers was with both Dexter Gordon and Randy Weston. We know that she suffered insult and abuse, but we also know that she did not let anything or anyone stop her from her music. In Jamaica, she was "Mama" again. Her students revered her, and one of them, the renowned reggae saxophonist Dean Fraser, wrote and recorded the song "This One's for Melba Liston" after her death in 1999.

There are diverse layers and aspects to the "Mischievous Lady" recording session and Dexter's tune written for Melba. This close focus on that day in 1947 illustrates the importance of musical apprenticeship, jazz culture, and the friendship at the heart of it all. The trajectory of Melba's career was forecast on that day: musicianship will trump gender stereotypes.[9]

CHAPTER 9

Central Avenue Bop

I remember my first time seeing Dexter. I was young, early
teens, and I just got my first tenor. My mother had gotten
me an alto, but I always wanted to play tenor, so finally she
saved enough money and bought me a tenor. There was a
place up in the Bronx, New York, called the Hunts Point
Plaza, where they put on sessions. So I went up there and
the guy in charge, a friend named Ray Pino, said that
Dexter didn't have his horn. Would I lend him my horn? So
I lent Dexter my horn, you know, and of course in those
days it was always a dangerous thing to do, to lend
musicians your horn. I wasn't unaware of that, you know,
as a young guy just coming along. But I felt quite secure in
doing it for some reason. Anyway, that worked out fine.
Dexter played my horn and I got it back, and that was that.

—Sonny Rollins[1]

Jazz history is often recounted as a sequence of turning points, a journey
from one seminal moment to another, lingering at the milestones where
everything—cultural, aesthetic, and even political—supposedly coalesces
into "the new." One of these moments occurred at the Elks Hall on Central Avenue in Los Angeles on July 6, 1947. On that evening, Wardell
Gray and Dexter Gordon locked musical horns, battling each other and
driving the audience into a furious frenzy with their tenor saxophones.
Portions of the night's playing were released on a series of four 78-rpm
discs on the Bop! Records label. Appropriately titled "The Hunt," this
two-tenor duel, with Wardell and Dexter alternately chasing and outdo-
ing each other, was spread over eight sides of three minutes each.

Apart from the sheer excitement of the battle, why was this concert
so mythological and historically significant? After all, the two musicians

had dueled before; one month earlier they had recorded "The Chase," a much more commercially successful recording, which was released on Dial Records on two sides of a 78. "The Chase" was so successful—it outsold all of Dial's other titles at the time, even Charlie Parker's—that "The Hunt" was marketed primarily as a Gray-Gordon duel, although their session was only part of a full night's gig that included musicians such as Howard McGhee, Sonny Criss, and Hampton Hawes, playing brilliantly on trumpet, alto saxophone, and piano, respectively. The 1947 musical battle-cum-duet that followed two nights of Independence Day celebrations has become a deliverance moment for that ubiquitous postwar jazz style, bebop. That the concert has become sanctified should be no surprise, though, given the quality of the playing, the mythic quality of the venue, and the stature of the other players who were on hand that night.

The two-tenor battle has been a key element in jazz performance ever since, but Dexter and Wardell were the quintessential bebop tenor-battle musicians. (Al Cohn and Zoot Sims, Sonny Stitt and Gene Ammons, Eddie "Lockjaw" Davis and Johnny Griffin, and John Coltrane and Sonny Rollins carried on the tradition.) Dexter:

> It wasn't like somebody would say, "I can play better than you, man," but actually . . . that's what it was. You'd think, damn, what the fuck was he playing? You'd try to figure out what was going on. To a degree, that was one of the things—to be fastest, the hippest. The tenor player with the biggest tone—that takes balls, that takes strength.

The classic form of the duel, following call-and-response tradition, calls for the tenor players to first trade choruses of thirty-two bars, then sixteen bars, then eight, then finally four-bar phrases flashing back and forth at breakneck speed. At just under seven minutes in length, "The Chase" was one of the longest jazz recordings of its day, but this did not seem to deter fans.

Dexter and Wardell recorded "The Hunt" at the Elks Hall, also known as the Elks Auditorium, the Elks Ballroom, and the Elks Club. Mention the Elks or its street, Central Avenue, to a jazz fan of a certain age and you will likely elicit a knowing bebop nod of the head and an insider's smile. The mythology has immortalized the place and its better events. When you listen to the entire recording of the concert on Savoy's three-CD set, *Bopland,* you can hear that "Cherokee" (also referred to as "Geronimo" and "Cherrykoke") sends the crowd into a frenzy—and rightly so. The playing is electrifying, not least because of Dexter's sinu-

ous lines that carry most of the song until Wardell joins in and intensi-
fies the heat for the last two or three minutes. It was sheer delight for the
crowd then, as it is for listeners now. The concert recording is a reminder,
though, that this music—bebop—emerges out of a thriving cultural
community. Two thousand people in sync *with* the music and *with* the
musicians, listening and dancing. It was a bebop moment, all right, Sunday, July 6, 1947. But what do we really know about that night?

From a notice in *Down Beat* on July 2, 1947, we know that this was
"the first in the Jack Williams Presents Jazz Concert Dance Series" and
that Williams was "out to prove that the same kind of music that draws
people to jazz concerts will pull customers who are chiefly dance-
minded." And draw a crowd it did.

Record producer Ralph Bass recorded the event and then made an
offer to Herman Lubinsky of Savoy Records to release the material on
Bass's newly formed label, Bop![2] "The concert was one of the best that
I have ever heard," Bass wrote in a letter to Lubinsky on July 10, 1947.
"And the recordings should make history. For the first time a Jazz Concert was given in a dance hall so that people could dance as well as listen. It was held in the heart of the 'Black Belt' in Los Angeles, and was
attended principally by colored people. Instead of being a formal and
stiff affair as conducted by Norman Granz and other impresarios, this
one was held before an audience that was standing or dancing and
inspired by 2,000 people who were shrieking encouragement to the
musicians, so that the results were clearly felt by the musicians."

While we are celebrating the joyous beauty of Central Avenue in
1947, however, we must mention that it was not until 1948 that the
U.S. Supreme Court finally ruled against restrictive and discriminatory
housing covenants, which had been strictly enforced in Los Angeles.[3]
Ralph Bass's live recording, then, is a testimony to celebration and resil-
ience in the midst of oppressive social circumstances.

Bass went on to write, "Particularly, there is one album in which
Wardell Gray and Dexter Gordon battle for 10 minutes with their ten-
ors." He is referring here to "The Hunt," which was based on Benny
Goodman's "Stompin' at the Savoy." "There is so much excitement in
this particular set that you cannot help but feel the intense rivalry
between these two who are continually encouraged by their followers,
and in my opinion, as well as others, this is wilder than the Illinois Jacquet solo in the 'Jazz at the Philharmonic' album now currently selling
so well." While clearly a promoter of his own recordings, Bass does not
exaggerate when he describes the crowd's response.

The Elks Auditorium (aka Ballroom, aka Club) was on the first floor of the Elks Hall (also called the Elks Temple) at 4016 South Central Avenue.[4] (Indeed, no small amount of confusion has arisen from the multiple names.) The auditorium had a beautiful stage and with its balcony was large enough to hold the crowd of two thousand that filled the place on July 6. On the second floor was another, smaller auditorium, where Saturday and Sunday matinee dances were held.[5] The third floor would open as the Elks Hawaiian Cocktail Lounge in April 1947.

The night before the historic July 6 concert, the Elks Hall held a dance called the "Freedom Fling," heralded in an ad in the *California Eagle* as the "hottest jam session in town—midnite on," featuring a "12-piece Unity Band; Fun, Refreshments, Friendliness; Spirit of '76 Decorations." The dance was sponsored by the Los Angeles Communist Party, which was both active and popular in Los Angeles' Black community at the time. Tickets were $1.20 (tax included).

The Elks Hall was constantly jumping. Various dances there were sponsored by Marcus Garvey's United Negro Improvement Association, the Mona Lisa Girls' Bridge Club, the Royal Syndicators, the Eleven and One Charity Club, the Original Calvarette Social Club, and Les Bonboniere. Women's social and charity clubs would also meet there, at the center of life in the Central Avenue neighborhood. Not all of the life on Central Avenue was nightlife.

The three-hour concert and dance at the Elks Hall on that historic Sunday, July 6, 1947, was released by Savoy years later.[6] Ralph Bass made the recording on two portable disc cutters, with the sides overlapping to capture and preserve all of the music and announcements. The sound quality is poor compared with today's superior technology, but the playing is no less impassioned or infectious than any ever recorded. It is worth listening to the recording to understand what jazz musicians were doing at that time and how involved the audience was in defining this "bebop moment."

The recording of the entire evening at the Elks Hall captures a full series of sets featuring the top jazz talent of the day. But for years the only segment that was deemed worthy of marketing on record was "The Hunt." Jazz fans who love the music from that period have fought it out over whether Dexter or Wardell won the contest on that Sunday. Dexter said he would have to give it to Wardell (but then again, Dexter was a very generous man). Subsequent reissues and compilations that featured that rendition of "The Hunt" implied that the recording was made at a Dexter-Wardell date. Of course, this was not the case at all.

FIGURE 10. The recording of "The Chase" for Dial Records set the standard for the popular tradition of "battling tenor saxophones." Wardell Gray and Dexter Gordon, June 12, 1947. Courtesy of the Ross Russell Collection, Harry Ransom Collection, University of Texas, Austin.

Both musicians were in fact playing at the Elks as members of Howard McGhee's band. My personal favorite from that recording is "After Hours Bop," because of Dexter's amazing solo—it foreshadows his unique sound and style that would become so immediately recognizable over the years—not to mention those of Howard McGhee's trumpet, Sonny Criss's alto saxophone, Trummy Young's trombone, and Red Callender's bass.

There was more than one style of jazz played in this concert, just as there was more than one style of music being played along Central Avenue. You can hear the young beboppers stretching out into new territory, and the older musicians—tenor players Wild Bill Moore and Gene

Montgomery, guitarist Barney Kessel, and trumpeter and bandleader Al Killian—playing in what was considered the hip and modern style of the times. One of the most remarkable things about this music is that the "older" musicians were only in their thirties at the time and the younger ones were indeed very young. Hampton Hawes was nineteen, Sonny Criss was twenty, Dexter was twenty-four, Wardell was twenty-six, and McGhee was only twenty-nine. When we limit our ears to narrow categories, we miss out on all kinds of great music.

No particular moment can be singled out as the one at which bebop arrived in Los Angeles, but there was a series of events that led up to this July 1947 event at the Elks Hall. The arrival, late in 1945, of the train from New York into Los Angeles' Union Station is a story that many jazz fans know well. It was the train that carried Dizzy Gillespie, Charlie Parker, Milt Jackson, Ray Brown, and Stan Levey to L.A. for their legendary December 10 opening-night appearance at Billy Berg's Club in Hollywood. As the legend goes, that was the night the West Coast was introduced to bebop. They were to perform over a two-month residency. We know that Dizzy stayed in Los Angeles until February 1946. Parker's stay in the California sun is worthy of several books on the subject alone. The gig at Billy Berg's Club marked the beginning of a period for Parker that is well documented, with his supposed erratic behavior at jam sessions and causing great havoc in public places. Jazz mythology has focused on Bird's addictions and his forced stay in the Camarillo State Mental Hospital in Ventura County, not far from Los Angeles. But he also made several remarkable recordings for Dial Records during that period. Dexter always believed that Bird's time in the hospital was the only break from a hard and hectic life that Parker ever had. At Camarillo, Bird tended the lettuce patch and played in the Saturday afternoon jazz concerts. He returned to New York in early 1947 and soon recorded "Relaxin' at Camarillo" for Dial Records.

But that December 1945 train with Dizzy and friends could not have brought the first beboppers to Los Angeles. In fact, there had been a packed auditorium ten months earlier, on February 11, 1945, at the same Elks Hall on Central Avenue, to listen and dance to the Coleman Hawkins band, featuring McGhee on trumpet, Sir Charles Thompson on piano, Oscar Pettiford on bass, and Denzil Best on drums.[7] If it is true, as McGhee has said, that "Coleman was the one who opened the West Coast up as far as modern sounds in jazz," we may consider the scope of Hawkins's influence in an entirely new way. But what about Billy Eckstine's band with Fats Navarro, Gene Ammons, Leo Parker,

Tommy Potter, Art Blakey, and Sarah Vaughan? They played an engagement in February 1945—without Dexter—at the Plantation Club in Watts[8] and had recorded for the Armed Forces Radio Service "Jubilee" programs some time before Hawkins arrived in Los Angeles. For that matter, are single dates or moments sufficient evidence for the *arrival* of this new music in Los Angeles, or should we consider something more?

When Coleman Hawkins left Los Angeles for New York in July 1945, following his engagement at Billy Berg's and appearances in Norman Granz's new Jazz at the Philharmonic concerts, Howard McGhee stayed on in Los Angeles, forming a band with Teddy Edwards, whom he convinced to switch from alto to tenor saxophone. These young musicians were at the center of a scene that developed in the after-hours spots and clubs along Central Avenue. To McGhee this scene was so wonderful that, in spite of the social conditions, he thought California "was like heaven on earth." (Some musicians referred to Los Angeles during that period with somewhat less admiration as "Mississippi with palm trees.")[9] McGhee's paradise was mainly the clubs where he and his peers played to everyone's delight.

On July 10, 1947, the *California Eagle,* one of the oldest Black-owned newspapers in the United States, reported the arrest of McGhee and his wife, Dorothy, "on charges of possessing marihuana cigarettes and residue of marihuana ashes about the premises." The article said that "McGhee and his wife were first apprehended while seated in a downtown theater by officers who evidently didn't like the Negro–white association. They were taken to Central Division jail where officers asserted Mrs. McGhee resembled a blonde woman suspected of robbery." So much for McGhee's "heaven on earth."

The new music came to musicians and fans over the radio and from the 78s that were like gold out West. There was a shoeshine stand near Central Avenue run by an infamous character known as Moose the Mooche—for whom the classic bebop composition by Charlie Parker is named—where patrons could get all the latest recordings. Moose's given name was Emery Byrd. According to legend, he was a former honor student at Jefferson High School (Dexter's alma mater) who contracted polio and later became a drug dealer and then a friend to Parker, who gave Moose half of the rights to his publishing income. The story has it that Moose obtained the records he sold from the Pullman porters riding the Santa Fe *Chief* between Chicago and Los Angeles. In his later years, Moose sent a letter to Ross Russell at Dial Records, giving his forwarding address as San Quentin Prison.

There was also a roving record seller known as Bebop, who operated with a portable record player that he would set up in cafeterias or on sidewalks—anywhere he could tap into an electrical source—playing discs he would carry in a fiberboard case. All the barbershops along Central Avenue had record players; Dexter described musicians walking in with their valued 78s and playing them for the barbers and their customers. As Dizzy Gillespie said, "This music was being played everywhere there were young musicians. It was the music of the time and we were always working on it." The image of musicians and patrons, including Dexter, gathered excitedly in the L.A. barbershops to hear and discuss the latest tunes calls to mind Dexter's paternal grandfather, Frank L. Gordon, entertaining many patrons in his "tonsorial establishments" in North Dakota a half century earlier.

Any discussion of Central Avenue and the legendary jam sessions in the late 1940s usually brings the talk around to Dexter Gordon and Wardell Gray. The two had first met in Detroit in 1943 when Dexter was with Lionel Hampton's band and Wardell was playing at the Congo Club there. They became friends, and the next time they saw each other, Wardell was playing with Earl Hines in Chicago. When Dexter moved from New York back home to Los Angeles in 1946, he and Wardell started playing together at nightly jam sessions. At the time, a curfew required L.A. clubs to close at midnight, but the after-hours scene on Central Avenue was thriving. There was Jack's Basket Room (also known as Bird in the Basket, and owned by champion boxer Jack Johnson), Lovejoy's, Brother's, the Brown Bomber, Club Alabam, the Downbeat, the Finale, and of course, the Elks. About this period of the late-night sessions, the record producer Dootsie Williams said, "Central Avenue was black. Black people dominated, and white people had to come and sit where they could. So it was really like a homeland, like a country, like another country." Dexter:

> At all the sessions, they would hire a rhythm section . . . but there would always be about ten horns up on the stand. Various tenors, altos, trumpets and an occasional trombone. But it seemed that in the wee small hours of the morning—always—there would be only Wardell and myself. It became a kind of traditional thing. Spontaneous? Yeah! Nothing was really worked out . . . We were coming out of the same bags—Lester and Bird. Bird was never really a mystery to me because he was coming out of Lester. And others, too . . . But it was the same lineage. That's where I was. That's where Wardell was.[10]

The reedman Buddy Collette remembered Dexter and Wardell sounding in their battles quite a bit like their personalities. Dexter could blow like he was blowing the house down, heavy, just like he looked. And Wardell was quick. Most of the times it would end up with Wardell more or less winning because he was faster and more consistent. Wardell could play about the same way every night, which was good. Dexter would be kind of out of it and he couldn't always find things . . . [But] every three or four nights Dexter could hit it. He had that knockout punch, like Joe Louis when you caught him right . . . Dexter'd just found his combination. He was always looking for things. [There's that Joe Louis reference again.]

Wardell joined the Benny Goodman band in 1948 and moved on to the Count Basie Orchestra in 1950. In 1955 he went to Las Vegas for a gig with Benny Carter at the newly opened Moulin Rouge, the first Las Vegas casino to integrate, and he was working there when he met his tragic death. Wardell was extremely intelligent, well-read, and worldly. "Interviewing Wardell Gray is more like attending a literary tea . . . with copious comments on chess, Shakespeare, James Jones, Norman Mailer and other Gray favorites," wrote Ted Hallock in an article for *Melody Maker* in 1954. Mystery continues to blur the details of Wardell's death. His body was found, his neck broken, dumped in the desert. The police ruled that he had died of a drug overdose. How he ended up in the desert remains unknown.

Dexter never believed the overdose story. In 1988 he went to Las Vegas to act in an episode of the television series *Crime Story*, which was set, as fate would have it, in the Moulin Rouge. He spoke with a doorman there who remembered Wardell and his untimely death. Dexter refused to accept the police report and believed that others were involved. A 1995 mystery novel by Bill Moody, *Death of a Tenor Man*, speculates about what might have happened (it's complicated), but of course we will most likely never know the truth. The year 1955 was a particularly painful one for Dexter during his own most difficult decade, with the death of Charlie Parker on March 12 and then Wardell Gray on May 25. They were both thirty-four years old. Dexter was thirty-two.

The great tenor battles between Dexter and Wardell were immortalized not only in recordings but also in literature. "The Hunt" gained something close to mythical status after it was singled out in two best-selling books by iconic Beat writers. From *Go*, by John Clellon Holmes:

> The Hunt: listen there for the anthem in which we jettisoned the intellectual Dixieland of atheism, rationalism, liberalism—and found our group's rebel streak at last.[11]

From *On the Road,* by Jack Kerouac:

> Moriarty stands bowed and jumping before the big phonograph listening to
> a wild bop record . . . "The Hunt," with Dexter Gordon and Wardell Gray
> blowing their tops before a screaming audience that gave the record fantastic
> frenzied volume.[12]

At midnight on December 31, 1947, the second recording ban began.
All union-member musicians were forbidden to record. The inciting
issue was the demand from the American Federation of Musicians that
record companies pay a percentage of sales into a union fund which
would help support unemployed musicians. The notion, held by the
record companies, of music as labor was critical at this time, and the
response to the strike was particularly vitriolic toward James C. Petrillo,
the union president. Personal attacks called him the czar, dictator, or the
Mussolini of Music.[13] The recording ban lasted for one year, until
December 1948. During the period of the ban, the long-playing 33-rpm
record was introduced, followed by the 45-rpm disc. These formats
changed jazz recording completely. The older 78-rpm record limited
recordings to three minutes per side. But the new ten-inch LP allowed
for fifteen minutes per side, and the twelve-inch format could hold up to
22½ minutes per side. The 45-rpm disc was for single songs but was
much smaller than the 78 disc and able to reproduce sound with higher
fidelity. With its oversized center hole, the 45 was particularly well
suited to coin-operated jukeboxes, which soon were everywhere, vastly
expanding the market for record sales. The new technology would in
time be great for musicians, but the price they paid, a year with no
recordings, made 1948 a very difficult year for jazz musicians who
depended on record sales and radio air play to support their bands and
their families.

Dexter went on the road in the early part of 1948 with Tadd Dameron (piano), Kenny Dorham (trumpet), Curley Russell (bass), Roy Porter (drums), and singer Earl Coleman. They played at the Pershing
Lounge and the Hotel DuSable Lounge in Chicago, as well as the Sunset
Terrace Ballroom in Indianapolis. After returning to New York, they
played at one of Fred Robbins's ongoing series of concerts at Town Hall
along with Machito and his Afro-Cuban Orchestra. This may be the
first time that Machito referred to Dexter as "Desiderio," a name Dexter liked to use for many years to come. The next day they were part of
a marathon show at Club 845 in the Bronx. Finally, the group played at
the Three Deuces on Fifty-Second Street, probably from February 19

through March 3. After that, the group disbanded. It was said that Dexter's drug habit started to get in the way.

Later in 1948 Dexter worked at the Royal Roost in New York, a club that Ralph Watkins originally opened as a chicken restaurant. After a difficult start, Watkins was persuaded by Sid Torin (better known as the radio disc jockey Symphony Sid) to try presenting modern jazz at the club. Beginning in 1948 the club began to showcase bebop musicians including Charlie Parker, Dizzy Gillespie, Fats Navarro, Tadd Dameron, Art Blakey, and Max Roach. It was while Dexter was playing the Royal Roost that Herman Leonard took the iconic "smoke" photo (see chapter 1), with Navarro and Blakey in the background.

In his book, *Miles: The Autobiography,* Miles Davis remembers a concert that Symphony Sid produced on an off night at the Royal Roost:

> Sid picked Tuesday night and did a concert with me and Bird, Tadd Dameron, Fats Navarro, and Dexter Gordon. They had a non-drinking section in the club where young people could come and sit and listen to the music for ninety cents. . . .
>
> This was the time when I got to know Dexter Gordon. Dexter had come east in 1948 (or somewhere around that time), and he and I and Stan Levey started hanging out. I had first met him in Los Angeles. Dexter was real hip and could play his ass off, so we used to go around and go to jams. Stan and I had lived together for a while in 1945, so we were good friends. Stan and Dexter were using heroin together but I was still clean. We would go down to 52nd Street to hang out. Dexter used to be super hip and dapper, with those big shouldered suits everybody was wearing in those days. I was wearing my three-piece Brooks Brothers suits that I thought were super hip, too. You know, that St. Louis style shit. Niggers from St. Louis had the reputation for being sharp as a tack when it came to clothes. So couldn't nobody tell me nothing.
>
> But Dexter didn't think my dress style was all that hip. So he used to always tell me, "Jim ('Jim' was an expression a lot of musicians used back then), you can't hang with us looking and dressing like that. Why don't you wear some other shit, Jim? You gotta get some vines. You gotta go to F&M's," which was a clothing store on Broadway in midtown.
>
> "Why, Dexter, these some bad suits I'm wearing. I paid a lot of money for this shit."
>
> "Miles, that ain't it, 'cause the shit ain't hip. See, it ain't got nothing to do with money; it's got something to do with hipness, Jim, and that shit you got on ain't nowhere near hip. You gotta get some of them big-shouldered suits and Mr. B shirts if you want to be hip, Miles."
>
> So I'd say, all hurt and shit, "But Dex, man, these are nice clothes."
>
> "I know you think they hip, Miles, but they ain't. I can't be seen with nobody wearing no square shit like you be wearing. And you playing Bird's band? The hippest band in the world? Man, you oughta know better."

I was hurt. I always respected Dexter because I thought he was super hip—one of the hippest and cleanest young cats on the whole music scene back then. Then one day he said, "Man, why don't you grow a moustache? Or a beard?" . . .

So I saved up forty-seven dollars and went down to F&M's and bought me a gray, big-shouldered suit that looked like it was too big for me. That's the suit I had on in all them pictures while I was in Bird's band in 1948 and even in my own publicity shot when I had that process in my hair. After I got that suit from F&M's, Dexter came up to me grinning that big grin of his and towering over me, patting me on my back, saying, "Yeah, Jim, now you looking like something, now you hip. You can hang with us." He was something else.[14]

The relationship between Dexter and Miles continued for the rest of Dexter's life. Whenever I would hear them speak on the phone, there was never any gap of years in the conversation. They had a way of continuing a conversation no matter how long it had been since they last spoke. Dexter did not take it well when Miles's music was criticized by musicians who thought he should be playing the Miles Davis music that they loved and that they had grown up with. Dexter told one young musician who had publicly criticized Miles that when he could play a solo like Miles played on "Bye Bye Blackbird," he could comment; but until then, Dexter suggested he go home and practice. At the Hollywood Bowl during a tour that followed the release of the film *Round Midnight,* he asked Miles when he was going to play a ballad again. Miles said, "Man, *you* play a ballad. It's too hard. I'm done with that." Dexter laughed and said he knew what Miles meant. These lifelong friendships among musicians are remarkable and beautiful. To be in their presence taught me so much about what this music is really about. When Dexter died, Miles called me more than once to ask if I needed anything at all. I assured him that I was okay and thanked him.

On January 18, 1949, with the recording ban finally over, Dexter went into a New York studio with Dameron and his orchestra for Capitol Records. They recorded "Sid's Delight" and "Casbah." He then returned to Los Angeles, and as the 1940s came to an end, Dexter's "lost decade" would begin.

CHAPTER 10

Trapped

The first time I heard Dexter was in a record store. I went
to buy another Coleman Hawkins record 'cause I had one
Coleman Hawkins and I wanted to hear some more. I went
in the store and the guy said, "You should listen to this
record, because this cat's really happening," so he put the
record on. It was "Dexter's Deck" and I fell in love with it.

—Hadley Caliman[1]

When Dexter began to write his life story in earnest while we were living
in Cuernavaca, he would take out his yellow legal pads and his sharpened
pencils and make notes. He wanted to begin with the history of his family
before he was born. He wanted to write about his grandfather, Edward
Baker, his French great-grandfather Boulanger, and his father's family
from the unlikely locale of Fargo, North Dakota. He wanted to write
about his childhood in Los Angeles; his father, Dr. Frank Gordon; and his
mother wearing white gloves and pearls attending St. Philip's Episcopal
Church where he was an altar boy. He was definitely going to write about
Jefferson High School and Sam Browne, Melba Liston, and Hampton
Hawes. The first gig outside L.A. with Lionel Hampton's band was a big
chapter, and then there was New York City, Fifty-Second Street, L.A.'s
Central Avenue, Dial Records, Louis Armstrong's band, and the Billy
Eckstine band. All these experiences, from the late 1920s through the
1940s, were to be included. We looked at photos together, and when we
got to Herman Leonard's famous "smoke" photo of Dexter at the Royal
Roost in 1948, he started to get a bit glum. I asked him why.

He said, "Things didn't go too well after that. There was a rocky
road ahead for a while."

He then moved straight to 1960, when he got a job in Los Angeles
with the play *The Connection*, writing the music for the production and

recording it for Riverside Records at Cannonball Adderley's insistence. He then started to write about getting his passport, being invited to London by Ronnie Scott, and his fourteen-year sojourn in Europe.

I said, "Dexter, you left out a decade from the outline."

"I know," he said.

I pointed out that one could not write an autobiography and exclude an entire decade. What about the 1950s? He just looked far away with a kind of wistful expression, and then turned to me and said, "If you want the fifties in the book, you will have to write it yourself. I don't want to think about it or talk about it or write about it." That was the end of the conversation.

When Dexter was adamant about something, when he had a certain expression on his face and a certain tone in his voice, there was absolutely no possibility of changing his mind. There was no space for nagging, cajoling, convincing, arguing. The discussion was over. He was not going to talk about the 1950s and that was that. (Of course, over the years Dexter did speak occasionally about some of his experiences in the 1950s, including his times in prison, but he still never wanted any of it to be in his book.)

Okay, so . . . "If you want it in the book, you will have to write it yourself."

I could not have written this part of the book without the help of Hadley Caliman. Born in Oklahoma in 1932, Hadley moved to Dexter's Los Angeles neighborhood in 1940 when he was eight years old and Dexter, at seventeen, was just starting out in the Lionel Hampton band. Hadley was so enamored with Dexter's playing that he also took up the tenor, studied with Dexter, and lent Dexter his horn when he needed it. Hadley even became known in the neighborhood as "Little Dex." Later, he became a regular on the Central Avenue scene, playing with Dexter, Wardell Gray, and many others.

But Hadley was not the only "Little Dex" in Los Angeles in the 1950s. Clifford Solomon was another player who was either given the nickname or who took it for himself. In his oral history interview for *Central Avenue Sounds*,[2] Solomon said, "After we discovered Dexter, all the guys wanted to play like Dexter, and everybody was a Little Dex. Hadley Caliman, Shedrick Carruthers, me, and a couple of other guys. Dexter was our idol. Then, when we met Dexter and he took us under his wing like we were disciples, we were hooked. You know what I mean? Dexter was our Christ."

Hadley taught for many years at Cornish College of the Arts in Seattle, Washington, and became a legendary figure on the Northwest jazz scene. He recorded several albums under his own name and appears on albums by Hampton Hawes, Freddie Hubbard, Joe Henderson, Gerald Wilson, Bobby Hutcherson, and Santana. He encouraged me to fill in the parts that Dexter wanted to leave out of his autobiography. Hadley said the whole story needed to be told and that he would help me. For many Mondays in 2010 I would call Hadley on Mercer Island, Washington, from my home in New York City. I would record our conversations and have them transcribed by the fabulous Jess Pinkham. His beautiful wife, Linda, helped us arrange these talks and worked with us on the transcriptions. Then in July 2010, Hadley said, "Max, I'm not buying any green bananas. I think you should come out here to see me." I had never heard that expression before and made some kind of joke about fried green bananas. Then he told me that he had liver cancer and didn't expect to live long enough for the bananas to ripen. I flew out to Mercer Island and we watched the film *Unchained* together—it was made at the Chino State prison while Hadley and Dexter were both inmates there—shared some delicious meals, took a walk, and sat by the water. He told me to keep going on the book and to explain to people what happened in Los Angeles to the musicians. Hadley Caliman:

> I was a huge Dexter fan and then the remarkable thing, the irony of the whole thing, was that Dexter lived within walking distance of where I lived, almost right around the corner.
>
> In the early fifties, Dexter had this green Torpedo Pontiac, and there were about seven people in the car. The police stopped us because of Dexter's driving. We didn't get busted that time. Don't let me ramble. Sometimes I get to rambling. One time, I went to Dexter's house to see if we could go find something to get high with, and we sat there and listened to Horace Silver a little bit and we talked about Hank Mobley and then we went and got some stuff, and we came back to his house and did it. When I started to go home, he said, "I'll walk you to the corner so I can get some Pall Mall cigarettes." I said okay, so we went to the store and on the way back the cops pulled over and put us in the car, and they started to harass Dexter about giving up somebody, and stuff he's been doing and all this kind of stuff. They talked real bad to us and took us all the way from Fifty-something Street to Seventh Street, downtown. By the time we got there, they had finished interrogating us and they told us to get out. Here I am, this little short dude with this big tall lanky guy, and we're walking all the way back, probably five miles, 'cause we didn't have enough money to get on the streetcar.
>
> I followed him around like a little puppy dog. When Dexter heard they were calling me "Little Dex," he said, "Gee, I hope Hadley doesn't do everything I did. He doesn't exactly need to be Little Dex."[3]

Hadley told me that all the other guys they called "Little Dex" were great players but that nobody ever heard of them because they were trapped in the web of persecution over their drug use, which ruined so many lives and careers. "Seventy-five percent of the musicians in L.A. were trapped there because of drugs," he said. "They were on parole and because of the law that allowed them to be busted for tracks and internal possession, they could never get out. It was a crime. Their careers were ruined. Their lives were stopped. For nothing."

Hadley's death on September 8, 2010, greatly saddened all who knew him. What he told me about Dexter's life in the 1950s, especially about people being jailed and held on probation for nothing more than having needle marks—tracks—on their arms, or showing signs, through a dubious test, of the presence of drugs in their system, made me dig ever deeper into Dexter's "lost decade."

The research into these painful years includes prison records, court documents, mug shots, and endless letters to various departments of corrections and prison inmate record archives requesting information. John Reid, in his master's research at Rutgers University, was very helpful in finding documents and sharing them with me.

The documents we found concerning Dexter's police record in Los Angeles indicate that he was arrested for the first time in 1946, at the age of twenty-three, and spent his first time behind bars in 1948 when he was twenty-five. The notation in his file reads: "Type of Institution to Which First Committed: Jail." Dexter never discussed the details of these first arrests. We do know that they were for "transporting drugs." In fact, all of Dexter's "crimes" derived from his drug habit. He never engaged in any sort of violence.

The first found mention in the press about Dexter's drug use was in the January 1949 issue of the French magazine *Jazz Hot*:

Gordon Privé de Saxo

Le sosie de Joe Louis, l'étoile du saxo tenor bop Dexter Gordon, reçoit deux années de prison pour vol. Il avait subi, il y a un an, trois mois de prévention pour trafic de stupéfiants.

Translation:

Dexter Gordon Deprived of his Sax

The Joe Louis lookalike, the tenor sax bop star Dexter Gordon, received two years in prison for theft. One year ago, he received a three-month probation for drug trafficking.

Dexter did not in fact spend two years in prison for theft as the article states. (And here again comes the Joe Louis comparison.) We know that he spent some time at the United States Narcotic Farm in Lexington, Kentucky. "Lexington," or "The Farm," as the facility was known by those who were either sent there by the courts or who signed themselves in, is infamous in jazz history. According to the Narcotic Farm's own description: "For nearly four decades, from the 1930s to the '70s, Lexington was a center for drug research and treatment. It drew addicts talented and desperate, obscure and celebrated, and provided free treatment and more: job training, sports, dental help, music lessons, even manicures. Research done there, much of it conducted with volunteer human subjects, yielded insights into drug addiction that still resonate today."[4]

Many jazz musicians chose to go to Lexington to take the "cure" rather than do time in jail or prison. The tap dancer Baby Lawrence wrote lyrical letters to the pianist Mary Lou Williams from there. Jazz musicians Howard McGhee, Tadd Dameron, Lee Morgan, Stan Levey, and Elvin Jones were among those who, like Dexter, spent time in and out of Lexington, sent there by the courts. It was said by many that all the great musicians at Lexington played in the greatest band that nobody ever heard, because as inmates they never were allowed to record. The documentary film *Narcotic Farm* tells of authors William S. Burroughs and his son, William Jr., spending time at Lexington, and both wrote about their experiences there. Burroughs Sr. describes the place in his book *Junkie,* detailing the grueling detox treatments but also suggesting that the food was excellent.

Since Dexter was reluctant (to put it mildly) to discuss this period of his life, we are forced to reconstruct it by examining two sets of documents: his discography and his California prison records. We know that Dexter was working at the Hula Hut in Los Angeles in August 1950 with Clark Terry (trumpet), Sonny Criss (alto saxophone), Wardell Gray, Jimmy Bunn (piano), Billy Hadnott (bass), and Chuck Thompson (drums), and that he recorded with vocalist Helen Humes in November 1950. Thanks to the great saxophonist, composer, bandleader, and educator Jimmy Heath, we know that Dexter played at Bop City (also known as Jimbo's Bop City) in San Francisco in 1950.

In February 1951 *Ebony* magazine published an article written by Cab Calloway under the headline "Is Dope Killing Our Musicians? Famed Orchestra Leader Sees Use of Narcotics as Dire Menace to Future of Band Business." Calloway wrote: "There are many alarmists among us who say that dope is slowly killing our musicians and that the jazz business is doomed to destroy itself in a poisonous cloud of mari-juana smoke to the sinister accompaniment of heroin hypodermic nee-dle 'pops.' I am not an alarmist. I know that the drug menace in music is very real, and that unless immediate steps are taken it will lead to the deterioration of a splendid art. I do not think, however, that the advance of the dope habit is irresistible. It can be checked."

Along with the article are photos of several musicians, including John Simmons, Miles Davis, Eddie Heywood, Gene Krupa, Billie Holi-day, Howard McGhee, Art Blakey, and Dexter. The caption beneath Dexter's photo reads, "Dexter Gordon, tenor sax star, was arrested sev-eral years back in the South for using dope while with a major jazz band." (There is no evidence that Dexter was ever arrested in the South.) Dexter's mother happened to be an *Ebony* subscriber, and she was humiliated when she saw the article. She told Dexter that she couldn't go to church or to her bridge club because she knew that everyone had seen it. Some thirty-five years later, when Dexter received a lifetime achievement award from the National Urban League, Cab Calloway was there as well. Dexter took the opportunity to tell Calloway that the article had been "uncalled for" and that it had upset his mother. Getting the anger off his chest after more than three decades made Dexter feel better, although he wasn't convinced that Calloway had any idea of what he was talking about.

In February 1952 a live recording was made of Dexter playing with Wardell Gray in Pasadena. In March he and Wardell worked at the Clef Club in Hollywood, and they recorded again in Hollywood in June. Then there is no evidence at all of Dexter's work until September 1955. Of course, there were good times for Dexter in the 1950s apart from his music. He married his first wife, Josephin A. Notti, known as Jodi, and they had two daughters, Robin (1952) and Deidre (1953). They all lived with Dexter's mother in the family home at 238 East Forty-Fifth Street on Los Angeles' Eastside. (Dexter and Josephin divorced in 1966.) But these were the years that Dexter wanted to leave out of his autobiogra-phy, and a look at his prison records from the California State Depart-ment of Corrections shows why, even if we can't know all of the details behind each entry.

His first significant incarceration began on May 19, 1953, when he was remanded to Chino Prison, about thirty-five miles east of Los Ange-les, to serve a sentence of one to fifteen years for second-degree burglary (entering a structure with intent to commit a crime). He was released on parole after serving fifteen months. According to his Inmate Record

Card, he had been arrested eight times before this conviction, and he had been on probation once. He was thirty years old.

Chino was built in 1941 on the site of a former sugar-beet ranch and was billed by the California Department of Corrections as "the first major minimum-security prison in the United States." Its former warden, Kenyon J. Scudder, called it California's "prison without walls, without guns, without guards, where the dignity of the individual is recognized and each is treated as a person." Although Dexter never talked about this period of his life in detail, he did say that his time at Chino had a profound effect on him and probably saved his life. The prison had a boxing arena on the grounds, and on holidays they would hold special concerts, boxing, wrestling, or weightlifting events. There were football and baseball games on Sundays with visitors welcome. Just as at Lexington, the band at Chino was as strong as any playing anywhere in California. With Dexter in the band were his old friend Hadley "Little Dex" Caliman and the drummer Roy Porter.

While most of the inmates had farm jobs, Dexter was able to work as a prison librarian because, he said, he was "just not fit for work in the fields." He said his feet were too big and he was too tall to pick strawberries and tomatoes. In the library he could read all day, and to make the best of his time he learned to read in French with the help of a dictionary and a donated collection of French books. He read *Les Misérables* by Victor Hugo and reread it many times thereafter. (Years later, after being detained at the Paris airport because of previous drug offenses, he told French minister of culture Jack Lang that he felt like Jean Valjean, who was imprisoned for nineteen years for stealing a loaf of bread.) Dexter was always proud to tell people that of course he could read French—he was part French, after all.

There were mandatory group counseling sessions at Chino, and at first Dexter thought he had no need for any such thing. But having no choice, he went. For years afterward he said that what he learned in those sessions helped him think about things in a different way. Hearing about the difficult lives the other men had lived and the problems they faced before getting locked up made him realize how privileged he had been as the only child in a stable home with a doctor for a father, a room of his own, enough to eat, and a structure that made his daily life free of stress and turmoil. He was also able to focus on the troubles he had caused for himself and his family, and begin to plot a way out. It didn't happen overnight, but he did often go back to what he had learned in those days about being self-reflective and nonjudgmental, and being careful not to blame anyone else for his circumstances. This experience could have been one of the worst for Dexter. But instead he said that Chino saved his life. He took a positive view of going to prison rather than the more obvious view. That was Dexter's way of surviving the worst of times. "It could always be worse" was one of his favorite expressions.

While Dexter was in Chino, a crew arrived to film the movie *Unchained*, which was based on Scudder's book, *Prisoners Are People*. The football star Elroy "Crazylegs" Hirsch played the lead character. The director was Hall Bartlett, and the cast also included Chester Morris, Jerry Paris, Peggy Knudsen, and Barbara Hale. Dexter appears in a scene in which the Chino band is playing. Because imprisoned musicians were not allowed to be union members, Dexter and the other band members are only seen and not heard on the film's soundtrack. When we see Dexter onscreen playing his tenor, the sounds we hear come from the horn of Georgie Auld. In later years, whenever Dexter would be asked to do a gig that he couldn't—or preferred not to—make, he would say, "Call Georgie Auld. He sounds just like me."

On my last visit with Hadley, he and his wife and I watched *Unchained*. He kept commenting on the background shots that showed real prisoners and the scene with Dexter in the band. Of course he did not like the fact that it was not Dexter playing in the film. He did think the film glorified the experience somewhat, but in the end he was glad to see that someone had taken the trouble to make a movie about prisoners as real human beings. Hadley was reflecting on his life, and just like Dexter he said that he had no regrets. He was grateful to have been a jazz musician. Then he went into his music room and began to practice. Just like Dexter.

Dexter always believed that his time spent in prison made him a better person. In an interview with journalist Pete Hamill, Dexter spoke about his time behind bars:

> Some people would go to jail [as a result of their heroin use], and as negative as that is, there's a positive side to it. You get some rest. You build your body back. And I have to say that has a lot to do with me making it, because during those years I would have those forced and periodic vacations. And after a while, when you see the same shit happening over and over again to your life, you finally say, Wow, man, this gotta stop. Bird and Fats and the other guys, it was continuously downhill. But jail saved my life.[5]

In 1955 Dexter recorded an album for Bethlehem Records called *Daddy Plays the Horn*, with Kenny Drew (piano), Leroy Vinnegar (bass), and Lawrence Marable (drums). For a period that Dexter wanted to forget, he sounds very good on this album, especially on Charlie Parker's "Confirmation." That same year he performed on drummer Stan Levey's album *This Time the Drum's on Me,* sounding in good shape on his composition "Stanley the Steamer." The album featured Conte Condoli (trumpet), Lou Levy (piano), Leroy Vinnegar (bass), and Frank Rosolino (trombone). One review of the album noted that "Stan brought in Dexter Gordon, his old pal from Harlem and one of the only guys in jazz as physically imposing as himself . . . Gordon was fresh off a two-year stint in Chino for heroin possession. He was grateful to Stan for a paying gig and a chance to regain lost ground." (Here again, the facts are stretched. Dexter was released from Chino on August 11, 1954, after serving fifteen months, not two years.)

One story Dexter did like to tell was about his very good friend and favorite drummer, Lawrence Marable. Lawrence had his own difficulties with drug use in the 1950s and at one point was wanted by police on an outstanding warrant. Marable stayed at large until Dexter was locked up for one of his stays in the L.A. County jail. At that point Lawrence turned himself in and accepted his own jail term. He admitted that he wanted to go to jail "to look after Dexter." Dexter considered that the greatest sign of friendship he had ever known. When I asked Lawrence about the story, he said, "I was afraid Dexter would find a better drummer inside, because all the best players were locked up." Then he laughed a huge raucous laugh. Lawrence also said that when he and his friends would go looking for things to steal out of unlocked cars to get drug money, they refused to take Dexter along because he was so tall and recognizable. But of course they would bring Dexter some of the ill-gotten cash. When things got better for Dexter in 1960 and he got the job in *The Connection,* a play about drug users, the first person he hired was Marable.

The years following his first prison term at Chino became very difficult for Dexter. An extremely harsh and notorious state regulation, Statute §11721 of the California Health and Safety Code, made it a misdemeanor punishable by imprisonment plus probation for any person to "be addicted to the use of narcotics." The California courts further decided that an "addict" could be prosecuted "at any time before he reforms, even if he never used or possessed any narcotics within the State and has not been guilty of any antisocial behavior there." Thus police were empowered to arrest people merely for having needle marks (tracks) on their arms or showing signs of having drugs in their system ("internal possession"). And courts routinely sent such people to jail.

Users of drugs were caught in a vicious cycle of arrests, jailings, paroles, and repeated jailings—first, perhaps, for merely having "tracks," then for violating their parole or probation, and maybe even again for having the same needle marks on their arms. It became a dreadful downward spiral that sapped years from the lives of many victims. Many of them simply did not survive.

Under this state regulation, Dexter was arraigned on a charge of having needle marks on his arms on January 18, 1956. He had been stopped by police while driving in a car with a friend. According to a report in the *Los Angeles Sentinel,* Dexter's friend said he had purchased twenty-five dollars' worth of heroin on Central Avenue. When the police questioned him about the needle marks on his arm, the friend replied, "That's my fifty-thousand-dollar arm—my golden arm." The friend and Dexter were each sentenced to ninety days in the Los Angeles County jail.

Dexter had entered his own vicious cycle. In July 1956 he was charged with stealing golf clubs from a parked car. According to the court record, "defendant [and associate] drove into the parking lot of the Broadway Department Store ... broke into a parked car and removed golf clubs and equipment valued at $310 and drove off ... The manager of the store was stationed on the roof with a pair of binoculars ... He wrote down the license number of the defendant's car which resulted in the arrest of defendants." It took more than a year, until September 1957, for Dexter to receive his sentence: one year in jail and three years' probation. After serving eight months in the county jail, he was released in May 1958, after which his three years' probation took effect.

On December 24, 1958, Dexter was in court once more, this time for violating that probation. In a plea for understanding, Dexter recounted the cascade of incidents and frustrations that got him in trouble yet again, and his attempts at straightening out. According to the court record, he told the judge, "We took golf clubs out of an open car in L.A [in 1956] ... I received 3 years' probation with one year in the county jail. I was released in May 1958. I went to work as a musician and did well. [Now I have been] arrested on a warrant [for petty theft] and [needle] marks. I received 30 days on the petty theft charge and 90 days on the marks." In a subsequent court appearance on the same charge, on February 25, 1959, Dexter was ordered back to Chino Prison. Dexter told the court that the punishment was excessive "for a bullshit probation violation ... This warrant was for a saxophone I had rented and pawned *prior* to receiving the [1957] probation. The warrant was issued on October 11, 1957, while I was incarcerated doing the 1-year sentence. I was released [in May 1958] and didn't know about [the warrant] until arrested 18 months later. My probation was revoked and I received the sentence of penitentiary on the original case."

Dexter did not have a lawyer representing him. But if he had, the lawyer might have argued that an arrest based on a warrant issued while Dexter was in jail and not revealed to him until months after his release was improper, at the very least. When Dexter said that he first learned about the warrant "18 months later," he must have meant eighteen months after the warrant was issued in October 1957, not eighteen months after his release from jail (since only nine months had passed when he made this remark in February 1959). In the many times that Dexter was arrested throughout his life, there is little or no evidence of him denying culpability. In this case he clearly felt blindsided by a warrant he didn't know existed.

After several months at Chino, Dexter was transferred to the maximum-security Folsom Prison on May 6, 1959. On February 25, 1960, after nine months, he was released and granted two years on parole. "That was the end of the line," he said. "You couldn't get any worse than that."[6]

Los Angeles led the nation in narcotics arrests in 1954, surpassing New York City by about 50 percent, even though it had only about one-tenth as many drug users. According to the Federal Bureau of Narcotics, it was estimated that Los Angeles had about three thousand "addicts," or about 5 percent of the nation's total heroin-using population.[7] The infamous Statute §11721 allowed a health and safety code violation to become a criminal offense and kept thousands of probationers trapped in Los Angeles and multitudes of musicians and other artists from pursuing their careers. They were arrested for having needle marks or for failing a so-called Nalline test, an injection that tested for "internal possession" of drugs. On June 25, 1962, the statute was overturned by the U.S. Supreme Court in the case of *Robinson v. California*. Lawrence Robinson had been one of the many who were stopped by police and arrested for having "tracks" on his arm. The Supreme Court decided that the California statute "inflicts a cruel and unusual punishment in violation of the Eighth and Fourteenth Amendments." The Eighth Amendment to the U.S. Constitution protects citizens from excessive bail, fines, and punishments. The Fourteenth, adopted in 1868 as one of the Reconstruction Amendments, addresses citizenship rights and equal protection under the law.

Cruel and unusual punishment as applied to people jailed for merely having what might be needle marks on their arms turned out to be quite an understatement. The Supreme Court likened the California law to one making it a criminal offense "to be mentally ill, or a leper, or to be afflicted with a venereal disease" and found that the state could not punish persons merely because of their "status" of addiction. The Court noted that the law was not aimed at the purchase, sale, or possession of illegal drugs.

The Nalline test emerged as a narcotic control measure in the late 1950s. Nalline is a trade name of Merck and Company for a synthetic opiate antagonist which counteracts the physical effects of opiates. After the injection of Nalline, dilation of the pupils would indicate the presence of opiates in a person's body. In Los Angeles a dilated pupil was enough to immediately consign a person to the county jail for ninety days for "internal possession" of narcotics. Many states rejected this testing procedure, but California continued its use into the 1960s. Nalline produces side effects such as dysphoria, anxiety, confusion, and hallucinations. For these reasons it is no longer used medically. We can remain grateful to Lawrence Robinson for pursuing this case, but unfortunately he did not live to see the decision. He died in 1961.

While Dexter was in Chino in 1959, he was devastated to learn of the tragic death, on July 17, of Billie Holiday, whose life and brilliant career had also been ravaged by drugs and persecution. He was so moved that he wrote a beautifully lyrical letter to *Down Beat,* which the magazine published in its edition of September 3, 1959, with this editor's note: "Tenor saxophonist Gordon's long letter is printed almost intact because of its summation of the feeling of countless persons, friends and fans, on the death of Billie Holiday. His outrage at her treatment is shared by all of us." The note did not mention that Dexter had mailed it from prison.

WORDS FOR LADY DAY, DOWN BEAT, SEPTEMBER 3, 1959

"My mother was 15, my father 18, and I was three years old when they got married." So says Lady Day in her book, Lady Sings the Blues.[8]

But today Lady sings the blues no more.

Tragedy surrounded Billie Holiday as an octopus surrounds its victim with its tentacles . . . [But] she wore it, tragedy, like a cloak of honor.

Even in the songs she sang, pathos reared its sentient head. The theme was invariably one of misuse: "My man, he beats me, too." "Jim never brings me pretty flowers." "Lover man, some day he'll come and he'll dry all my tears." The heart-rending "Gloomy Sunday," and "Strange Fruit." Happy songs, you ask? Sure, she sang them, but even these had an aura of gloom.

Lady sang out for all the world to bear witness to the suffering of womankind. Moreover, men and women both received her message. Someone I *know, very dear to me, while suffering in a hospital, heard repeatedly in her delirium the voice of Billie Holiday—her only consolation.*

After entering the hospital and being put on the critical list for complications, Billie was said to have been found with a bundle of heroin by a nurse, who was "happening by." From this, I deduce she was still fighting for her life. However, after the police, the notoriety, the inevitable court hassle to follow, she seems to have given up, and unlike old generals, just faded away. This, to me, is a sad note of our times, our society, in which something as heinous as this is allowed to happen. A thinking person can denote many other intangibles in a situation such as this . . .

Billie's contribution will always be near, for many singers carry her style on today. One vocalist in particular not only sings like her, but snaps her fingers, taps her feet, holds her head to one side like Lady Day. Lady's voice, while very sophisticated, was coarse, soft, yet earthy. Her style and delivery were unique, all her own. The contribution she made in the American art form, jazz, was infinite and immeasurable and meant many things to many people.

Generous to a fault, Billie was misused by people, many people. Loving well but not wisely, that is the story of Billie Holiday's life. Although regal, but not "pale," Lady to me was a queen.

Dexter Gordon, Los Angeles

This touching letter gives us an example of Dexter's literary flair and use of language. In the first lines, he refers to a quote from her book, *Lady Sings the Blues*. The actual lines are these: "Mom and Pop were just a couple of kids when they got married. He was eighteen, she was sixteen, and I was three." Later in the letter he refers to a line from *Othello:* "Of one that lov'd not wisely but too well." This is something Dexter would often do in letters, and readers would wonder about the phrase that seemed to come out of nowhere. He did something very similar when he dropped musical quotes into his solos. He would hear them in his head and include them in his playing, and though they might seem random to some listeners, there was always a reason for them. When he describes Billie at the end of the letter as "regal, but not pale," I interpret that to mean that all others "pale" in comparison. Of course his words and his meanings are open for discussion, but when he had something important to say, as he did in this letter, there were always layers of meaning.

All too often in the 1950s and 1960s the persecution of drug users was a kind of sport to some law enforcement types. In 1974 John O'Grady (with Nolan Davis) published a book entitled *O'Grady: The Life and Times of Hollywood's No. 1 Private Eye*.[9] In it, O'Grady delights in recounting his adventures in chasing down prey, the more famous the better:

The year was 1948 and the use of heroin, smuggled up from Mexico, was already pretty widespread in Hollywood . . . I resolved to wage a one-man war on "stuff," also known in certain circles as "shit." It was apparent to me even in the late 1940s that heroin was going to sweep the country unless it could be stopped. I did my damnedest to stop it . . . I was put in charge of the Hollywood narc squad . . . At the time I was working drugs, the biggest peripheral contributor to narco traffic was the jazz crowd. I set out to destroy that crowd and damn near did. I ran Charlie "Yardbird" Parker, the great saxophonist, out of town. I could have nailed him. His arms were covered with track marks from heroin needles. But he was too old and too drunk and I decided it wasn't worth wasting the time nailing Parker just so the City of L.A. could pay for his keep. As a cop, mine was not to reason why addicts took drugs, mine was to bust their asses.

One of Dexter's L.A. friends, the jazz singer Ed Reed, who survived years of his own entanglements in the prison system to achieve a successful recording and international performing career, recalled an incident at the end of Dexter's decade of troubles in a conversation with me:

The parole officer and the cops kicked in our door in Watts and caught Dexter and me. They accused us of a parole violation. They were going to take us to San Quentin. It was a two-day trip by bus, so first they took us to Soledad Prison (about four hours north of Los Angeles) to spend the night. The next morning I got back on the bus, looked around and said, "Hey, where's Dexter?" He wasn't there. I never did know what happened to him. Did he escape or just disappear? Next thing I knew, I read in *Down Beat* that he was in Europe. Good for him. He got out of that life.

In the spring of 1961, after his last detention, Dexter was finally allowed to travel outside of Los Angeles. And February 25, 1962, was the day that Dexter—having satisfied all the requirements of his parole and probation—was finally formally discharged from the California penal system. He never forgot that date. He was two days short of his thirty-ninth birthday.

CHAPTER 11

Resurgence

*I was never really away from jazz [in the 1950s]—not a
final, absolute separation. It's just that there were so many
other things that put great demands on my time that I
wasn't able to function jazz-wise as much as I would have
liked—or should have been doing. I wasn't always available
for public appearances but inside of me it was still swinging.
I kept hearing the changes. As the song says, "They can't
take that away from me." Nineteen sixty-two was the year
I was able to stand up straight and breathe, and not have to
always be looking over my shoulder for the police or danger.*

—Dexter Gordon

In Dexter's life story, every so often there would come a year that was
pivotal. He called these "phoenix rising" years. The year 1960 was certainly one of those. Dexter:

> *I guess the start of it all was the play,* The Connection. *I was asked to write the
> music and to act in the production. I played the part of what the script called
> the Number One Musician—the bandleader, in fact. This was quite a challenge
> for me. The themes had to be specific to the plot or the scene. It really built up
> my self-confidence and at that time I really needed it. It did a lot for me.*

In another ironic moment in Dexter's life, he wasn't using drugs when
he acted the part of a drug addict in a play. But as he said, "I could definitely understand the character and play the part." *The Connection,* written by Jack Gelber, was originally produced by the Living Theatre in New
York City in 1959, directed by Living Theatre cofounder Judith Malina,
and designed by cofounder Julian Beck. It is the story of a producer and
a writer who are attempting to stage a play about drug addicts, some of
whom happen to be musicians. What the addicts have in common is that

they are all waiting for Cowboy, "the connection," to bring them drugs at the apartment of one of the characters. Live jazz is performed between scenes by the musicians onstage. In the New York production, the music was composed by pianist Freddie Redd. Jackie McLean acted and played saxophone in the play, and the actor Carl Lee played the role of Cowboy. (In later years, Carl Lee was the bartender at the New York jazz club Slug's. He is the son of legendary actor Canada Lee.)

In the Los Angeles production, the play featured actors Robert Blake and Gavin McLeod and was produced by Albert "Cubby" Broccoli, who went on to produce more than a dozen James Bond films among many others. The musicians included Dexter's very good friend Lawrence Marable on drums, Gildo Mahones on piano, and Bob West on bass. Dexter loved to tell a story about Marable. For the first week of the production, the musicians were paid with checks that had "The Connection" printed on them. Lawrence took one look at his check and said, "They must be joking. No one is going to cash a check from *the connection*! Get cash." Dexter assured him that the check would be fine and they drove to the historic Farmers Market on Third and Fairfax, where musicians normally cashed their checks, and had no problem. Dexter and Lawrence laughed about that for years.

Morgan Ames, the singer, songwriter, and producer, wrote the lyrics to "Ernie's Tune," one of Dexter's compositions for the play. Dexter's character, the Number One Musician, was meant to be "soft-spoken, talented, lost, attractive," and Ames thought that Dexter was perfectly cast. Dexter's compositions were written to fit into the production in exactly the same way Freddie Redd's tunes did in the New York version. Freddie's songs are included in the Blue Note album *The Music from the Connection*. Dexter's tune "Soul Sister" is the counterpart to Freddie's "(Theme for) Sister Salvation"; Dexter's "I Want More" was heard in L.A., whereas Freddie's "O.D. (Overdose)" was heard in New York; Dexter's "Ernie's Tune" parallels Freddie's "Music Forever." This was the first time Dexter had written music for a play, and he found the challenge very exciting. The timing was perfect for him and he often talked about the moment as another turning point in his life.

The journalist Steven Cerra recalled:

A quick stroll west would bring you to Cahuenga Blvd. and Shelly's Manne Hole and on your way over on Selma Street from Vine you'd pass the Ivar Theater. Although I had both walked and driven by it a number of times, I had never been inside the Ivar . . . That was about to change when I noticed tenor saxophonist Dexter Gordon's name on the marquis announcing his appearance in the West Coast version of Jack Gelber's *The Connection,* a play that had premiered in New York City in July 1959.

> I stopped at the Ivar's box office to pick up some tickets . . . This was going to be my first opportunity to hear "long tall Dexter" in person which was reason enough for me to check out the play . . . I met Dexter after the performance in the theater's "green room." Among the well-wishers was the drummer Stan Levey. I knew him from his time at The Lighthouse. Dexter was very, very happy to see Stan . . . Afterwards, as we were walking to our cars, I remember Stan saying that "it was good to see him (Dexter) so happy." Stan knew from personal experience what Dexter had been through and he was glad to see him so together.[1]

During the run of *The Connection,* Dexter took a group to play at the Zebra Lounge in Los Angeles. Cannonball Adderley heard them there and wanted to record the group for the Jazzland label. At first Dexter was reluctant to say yes, because he hadn't recorded anything since 1955 and was still recovering from his years of incarceration. He was on parole and working in *The Connection,* but Cannonball persisted. On October 13, 1960, Dexter went into the studio with Martin Banks (trumpet), Richard Boone (trombone), Dolo Coker (piano), Charles Green (bass), and Lawrence Marable (drums). The album that came out of the session was *The Resurgence of Dexter Gordon.* It was prophetic way beyond its title. Dexter remained ever grateful to the brilliant and very loyal Cannonball Adderley for giving him this chance.

During the time that Dexter was performing in *The Connection* and recording *Resurgence* for Cannonball, correspondence began between the agent Bob Leonard and Alfred Lion, the cofounder of Blue Note Records, about signing Dexter to a contract with Blue Note. A letter from Leonard to Lion dated October 27, 1960, suggested that there was renewed interest in Dexter, because it included a set of terms being offered by Prestige Records, a Blue Note competitor. On October 30, Blue Note made its offer for Dexter.

The terms of the deal, apparently standard for the time, were minimal to say the least: a 3 percent royalty for each LP album sold. A musician could not expect to make a living from an income of 14¼ cents per record (3 percent of the $4.76 retail price), especially since there was no accurate way to track sales. The musician's benefit from this exclusive contract was exposure to a jazz audience, the hoped-for increase of club bookings, and the recognition of being associated with a label that presented some of the most popular jazz artists of the day, including Miles Davis, Sonny Rollins, and John Coltrane. For Dexter this was an opportunity that he could not pass up, especially after the very lean years following his recordings on Savoy and Dial. He remained grateful to Alfred Lion and his partner Francis Wolff, and as the years went by, the musical value of the Blue Note recordings became apparent, their longevity proving that jazz fans are loyal and know how to discern a great recording from a mediocre one.

Dexter signed the contract on November 7, 1960. He would go on to make several of his classic and most beloved recordings for Blue Note. His relationship with Lion and Wolff is documented by the letters they exchanged while Dexter lived in Europe and by the iconic photos taken by Wolff. They give us a rare opportunity to share this time with Dexter and unique insight into the ways he was thinking about his career and his future. Years later he would say that he always believed the Blue Note recordings would stand up over time, and he was pleased that so many people were able to enjoy the music for so long.

The year 1961 was a transitional one on many levels. The Berlin Wall went up. President Kennedy ordered a CIA-led militia to invade Cuba's Bay of Pigs. A man flew in space for the first time (Russian Yuri Gagarin). The dictator Rafael Trujillo was assassinated in the Dominican Republic. Roger Maris broke Babe Ruth's "unbreakable" record of sixty home runs in a single baseball season. And Dexter Gordon, an avid reader of newspapers, a great baseball fan, and a now nearly forty-year-old jazz musician who had just come through a decade of terrible troubles with drug addiction and the justice system, was finally allowed to leave Los Angeles. His last detention ended on April 14; he was off parole and allowed to get on with his life.

Dexter arrived in New York City in May and began his recording tenure with Blue Note Records. Lion, who had founded Blue Note in 1939, and Wolff knew what kind of music they wanted to hear, and it had to swing. Dexter was happy to oblige. Before Dexter left California, Lion wrote a him a letter saying: "The rhythm section has been recording steadily behind [alto saxophonist] Lou Donaldson and now with tenor saxophonist Booker Ervin. I don't want any complicated music; but rather some good standards in medium, medium-bright and medium bounce tempos. I'd like to make something that can be enjoyed and played on jukeboxes stationed in the soul spots throughout the nation."

On May 6 Dexter went into Rudy Van Gelder's studio in Englewood Cliffs, New Jersey, to record with twenty-three-year-old Freddie Hubbard on trumpet, Horace Parlan on piano, George Tucker on bass, and Al Harewood on drums (the rhythm section mentioned in Lion's letter).

FIGURE 11. Alfred Lion (left) and Francis Wolff were important supporters of Dexter, not only as Blue Note executives but also as friends. 1961 image. Photograph by Rudy Van Gelder. © Mosaic Images LLC.

The album was released as *Doin' Allright,* which was also the title of one of Dexter's compositions on the LP. I always wondered about the use of "Allright" as one word instead of "Alright" or "All Right" for the album's cover. Perhaps it had something to do with Lion and Wolff's idea of hip English usage at the time. On this recording Dexter plays his composition "Society Red." As he explained:

> *In the forties, when some of us konked our hair, it would turn decidedly red. Malcolm was "Detroit Red" and I was "Society Red." That name stayed with me over the years with the cats who knew me then.*

Malcolm, of course, was Malcolm Little, who became Malcolm X.

On May 9 Dexter went back to Van Gelder's studio to record the album that would become *Dexter Calling.* This LP had Kenny Drew on piano, Paul Chambers on bass, and Philly Joe Jones on drums. The original tunes on the album include several of Dexter's compositions from *The Connection:* "Soul Sister," "Modal Mood," "I Want More," and "Ernie's Tune."

We know from Dexter's good friend and the ultimate Blue Note expert Michael Cuscuna that the bands recording for the label would usually rehearse for two days before a session at a space across the street from Birdland, the legendary New York City jazz club located at 1678 Broadway, which opened in 1949 and closed in 1965. According to Michael Cuscuna, sessions at Van Gelder's studio usually lasted about six hours. A cab would pick up the musicians in front of the Empire Hotel on West Sixty-Third Street, where Blue Note had its offices, and take them across the Hudson River to Englewood Cliffs. They invariably used Babe's Taxi out of Fort Lee, New Jersey, because New York cab companies would charge double fare for the river crossing and Jersey companies did not. Many of the musicians requested a stop along the way at a certain deli on 113th Street to pick up sandwiches and other refreshments for the session. The logistics were arranged by tenor saxophonist Ike Quebec who was the A&R (artist and repertoire) man on the early Blue Note sessions until his death in January 1963. Ike was present at all the sessions and was an important recording artist in his own right.

After recording the two albums in May, Dexter played a gig in Chicago, then returned to Los Angeles where he worked until April 1962. Dexter said many times that he turned a corner in 1962 and never looked back. On August 27 of that year he recorded the album *Go* at Rudy Van Gelder's studio, with Sonny Clark on piano, Butch Warren on bass, and Billy Higgins on drums. *Go* would become Dexter's most popular Blue Note release. Years later, when he finally decided to answer the question he was so often asked—"Which is your favorite record?"—he listened to all his recordings and settled on *Go*. He chose it because of the rhythm section. The album includes his tune "Cheese Cake," which is considered the quintessential Dexter Gordon classic. It is his most recorded composition, and the ability to play it is practically a mandatory rite of passage for all young tenor players. About *Go* he said, "With that rhythm section, I could play anything and they were right there. We were four as one, and isn't that what we are always trying to do?"

Dexter loved Billy Higgins. Twenty-four years after *Go*, when Dexter starred in the film *Round Midnight*, he insisted that Billy be cast as his drummer. And in 1987 Dexter asked Higgins to join him on what would be his final tour. He called him "Smiling Billy" and said that when he looked over at him, he knew everything was going to be all right.

On August 29 Dexter went into Van Gelder's studio once more and recorded *A Swingin' Affair* with the same rhythm section. That album included two of Dexter's compositions, "Soy Califa" ("I am from

California" in Los Angeles Spanish) and "McSplivens" (named for his dog). Earlier in 1962, Dexter had been a sideman on the first recording by the twenty-two-year-old pianist Herbie Hancock, *Takin' Off*. Herbie was joined on his album by Freddie Hubbard, Butch Warren, and Billy Higgins. (Herbie and Freddie would also play roles in *Round Midnight*.) It includes "Watermelon Man," which would become Herbie's hit tune after Mongo Santamaria recorded it and made it a big success. Dexter also did a session with Tommy Turrentine on trumpet, Sir Charles Thompson on piano, Al Lucas on bass, and Willie Bobo on drums, and a few tunes including Sonny Stitt on alto sax. Then he did a date with Dave Burns on trumpet, Sonny Clark on piano, Ron Carter on bass, and Philly Joe Jones on drums. These two recordings were rejected by Alfred Lion and collected dust until 1981, when Michael Cuscuna began to go into the Blue Note vaults and released the tracks as *Landslide*.

Dexter continued to record for Blue Note through the first years of his fourteen-year sojourn in Europe. To this day, those classic recordings are still collected by all serious jazz fans throughout the world. Dexter was right when he said that he believed they would hold up in the history of jazz.

CHAPTER 12

New Life

He says, "Hello," and then the sparkles pour out of him
like a tail, a comet, a fire, and his tone and energy forces
us back so we must hold onto the table, not to be blown
away.

—Henrik Wolsgaard-Iversen[1]

While Dexter was in New York City recording for Blue Note in 1962,
he ran into the British tenor saxophonist Ronnie Scott in the midtown
musician's bar Charlie's. Scott owned and operated Ronnie Scott's
Club, an extremely popular jazz club in London's West End. In what has
become one of the most famous of all Dexter Gordon moments, Scott
walked up to Dexter and said, "Would you *fahncy* coming to London to
work?"

Other than over-the-border visits to Mexico, he had never been out
of the country and did not yet have a passport. His answer to Scott was,
"Oh yes. That would be grand." They shook hands and the deal was
made. Dexter wrote down the address of Scott's club, got a haircut, collected a passport, bought some reeds, and went shopping for a few new
things to wear, including a new pair of shoes. He said goodbye to friends
and family and took off for London. At the age of thirty-nine he was
ready for new adventures. Nat King Cole had told Dexter about the
grand reception he had received when he first went to Europe. Nat said
that he even was given bouquets of flowers after his concerts. "Who
ever heard of a dude getting flowers in this country?" he told Dexter. He
advised Dexter to try to get over there, but it took a long time before
such a trip could be a reality for him. He had read many books about
European history, had learned some French while in prison, and knew
that his great-grandfather was French. He wanted to go to Paris, but his

FIGURE 12. Dexter arriving at Ronnie Scott's Club in London, 1962.
Photograph courtesy of Francesca Nemko.

troubles in the 1950s had put a hold on that dream. Now he was ready
to move into his future life.

Enthralled after his arrival in London, Dexter wrote an exuberant
letter to Alfred Lion and Francis Wolff from Ronnie Scott's Club on
September 12, 1962. This was the beginning of a fascinating correspondence between the three of them during Dexter's first years in
Europe, detailing his work and social activities, thoughts about his life,
his career and future. At the very end of this letter, Dexter sneaks in an
interesting suggestion for the title of his next album, *Very Saxily Yours*.
Dexter took to finishing many of his letters with that phrase. He

chose the words as a tribute to Louis Armstrong, who would often sign his letters "Red Beans and Ricely Yours."

> *Sept 12, 1962*
> *D. Gordon*
> *39 Gerrard St*
> *C/O Ronnie Scott Club*
> *London WI, Eng.*
>
> *A. Lion + F. Wolff*
> *Blue Note Records*
> *43 W. 61 St.*
> *NY 19 NY*

Hi Gentlemen.
    This is really a beautiful and worthwhile trip. I'm really having a ball.
    I'm working with a nice rhythm section and they really try very hard to please me. They're much better than some of sections I was into at home.
    The audiences have been tremendous and it is certainly good for my ego. Standing ovations, write-ups, magazine covers and chicks. I hope I'll be able to tear myself away when it comes time to split (smile?).
    I'm going to the Blue Note² in Paris—Kenny Drew and Kenny Clarke are there. Very good.
    I met the [Blue Note Records] distributor here and he is very nice guy and evidently is trying to push the album.
    I'm going to do a morning autograph scene at Dobell's Record Store (the best).
    Everyone waiting for the new one. Met Tony Hill, but haven't seen him since.
Regards to "One" + the rest of the "girls."
Very Saxily yours,
Dexter
Album Title: Very Saxily Yours

Alfred Lion's reply:

> September 26, 1962
> Mr. Dexter Gordon
> c/o Ronnie Scott Club
> 39 Gerrard Street
> London W. 1
> ENGLAND

Dear Dexter,
    I wish to thank you for your kind letter and I'm glad to learn that you arrived well and that you like the country and the British musicians as well.

I know you're going to have a good time as there is no shortage of pretty girls in England nor in your next stop in France. You should be in for a very good time during the next three months.

That album title of yours was very sexy, but I'll have to use it on something else, because the one that is coming out is by now far advanced. I'm enclosing a cover sheet for you.

Nothing too much happening here—same old story. Dexter, remember that when you come back this time I want to go on a well-planned recording schedule with you. I definitely want to make the Afro-Cuban date, and after that we go on another bag. Keep your eyes and ears open and don't knock yourself out, because nothing is worse than a physical breakdown. Then everything goes.

I have lots of friends in England who like me and the company. They can do things for you. Don't forget to write me in between. I like to hear from you and what's happening. Do I have to tell you that I find very little time to sleep and eat? This business as you must know by now can be very taxing on everybody's nerves. So, Dexter, thanks a lot again for everything and best regards from Ike [Quebec] who is up and down, down and up—well you know.

So best regards from Frank and myself. Write soon.

Very truly yours,

Alfred W. Lion

BLUE NOTE RECORDS INC.

While Dexter was at Ronnie Scott's Club in London, Harold Goldberg, one of the owners of the Jazzhus Montmartre in Copenhagen, Denmark, called Ronnie or perhaps Pete King, the club manager, to arrange for Dexter to come to Copenhagen following his engagement in London. Dexter agreed to make the trip but, as it turned out, not before he ran into his old friend, the trumpeter Chet Baker, in London. Chet knew all the doctors in town who would readily write out prescriptions for morphine, and then all you had to do was go to a pharmacy and get your supply. It wasn't a crime to be a drug user in London at that time. Apparently that kind of freedom appealed to Dexter, and he fell off the wagon.

On the October night he was supposed to play his first gig in Denmark, the Jazzhus Montmartre filled with fans who had heard Dexter's records. Many of those fans who waited that night, and several more nights, still love to talk about the anticipation and wonder over whether he ever would arrive at all. The Jazzhus Montmartre was already a legendary jazz site because as early as 1959 the club presented top jazz artists, including Oscar Pettiford and Stan Getz. Many musicians chose to make Copenhagen their home, including Thad Jones, Ernie Wilkins,

Sahib Shihab, Kenny Drew, and Horace Parlan. The jazz scene there was surely central to their decision to remain, as was the city's convenient airport and train station, which allowed them a way to travel easily for work throughout Europe. The club was run by Herluf Kamp-Larsen who remained in charge through most of the years that Dexter was in Copenhagen, until 1974. The club changed locations in the 1970s and closed in the mid-1990s, but in 2010 it reopened at its original location and is again an important jazz cultural center in Copenhagen.

The story of Dexter's belated arrival in Copenhagen, on October 9, 1962, is one of those jazz legends that changes in shape and detail over the years, but the essential excitement remains. Here is how the legendary Danish jazz supporter and author Henrik Wolsgaard-Iversen remembers the arrival in his book, *Montmartre* (translated from Danish):

> Dexter Gordon should have arrived that night in October 1962 and we were all ready, but he didn't arrive. Shit. Maybe tomorrow. He was on his way from Ronnie Scott's in London to Montmartre, Harry Goldberg explained. Harry Goldberg was one of the owners of the Montmartre club. He had talked to Dexter Gordon on the phone and he said he was on his way. He didn't know when, but tomorrow, quite surely. We listened to the trio instead, also the next day when the American tenor also didn't turn up, and there was a strange excitement in the room. Does he exist? Is he in jail? We heard one or two things. Yes, it was a bit exciting.
>
> In the newspaper, it says that Gordon is delayed, and there are several small bulletins on the way. The jazz press is impatient. The week after, he's there, on October 9. Goldberg introduced him and suddenly the long man is on stage and putting his hat into the horizontal light bulbs.
>
> He says, "Hello," and then the sparkles pour out of him like a tail, a comet, a fire, and his tone and energy forces us back so we must hold onto the table, not to be blown away. The tempo is tough, hard-driving bebop on "All The Things You Are," and that's the longest number I ever heard, over half an hour. And the world of improvisation in its utmost consequences opens itself to me, in this compact and yet so open form. He's in a dark, slim suit, white shirt, and dark tie with knots, conservative but also very hip. The trio behind him is Atli Bjørn on piano, Marcel Rigot on bass, and William Schiöpffe on drums. And they get slowly accustomed to this great canvas that Gordon is painting. There are colors that you can almost taste, salt and pepper, curry, mustard, sweet fruits, dry cinnamon. If Coltrane comes from the stars, it is obvious that Gordon comes from the earth, the good earth.
>
> The water is never quiet around Dexter. There's always drama on the way, something chaotic which he either stages or that the circumstances create. Like he doesn't want the peace and quiet he came for. You see him now,

now you don't see him. Sometimes he's far away and you think he's not listening, not seeing, but he is perceiving everything. And he can play and play well and longer than most people, even when the knees are clashing together and the hands are fluttering . . . Dexter is like Peter Pan who flies freely and provokes the habits in others, who draws on our patience but all the same he is still there where he should be, with his fabulous timing.

The three first weeks Dexter lived in a hotel and when he returns in '63 he moves into the Pensions-Teller in Brødeke, a good place for musicians and other artists. Anders Stefansen, the booking agent, has taken Gordon in his stable and books him around Scandinavia even before Dexter has become hot in these areas. And there are plenty of open spaces in the start—if there was nothing at all, Stefansen and Gordon had an emergency gig in Bergen at a hotel. Here there were always jobs for no money, 150 kroner per night, but all was paid for: good, healthy Norwegian food, nice hotel rooms, sax playing, and Gordon played here for many weeks in his first time in Scandinavia.

At Pensions-Teller he lived in the same place as the older American journalist Ed Reeves, who for many years wrote for the Afro-American newspaper the *Chicago Defender*. A nice and very knowledgeable man who had his way with us, sometimes with his American cat, Muggles. Reeves is a Republican which is very unusual for Black Americans, who were almost always born to be Democrats. Reeves has strong opinions on the Democratic failure towards the Black American population in the United States. He has political literature, articles, documentations for these allegations and he and Dexter have long conversations and it is through Reeves that I got to know Dexter outside the jazz milieu. And it is also here that Leonard Malone, the journalist and the writer, got contact and a lifelong relationship with Gordon. Malone lived with us in 1962, his first year in Denmark, and it is as if we became family. Gordon is 39, Reeves is 50, Malone and I are 25.[3]

Torben Ulrich, the Danish writer, musician, filmmaker, painter, director, performer, and former champion professional tennis player, was also there at Jazzhus Montmartre on Dexter's first night in Copenhagen. His recollection:

And then finally to stand there, just five yards away! We thought all the music we'd been listening to here at home was great, but this opened up another world. They had to carry me out into the street because I was so overwhelmed. It was powerful. Before then, a tune had been a tune. But here, a tune was a trip.[4]

Ulrich and Dexter became very good friends, and Torben asked Dexter to be godfather to his son, Lars Ulrich, who grew up to become one of the founding members of the heavy metal band Metallica.

Dexter had planned to stay in Europe for three months, but two months later, on November 27, 1962, he wrote to Alfred Lion from the Copenhagen address of Lotte Nielsen, a woman with whom he was living at that time.

november 27, 1962
27/11/62
andreas bjorngade 22
kobenhavn
danmark

dear alfred,
    i've been hoping to hear from you but since i haven't i thought i would write. excuse the lack of capitals in this letter but this machine sticks if you use the capital key, so—no capitals.
    is the new album out yet? i received the album sleeve that you sent. very sharp. also, while listening to a jazz program in london, they mentioned me in connection with those artists that had used the bossa nova which made me think the new one was out.
    they really are going for me big here in scandinavia and the albums are going like lox and bagels, yeh. however they say your distributor in stockholm is a blanck. in fact, i broke the house records at the "gyllene cirklin," in stockholm, and they've brought me back here at the monmartre jazzhus, for the whole month of december. calo, and london, want me back too. i really need a manager now. it's a gas, alfred, a gas.
    well, give my utmost regards to el frank, and ol' "que" [Ike Quebec], and i guess i will hear from you soon.
very saxily yours,
dexter g.

Dexter settled into life in Copenhagen quite swiftly, made friendships that lasted his entire life, found a way to communicate and studied the language, liked the food and the people, and took time to get himself together. As he put it, *I finally stopped looking over my shoulder when I walked down the street.* Dexter:

> I stayed at Montmartre for about a month and did a tour—Goteborg, Stockholm, Oslo—and came back to Montmartre. And so this kept going on and on until finally about two years later I saw an article, I think it was by Ira Gitler and he referred to me as the expatriate Dexter Gordon. And then it hit me and I said to myself: Well, have I really been here that long? But I was happy, everything was going nicely and I had not been thinking in terms of time. But as it turned out, it was a very good move—to me anyway.[5]

Dexter began the year 1963 working through most of January at the Montmartre with Atli Bjørn, Marcel Rigot, and William Schiöpffe. Don

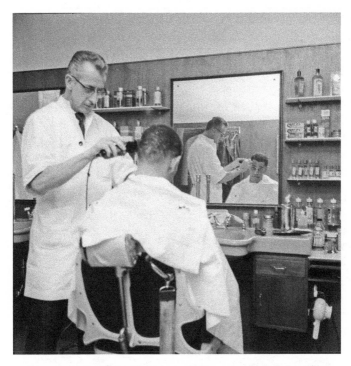

FIGURE 13. Barbershops, like this one in Copenhagen in 1962, played a key role in Dexter's life. His paternal grandfather was a barber, and it was in the Los Angeles barbershops of the 1940s that Dexter and many jazz fans listened to and discussed the latest records. Photograph © Kirsten Malone.

Byas was in town for a few days, which was always a big thrill for Dexter, and he was honored to sit in with Don's band. In February Dexter played another twenty-three dates at the Montmartre, including his fortieth birthday celebration on the twenty-seventh. It was during this time that Dexter first began playing with the bassist Niels-Henning Ørsted Pedersen, who was just seventeen years old. Dexter had first heard Niels as a fifteen-year-old and knew even then that he would be one of the great bassists in jazz. Niels played with Dexter and other visiting musicians until he joined the Oscar Peterson Trio in 1973, with which he stayed through much of the 1970s and 1980s. When Peterson resumed playing in the late 1990s after suffering a stroke, Ørsted Pedersen was with him, offering the musical support needed to make Oscar's return a success. Oscar Peterson wrote in his 2002 autobiography, *A Jazz Odyssey: The Life of Oscar Peterson,* "Niels Pedersen is the type of player whose talents on his instrument are such that he is almost unaware of what he does. His virtuosity on the bass surpasses anyone else that I have known. His melodic sense is impeccable, his choice of harmonic sequences is a pure delight to play with, and his time is flawless . . . He is now arguably the most inventive bassist in jazz."[6]

February also brought some very bad news for Dexter. Francis Wolff wrote on the thirteenth to tell him that his friends Sonny Clark and Ike Quebec had both died in the same week:

> Sonny died suddenly, while Ike had been in the hospital for about five weeks. Ike suffered from lung cancer which was incurable. Last Monday there was a big benefit for Sonny Clark at the Village Gate. Horace Silver, Jackie McLean, Kenny Dorham, Freddie Redd and many others played. Billy Higgins was there too and he told me that he played with you and you were well . . . Now take care of yourself and be careful.
> With best regards also from Alfred, sincerely,
> Francis Wolff

This news must have hit Dexter hard, as he was already outliving many of the musicians he loved, and would always reflect on what might have been if they had lived longer. He replied to Wolff's letter shortly after he received it:

> dear alfred, and dear frank,
>   was ich los? and all that jazz, continental, that is. seriously though, i wanted to express my shock at hearing about sonny and quebec. although, it was pretty obvious even to me, that it would happen in the near future, it still set me back on my heels. oddly enough, i told sonny this summer that it was going to happen soon if he didn't or couldn't change his pattern and start taking care of himself. but, he had almost totally given up, i think.
>   quebec didn't seem at that time so precarious. but, little did I know. things must be a little blue around blue note these days.
> as always,
> dexter

Tenor saxophonist Ike Quebec was born on August 17, 1918, in Newark, New Jersey, and was forty-four when he died on January 16, 1963, in New York City. He began his recording career in 1940 with the Barons of Rhythm and went on to record and perform with Frankie Newton, Hot Lips Page, Roy Eldridge, Ella Fitzgerald, Benny Carter, and Coleman Hawkins. He recorded several albums for Blue Note Records and then began a relationship with the label as an A&R man.

According to Dexter, Ike was often called upon to help out with arrangements at recording sessions.

Pianist Sonny Clark (Conrad Yeatis Clark) was born on July 21, 1931, in the coal-mining town of Herminie No. 2, Pennsylvania, and was only thirty-one when he died on January 13, 1963, also in New York City. When he was twenty years old, he moved to Los Angeles and worked with Wardell Gray. Then he toured the United States and Europe with the clarinetist Buddy DeFranco. He returned to New York in 1957 with Dinah Washington and began his association with Blue Note, recording with Kenny Burrell, Donald Byrd, Paul Chambers, John Coltrane, Art Farmer, Grant Green, Jackie McLean, Hank Mobley, and of course, Dexter. His 1958 album *Cool Struttin'* remains one of the top-selling and iconic Blue Note titles.

Dexter worked at the Montmartre throughout the month of March 1963, and in early April he sat in as a guest with Cat Anderson. In May he went to Paris, where on the twenty-third he recorded for Blue Note. The album was *Our Man in Paris* with Bud Powell on piano, Pierre Michelot on bass, and Kenny Clarke on drums. This was to become one of Dexter's most popular recordings and it remains a classic album to this day. Francis Wolff went to Paris to supervise the recording at CBS Studios. The next day Wolff wrote all about it to Alfred Lion:

Dear Alfred, Had the session yesterday, it went well, from about 3:45–9 P.M. We made standards, Dexter's originals were not so good, besides Bud has great trouble learning new tunes. Here's what we made:

Our love is here to stay (medium)	6.28
Broadway (medium)	6.30
Stairway to the stars (slow)	6.40
A Night in Tunisia (medium)	8.13
Willow weep for me (med. Slow)	8.45
Scrapple from the apple (up)	7.17 or 8.21
X Like someone in love (medium)	6.15
X (Bud Powell Trio only) ——	
[total]	50.18

I'm going over to the studio tomorrow and have a duplicate tape made to send to N.Y. I'll leave the original tape at the studio as a safety. Dexter had a good day, only on the last take he got a little tired. Then he had it. The rehearsals were a hassle, Dexter was dragged but he snapped into it at the session.

Please make the following money transfers:

EARL POWELL, Hotel de Seine, 60 rue de Seine, Paris—$460 (I paid $40. on acct.)

PIERRE MICHELOT, Immeuble de la tour, 9 rue Jean Moulin, Gagny (Seine & Oise), France—$200

LIAQUAT A. SALAAM*, 142 bis Rue de Rosny, Montreuil s/Bois, Seine, France—$350.

*This is Kenny Clarke. Please transfer this in Dollars to the American Express Co., Paris, for him. Use his Muslim name.

I'll let you know about Dexter. I guess we'll send his money to Copenhagen. ($300 for the session and $550. Advance on royalties).

I'll get the bill from the studio tomorrow and send it to you.

I'm leaving tomorrow Sat'day and will be at the Stephen Court Hotel, London, till Tuesday or Wednesday.

Not only Dexter, Bud was in good shape and played very well. Rained all day yesterday. Today's a little better.

Feeling pooped today, it was a job making this session.

Take it easy and don't get nervous. Best, Frank

There is so much to learn from Wolff's letter to Lion. The sums paid for the sessions look so very small considering that Bud Powell was one of the creators of modern jazz and that Kenny Clarke was the first bebop drummer. Even though these were the accepted rates at the time, they represent every dollar Powell and Clarke ever made for a recording that is still in print and is considered a classic after more than fifty years. We learn that Kenny Clarke was using his Muslim name, which makes me wonder about his embrace of Islam in the late 1930s. Kenny had first gone to Europe when he was in the army and then settled in France in 1956. He remained there, living in Montreuil until his death in 1985. On Dexter's first visit to Paris, he took a cab from the train station to Saint-Germain-des-Prés. When he saw two Black men sitting at a café, he asked the cab driver to stop. He leaned out of the window and said, "Hey, do you know where I can find Kenny Clarke?" One of the men replied in French, clearly not knowing what Dexter was asking. Dexter often told the story because he later realized that they were either West African or French Caribbean and he had assumed that anyone Black must be from the States. He said he realized at that moment how unsophisticated he was.

At the time of this recording, Bud Powell was in Paris, playing at the Parisian Blue Note and staying at the Crystal Hotel. All of this would later become part of the 1986 film *Round Midnight,* in which Dexter plays the fictional lead character, a musician drawn from characterizations of Powell and Lester Young, and for which he was nominated for an Academy Award. So many confluences occurred around Dexter's life. Bud remained in Paris from 1959 until his return to New York in 1964. He died there in 1966. Bud's playing on *Our Man in Paris* is very good indeed, and it would become very important as one of his best late recordings.

Pierre Michelot was the house bassist at the Blue Note in Paris with Bud Powell and Kenny Clarke. Twenty-three years later, when it came time to make *Round Midnight*, Dexter recommended Pierre to play in the film, and then they went on tour together with the Round Midnight band in 1988. He was a marvelous musician and Dexter said he was reliable in all ways. He was so very fond of Pierre.

In June, Dexter was back in Copenhagen at the Montmartre for most of the month. Bud Powell came to town and they worked together on June 18, with Niels-Henning Ørsted Pedersen on bass, and then again on June 19–23. When Abdullah Ibrahim (Dollar Brand) came to Copenhagen in 1963, he brought along the drummer Makaya Ntshoko. Ibrahim and his group worked often in Club Montmartre until he left for New York in 1965. Dexter loved Makaya's playing and said that he was just like some of the best drummers in the States. It seems Makaya remained in Copenhagen, since we know he worked with Dexter in 1966 and also with other musicians who appeared at the Montmartre, including Rex Stewart, Yusef Lateef, and Brew Moore. It is also during this period in 1963 that the pianist Tete Montoliu started performing with Dexter. Tete was born in the Eixample district of Barcelona and began his career with Lionel Hampton, which provided Tete and Dexter with a great subject for discussion and much laughter. Tete had a tremendous European career, recording and performing with many of the top names in jazz, including Elvin Jones, Johnny Griffin, George Coleman, Anthony Braxton, and Joe Henderson. He appears on seven albums on SteepleChase Records with Dexter.

Dexter was at the club for the entire month of July and then again in August. Bookings like these would have been exceptional for any jazz musician. Dexter would hardly have been able to work more than a Sunday matinee had he remained in New York, since he had been denied a cabaret card, a required license for work in nightclubs. The cabaret card was not abolished until 1967. We can see that staying in Copenhagen afforded benefits for Dexter that no other place ever offered him musically. He practiced and performed and lived peacefully. As he recalled, this was the first time he could breathe and be accepted as a jazz musician, and treated as an artist.

On October 25 John Coltrane and the Quartet with McCoy Tyner, Jimmy Garrison, and Elvin Jones came to play at the Tivoli Concert

Hall in Copenhagen. Of course Dexter attended the concert, and that was when the famous "Dexter and Trane Mouthpiece Story" unfolded. According to Dexter, he told Trane how much he loved the band and his sound but thought that he wasn't quite projecting the way he should. So Dexter gave Trane one of his Otto Link mouthpieces. Years later, he said that maybe he should have kept that mouthpiece because Trane sounded so good. When I told Dexter that I thought he sounded very good, he laughed and said, "Not as good as Trane."

When Dexter told this story about hearing Trane in Copenhagen, I had my own John Coltrane story. When I was living on New York City's Lower East Side in the early 1960s, Elvin Jones lived one block away. To get to Elvin's apartment I would walk through a bus garage, and there would be Elvin looking out the window, watching the neighborhood and the kids who were practicing drum rudiments on metal garbage cans. He had given them drumsticks and showed them what to practice. This made him very popular with the kids but not so popular with the older neighbors. Other musicians lived in the same building as Elvin and many lived in the neighborhood, including Lee Morgan, Pepper Adams, and Sun Ra. Elvin Jones was the "mayor" of the Lower East Side. Everyone knew him and he greeted them all when he walked across town. Elvin was one of the most brilliant human beings I have ever met and one of the kindest. We went to hear him play with Harry "Sweets" Edison at a gig where they served dinner to the musicans and their guests. Elvin thought that was such a good idea at a time when money was scarce, to say the least. Elvin played brushes during the first set, and Sweets said he was perfect at swinging on brushes. I went upstairs to see Elvin and his girlfiend Joy, and while I was there Trane came in with Dexter's album, *Dexter Calling*. I looked at the LP cover and said, "Wow, he is so handsome." Elvin rolled his eyes and I recall that one of the musicians said, "That's Dexter Gordon. You need to listen to him." When I told Dexter years later about Trane carrying around that album, he was delighted and asked, "What did he say about me?" What I remembered was that they put the LP on the turntable, sat and listened to it—and then they listened to it again. That is how it was in those days.

For the rest of 1963, Dexter toured in Switzerland, Germany, and Norway. A glance at a map of Europe shows how convenient it was for Dexter to live in Copenhagen and travel easily by train all over the Continent. And there were so many places that welcomed jazz and the musicians who were playing it. One highlight at the end of the year was the visit by his very good friend Kenny Dorham. Dexter played with Kenny in Arhus, Denmark, and they spent time together laughing and telling their bebop stories, which always were told in a kind of coded language. Kenny had recorded for Blue Note with Joe Henderson and Tony Williams earlier that year, and Dexter loved that album, *Una Mas,* and often talked about the loss of Kenny Dorham at the age of forty-eight in 1972. He would get a wistful expression and say, "I really miss Kenny."

CHAPTER 13

Very Saxily Yours

When Dexter played, everybody listened. And he was
long-winded. Coltrane was not the first long-winded
saxophone player!

—Jimmy Heath[1]

In February 1964 Dexter performed with the Danish Radio big band in
Copenhagen. In March he went to Basel, Switzerland, to record a concert for Swiss television with George Gruntz (piano), Paul Rovere (bass),
and Daniel Humair (drums). This concert was released on a DVD by
Jazz Icons and is an excellent example of Dexter's playing at that time.

In the spring of 1964 Johnny Griffin and Arthur Taylor worked at
the Montmartre while Dexter did a short stint in an unsuccessful production of the play *The Connection*. It was the same play that Dexter
had performed in and composed music for in Los Angeles in 1960, but
it did not translate well for the Danish audience, which knew little
about the kinds of drug addicts portrayed in the play. Dexter would get
to the Montmartre as often as possible to sit in with Griff, whom he
called "the fastest horn in the West," for his lightning-speed solos. After
one set with Dexter, Griffin was heard to say, "Oh God, why do I have
to crawl up that mountain called Dexter every night?" Dexter and Griff
fought it out with their horns in much the same way Dexter had done
with Wardell Gray almost twenty years earlier. Dexter said that Griff
sparked a fire in him that sometimes was getting a little dim.

In June he went to Paris and recorded *One Flight Up* for Blue Note
with Donald Byrd, Kenny Drew, Niels-Henning Ørsted Pedersen
(NHOP), and Arthur Taylor. He had asked Alfred Lion and Francis
Wolff to let him record with this group when he started working with

NHOP in Copenhagen and was very pleased about the result. After that, Dexter worked at the Montmartre through July with Tete Montoliu, who became his very good friend and one of his favorite pianists, as well as with NHOP and the drummer Alex Riel.

On June 25 Dexter wrote from Copenhagen to Francis Wolff at Blue Note, mentioning a "situation" that is explained following the letter.

> *Hello Frank,*
>
> *Well, I hope you have survived your adventurous "holiday" in Europe and are now enjoying your calmer surroundings on 61st Street.*
>
> *Anyway, I've given the situation much thought and I believe I understand it pretty well and as you say, "experience gained."*
>
> *At any rate it was a little different and who knows, it might be a hit record, a collector's item yet!*
>
> *It was amazing how rapidly I went back into that old bag—from being depressed (Paris—Blue Note!) and being surrounded by old friends in a similar shaky condition. I think I have to watch myself!!*
>
> *I'm still planning to come to the Apple, probably in October and will have all the material ready for the date or dates.*
>
> *I guess this is all for now—so regards to all, and especially Alfred.*
>
> *Very saxily yours*

This letter to Wolff refers to the recording session in May 1963 for the album *Our Man in Paris*, which was released in December 1963. When Dexter mentions "the situation" and "old friends in a similar shaky condition," he is indicating that drugs were involved when he went to Paris to make the recording with Bud Powell and Kenny Clarke. "Experience gained" is his typical response to matters such as these. He was not one to beat himself up over a mistake and never denied the truth when he knew the music could have been better if he had been in better shape. Many people name *Our Man in Paris* as one of their favorite Dexter Gordon recordings. But Dexter felt it should have been better.

After the Montmartre run, Dexter took the group with Tete to perform at the jazz festival in Molde, Norway. In August they were all back at the Montmartre again.

On August 20 Dexter again wrote to Wolff:

> *Dear Frank,*
>
> *Overjoyed! That's the word—overjoyed for our latest release—A Swingin' Affair. It's a very happy sounding album and I think it's going to sell very well.*

You made no mention of my showing in the [Down Beat *magazine*] *Critics Poll—which when I think of 3 years ago I wasn't in anybody's poll is fantastic—last year the New Star and this year, No. 7 with the big boys!² Wow!*

I think I'm ready to do a big band album—with Dameron charts—what do you think about that?

As you probably noticed these last few months—almost all year—I've been very lethargic and without a real interest in anything but things have changed and once again I feel interest, enthusiasm, vitality. Maybe it's love. Ah! Love.

I shall be here until the end of the month and then to Stockholm and the Gyllene Cirkeln [Golden Circle].

In October, perhaps Spain for a holiday. I haven't had a holiday or a week off since Our Man in Paris, May '63. Fantastic, no.

I'm actually over-worked and I'm sleeping all the way to the bank (smiles, smiles)!

Best regards to Martha's Vineyard's favorite guest, Alfred, whom I hope is in the best of health, also, you.

Let me hear from you soon about our plans.

Very saxily yours,
Dexter

Dexter spent September and October in Sweden, where he wrote to Wolff on October 25:

Malmö, Sweden

Dear Frank,

Greetings and salutations to you and Alfred.

These last two months I have been working here in Sweden. The Golden Circle (Stockholm) in Sept. and one nighters from the top of Sweden to the bottom in October. Man, this is a long country.

We have played every little town and hamlet in the country. The first time I have done this since the big band days. Not much money but I think it is very good for me and for jazz!

So now, I have a few days off, to rest and I'm really enjoying it.

Malmö is in the south (the bottom of Sweden) and is right across the Sound from Copenhagen. They have several ferries daily between the two countries. From Nov 2–7 I shall be in Oslo, at the Metropole. Then I go to Madrid from the 8th to 31st.

So, I shall leave on the first (1) of December for N.Y.C. And, Frank, please don't have a brass band at the airport to greet me. After all that should probably be a little embarrassing—don't you think so.

Anyway, I would be able to stay in N.Y.C. until the 15th if we are able to record at that time. Because I want to go home to L.A. to spend the holidays with my family.

So, if we do not record then I could come back in Jan. or Feb. to do so.

Really looking forward to seeing the Skyline, Broadway, 125th St, 61st St, Rudy's, Birdland etc.
Very saxily yours,
Dexter

A few days after writing that letter, on October 29, Dexter was arrested at a hotel in Malmö, charged with buying several grams of narcotics that had been stolen from a dealer in Stockholm. His Danish girlfriend, Lotte Nielsen, and another Danish woman were with him at the hotel at the time of the arrest. At his hearing, Dexter admitted that he had bought narcotics in Stockholm, but he denied the charge of receiving stolen goods. He said it was no secret that he was an addict. According to the police report, Nielsen claimed that she had nothing to do with the drugs found on Dexter. She said she had been in Israel and Italy before joining Dexter in Sweden and that Dexter had lived in her apartment when he was in Copenhagen. He was released on November 3 and forced to leave Sweden. He went to Oslo, Norway, to play the Metropole Club and then to Madrid, where he appeared at the Whiskey Jazz Club through December 7.

Dexter then made a return visit to the States, wanting to find out if things had improved for him back home. Back in New York City for the first time since he had left to play Ronnie Scott's Club in 1962, Dexter played in a December 11, 1964, concert at Birdland that was described by the syndicated columnist Dorothy Kilgallen as "one of the biggest jam sessions ever held ... with some of the biggest names in the business—Cannonball Adderley, Gerry Mulligan, Billy Taylor and two dozen others." *Down Beat's* review raved that "Gordon, playing Jimmy Heath's horn, romped and stomped through a row of smoking choruses of 'Au Privave' and brought the house down. He then went home to get his own tenor, returning in time for the last number on the following set, a wailing 'Now's the Time,' on which his solo became the musical high point of the night."[3] Dexter next went to Chicago and then on to Los Angeles for a two-week engagement at the It Club, where he worked with Hampton Hawes and Philly Joe Jones.

The visit to Los Angeles also gave Dexter an opportunity to see his wife, Jodi, and their two daughters. In an interview with the cinematographer Chuck France for his film *Jazz in Exile*, Dexter reflected on the trip:

Well, I came for a couple of reasons. The first one really was a personal thing, because I had been separated from my wife for two or three years and we have two daughters who were just becoming teenagers at the time and I thought it possible, since things had changed a little bit, that there was a possibility of getting back together. Also, I was curious to test the wind and what was happening, and I was here for about six months on the East Coast and in Chicago and also in my home at Los Angeles, but everything was pretty negative—and positive too because there was a revolution going on and I just thought that my particular thing was to return to Europe and to live there and develop musically and as a human being, which I did, and I think that was for me the right move.[4]

On February 21, 1965, Malcolm X was assassinated at the Audubon Ballroom in Harlem. Dexter always remembered that date and talked about "Detroit Red" as he remembered him when they were young men in Harlem in the early 1940s. Malcolm was only thirty-nine years old when he was killed. Dexter often said that Malcolm's early death made his own decision to remain living in Europe through most of the 1960s and early 1970s seem like the right choice for his life. By May 27 Dexter was back in New York again. This time he went into Rudy Van Gelder's studio in New Jersey to record the album that became *Clubhouse* for Blue Note. The musicians on the date were Freddie Hubbard (trumpet), Barry Harris (piano), Bob Cranshaw (bass), and Billy Higgins (drums). The next day he went back and recorded the album *Gettin' Around* with Bobby Hutcherson (vibes), Harris, Cranshaw, and Higgins.

He was back in Copenhagen in June and July working at the Montmartre and wrote to Wolff about his six-month visit to the States. From this letter it is obvious that Dexter went back to his old habits, including using drugs,[5] most likely in Los Angeles. He is disappointed in his performances at the recording sessions and apologizes to Wolff and Lion for what must have transpired on the dates. He thanks Wolff for being so understanding.

Juli 13, 1965
Dexter Gordon
c/o Nielsen
Andreas Bjornsgade 22-V
Copenhagen K, Denmark

Francis,
  Good to hear from you, so promptly. Sorry, I couldn't answer likewise.
  Anyway, I've been working ever since I've been here, at the Montmartre with K. Drew, Niels Henning Ørsted Pedersen, and tromme Alex Riel.
  Now I've taken off for 2 weeks to finish up on my illness—it's too much strain to be doing everything at once. You know what happened

to my ticket, the one "I lost." My wife took it and tried to cash it. Pan Am just called me this morning to ask me about it. Isn't that fantastish? In fact, that's why I had to "escape" from reality + couldn't take care of business. But somehow we got through the dates which I think were O.K. Too bad I wasn't really in good shape because the albums would have been a "bitch."

Anyway, I really don't think I'll ever go for that again! SO I should be your best seller for many years to come.

Have you decided when you're coming to Europa—Copenhagen?

I'm really looking forward to that new fat contract you're offering me. It will probably be so generous I'll be reluctant to accept it. (smile?)

Anyway, you can send checks, statements, fan mail etc. etc. to this address.

So, many thanks for being understanding, etc. through my problems. Also to Alfred, Ruth for the same reasons.

I hope we can still do the next album here. There is supposed to be a very good engineer here and I'll try to have it all set up.

Regards,
Dexter

Dexter went to Berlin in October for several concerts, one of which, with Booker Ervin and Sonny Rollins, was recorded for a radio broadcast. He wrote to Alfred Lion from Brussels to say that he was in good shape again and that his health was like "honey dew melon." These letters help us understand Dexter's relationship with Lion and Wolff, how important and involved he was in Blue Note's business, and how encouraged he was about these recordings. These classic Blue Note discs are more than simply record sessions. This was a time when Dexter was trying to make a new life for himself and erase the stress and shame from the years spent in jail and on drugs. The battle wasn't won overnight, but his letters show that he was definitely in a fight to find a way out of his past life.

Octobre 19–65
Hotel Royale
Bruxelles
Belge

Alfred,
I forgot to mention, in my last letter, about the recording to be made at the Berlin Jazz Festival, Oct 29–31.

As you probably know the 1st night is going to be a tenor workshop: 6 tenor players with Ben, Don Byas, Booker Irvin, Brew Moore, Sonny Rollins + Very saxily yours.

And this part I know you'll dig, it's going to be recorded and
royalties are non-existent at Prestige, or so I've been told! Why don't
you write me and let me know if it is O.K. and/or what you think.
  I will be at the Paris address until the 29th of Oct:

Hotel Crystal
24, Rue St. Benoit
  My new horn is just beginning to sound for me—each time, I hear a
little more, a little more. It looks like "shiny stockings"!
  It was a nice letter you wrote to me this summer and I want you to
know Alfred that the health is like "honey dew melon." Happy days are
here again!!!
  Also, I'm anxious to hear the reaction to "One Flight Up." Has it
*been reviewed yet? Probably a * critic.*
  So, let me know as soon as—about the business at hand.
Regards
Dexter

The new horn he mentions in the letter, the one he refers to as looking like "shiny stockings," was a new Selmer Mark VI that he got in
Paris. The story about that saxophone, and the one it replaced, has been
told and retold so often that it is impossible to separate fact from fiction. Dexter's friend Leonard (Skip) Malone wrote about the new horn
in his book *More Than You Know: Dexter Gordon in Copenhagen:*

> When Dexter came to Denmark he always played on one of the famous old
> Conn tenor saxophones, known for their huge tone, their heavy sound and
> their dragging mechanics. Some years later he came home from a European
> tour and had replaced the old Conn with a brand new Selmer. I asked him
> why. Well, he had been in Paris, found a hotel, placed his baggage and went
> out on the town and had something to drink. In the morning he decided to
> return to his hotel but discovered he had forgotten where it was located, and
> what the name of the hotel was. He never found it. So he went to the Selmer
> factory and got a new tenor, which with its lighter tone and faster fingering,
> almost sounded like an alto sax when he played on it. Johnny Griffin had to
> show him how to open the keys to gain a fuller volume. Maybe at the same
> time the exchange heralded a shift from the barrel gravity of youth to the
> sophisticated elegance of mature years. Maybe he had an unconscious need
> to say goodbye to the old Conn. Maybe the tale about the hotel was—just
> a tale.[6]

Dexter had already been living in Copenhagen for three years when
Ben Webster arrived in late 1965. Ben had been living in Amsterdam,
but as Dexter put it, the town wasn't big enough for two tenor legends—
Don Byas was there and it was "his town." But apparently Copenhagen

was big enough for two. Dexter's life in Copenhagen would not have been as rich as it was if Ben hadn't been there also. I believe that having Ben there provided Dexter with a context by which to measure his own success in his life and his playing, as well as another perspective on the difficulties of being a jazz musician in the States. Ben's presence and friendship made Dexter grateful for having decided to live in Europe and for choosing Copenhagen as his home. Or rather, as he preferred to put it, for Copenhagen choosing him.

Dexter was thrilled to be around Ben, fourteen years his senior, and loved to hear him play and tell his stories about "the Guv'nor," as Ben called Duke Ellington. Dexter would describe Ben as being ever so charming and sociable as an evening would begin. Then, as more drinks were sent to him from admiring fans, other Ben personalities would appear. First he would be laughing and talking, then he would get somber and tearful about the past, then he might become angry and aggressive. Dexter always tried to get out the door before the last stages began. He often told stories about being on the road with Ben on a Wim Wigt tour. Wim was a booking agent from Wageningen, Holland, who was quite young and inexperienced when he began booking Ben and Dexter and other jazz musicians who were living in Europe. Of course as the years went by, Wim became quite experienced, had a record label, and employed American road managers, including me, which is how I met Dexter. Dexter liked to say that sending me on the road to Nancy, France, to travel with his band during a predicted train strike was the nicest thing Wim Wigt had ever done for him. (But that's another story, which comes along later.)

The story about Dexter and Ben playing "Body and Soul" has been told, retold, and written in many versions in books and articles with interpretations by Dutch musicians and jazz fans, but here is how Dexter told the story (and he did not force more meaning into the incident than it needs). Normally when they appeared on the same gig, Dexter and Ben would play a finale together. They began to play "Body and Soul" one night in a club in Holland. Ben said that it was impossible to add anything to the song after Coleman Hawkins's classic 1939 version, but it needed to be played and so it was the finale of their gig that night. Ben played his solo first and walked off stage. Then Dexter instructed the pianist, Rob Agerbeek, to play in the "Coltrane style." This meant that he should play different chords and a chromatic bass line and take a new approach to the standard. When Dexter began to solo, Ben started yelling, "Hey, motherfucker, how dare you, this is not how you play this piece, who do you think you are, what kind of shit is that . . . !"

Dexter always said that he just kept playing. Agerbeek has it all on tape in case the story needs to be verified. Afterward, Dexter tried to calm Ben down and explain that they were just trying to do their thing, but Ben wouldn't hear it. In the car ride back to their hotel, Ben sat in the front with Wim Wigt, and Dexter sat in the back with Wim's wife, Ria. Ben continued to berate Dexter and the tirade continued all the way back to Copenhagen. Ben refused to speak to Dexter for about six weeks, which was very upsetting to Dexter because he never wanted to hurt Ben or insult him. Ben said, "Got my phone number?"

Dexter said, "Yes, Ben."

Ben said, "Well, lose it."

Dexter wanted to play "Body and Soul" the way he heard Trane reinterpret it, and that was the way he played it until the end of his life. Dexter was first and foremost a jazz fan. Whenever any of the older musicians would be in town, he would be sure to be in their company and they treated him like the new kid on the block. The incident with Ben was worrying him until one night Ben came into the Montmartre where Dexter was playing. During a break, Ben came over to Dexter at the bar and handed him a box. Dexter opened it and found a gold Cartier cigarette lighter. Ben said, "Okay, let's forget it. But don't ever do that again." Dexter was so relieved.

Another time when Ben and Dexter were traveling together, Dexter was taking a solo that Ben thought was way too long. He said to a friend: "Are they showing *Gone with the Wind* around here? If so, I can go to see it and come back and Dexter will still be playing the same solo." *Gone with the Wind* is three hours and fifty-eight minutes long.

Ben died in Amsterdam in 1973, but his ashes were buried in Assistens Kirkegård Cemetery in Copenhagen. When his Selmer Mark VI tenor saxophone came up for sale, Dexter bought it and that became his horn. He played it until the end of his life and played it in the film *Round Midnight* as well. He said that he hoped playing that horn would help him to play ballads the way Ben did. I always wondered if he was joking or not. In Copenhagen there are streets that intersect named Dexter Gordons Vej and Ben Websters Vej in what they call "New Jazz City." I am sure both men would be very pleased about that. Jimmy Heath:

> Dexter had a way of playing ballads people don't talk about. He played ballads with full consciousness of the lyric. This is something that Ben Webster

had said before: If you don't know the words to the song, you can't sing it. What you're really trying to do, as an instrumentalist, is sing. That's why Ben Webster, Johnny Hodges, people like that, were so famous. They could sing a melody. But Dexter, he could do that also.[7]

CHAPTER 14

Trouble in Paris

They're building bigger and better prisons in the States
and they're getting fuller and fuller. But I don't really see
how that's helping the drug problem.

—Dexter Gordon[1]

When something really bad happened, or when someone asked Dexter about an event that he preferred to forget, or that roused a painful memory about a person who had died tragically (there were many in his life), he would get very quiet. So quiet that it could be frightening, in a way. The silence would surround his huge frame and move out to fill the room. Those who knew him well would move back because it felt like being near a volcano before it erupts. I once asked him about a lovely photo I had seen that was taken in back of the Jazzhus Montmartre in Copenhagen. He gave me that certain look and said, "That was a long time ago." That was the end of the conversation. I never brought it up again until after he had died, and then I asked his closest friend, Skip Malone, about the girl in the photo and the return address on his letters to Alfred Lion and Frank Wolff that had her home address in Copenhagen. He said, "Max, leave it alone. You don't want to dig this up. It's not a pretty story." Of course, his response made me even more curious about this short, happy girl in the photo, the same girl whose name is on the Christmas card to Blue Note Records in 1966: "Dexter and Lotte." Dexter's most trusted supporter in Denmark, the political cartoonist Klaus Albrechtsen, told me that Lotte had met a sad end and that her father blamed Dexter for her demise. But he did not want to share with me any of the correspondence he had with the girl's father.

Here is what we know about the story of Dexter and Lotte. On February 20, 1966, Dexter sent a postcard to Alfred Lion and his wife, Ruth,

FIGURE 14. Dexter and Lotte Nielsen with friends behind the Jazzhus Montmartre in Copenhagen. Photograph by Jesper Høm. From the private collection of Dexter Gordon.

in New York from the Drop Inn in Copenhagen. He wrote that he was just back from two weeks at the Gyllene Cirkeln (Golden Circle) in Stockholm and "Lotte and I dropped inn to have dinner. Thought about you and here we are." He wrote that he had a two-month gig at the Blue Note Club in Paris beginning March 1 and then would go back for the summer to the Montmartre in Copenhagen. The postcard ended with a note written in the hand of his Danish girlfriend, Lotte Nielsen: "So we're glad, nobody had stopped the world yet, cause we don't want to get off. How about you? Regards, Lotte." Things seemed quite upbeat for Dexter at the time. Unfortunately, there was a rather bad turn of events to come.

On March 26 Dexter wrote to Frank Wolff from 24 Rue St. Benoit, the site of the Hotel Crystal in Paris. It was a notable location, just off Boulevard Saint-Germain and around the corner from Les Deux Magots, the famous haven for Jean-Paul Sartre and the existentialists, and also around the corner from Brasserie Lipp, where Herman Leonard took the iconic jazz photograph of Johnny Hodges sitting at the table with his saxophone beside a glass of wine and being served by a waiter. From his hotel Dexter could walk to Café de Flore where James Baldwin had worked upstairs on *Go Tell It on the Mountain*. Dexter loved to be anywhere that Baldwin or Richard Wright had been in Paris. Baldwin moves in and out of Dexter's story in a way that explains many things about Black artists trying to live in Europe, and Baldwin gives voice to many things that Dexter talked about after he came back to the States in the 1970s.

Dexter's letter to Wolff (see below) mentions Mae Mezzrow, who had been the wife of Mezz Mezzrow, the notorious "Muggles King" ("muggles" was slang for marijuana, which Mezzrow was said to have sold to musicians), the saxophonist and clarinetist who proclaimed himself "a voluntary Negro," and whose 1946 jive-talking autobiography, *Really the Blues,* became legendary in jazz circles. Dexter says that Mae got a job as the cook at the Montmartre and eventually they hoped she would open a soul food restaurant in Copenhagen. He also incorrectly refers to vibraphonist Bobby Hutcherson as Teddy. Teddy Hutcherson, Bobby's older brother, was a very close friend of Dexter's when they were kids in Los Angeles. Dexter was most likely thinking of his friend when he referred to Bobby as "Teddy H." in the letter. Bobby and Dexter would meet up again in 1986 during the filming of *Round Midnight,* and they would share memories of Dexter's great friend, Teddy.

The album Dexter mentions in the letter, recorded on May 28, 1965, at Rudy Van Gelder's studio in New Jersey, became *Gettin' Around,* one of the classic Dexter Blue Note albums, with a cover photo of Dexter riding a bicycle in Copenhagen. The album was released in 1966, in time to help fund the ensuing legal difficulties that Dexter would encounter in Paris.

> *Sat afternoon*
> *En Paris*
> *26 of March, 1966*
> *24 Rue St. Benoit*
> *Paris 6*

Cher Frank,

I'm "ici" in Paris and you haven't popped up, what happened? It just doesn't seem right. I keep expecting to hear you on the phone etc.

Anyway, I'm here at the Blue Note working for smiling B. Benjamin. This time I got 2 months beginning the 1st of March which takes me into May.

May 11 + 12 in the Bologna Festival and then the last two weeks I'll be in Lisboa. There is a new club there which is located outside of town, a sea resort, which is serving sunshine and vinho verde!

And then, of course, my annual Copenhagen scene at Montmartre, with Kenny, Niels, and Alex, the drummer you don't dig. Incidentally, he went to Berkelee Jan 1, to study with Alan Dawson and he comes back for the gig this summer! It might help a little. Even so, he's the best I've heard in Europe, especially for me.

Also, I'm still hoping to get in the live one in the club—that's the place.

Too bad you couldn't come when I called you. It was really popping!!

I just heard I have a check in Copenhagen—this time through Private bankers instead of the other, which is my bank—it makes it simpler.

Incidentally, I got Mae Mezz the gig in the kitchen at Montmartre, with the eventual hope we could open up our own soul food restaurant up there. They don't have one there.

So now I have to start thinking about and working on coming home—I guess it will be in the fall. After the long, hot summer.

I was surprised to hear Al had rejected the date with Freddie H etc. So, very anxious to hear the date with Vibes with Teddy H. should be interesting to hear—what think you? When will you send me a copy? But to Copenhagen!

Well, the telephone etc is starting to ring, visitors and such, so I better go now.

Hear from you soon
All the best to Alfred and Ruth –
Very saxily yours,
Dexter

Unfortunately, things did not go at all well for Dexter in Paris. On the morning of May 4, 1966, police officers arrested him at his hotel, charging him with using narcotics. Lotte Nielsen was with Dexter and was also arrested. The story made headlines in Paris and Copenhagen. From the *New York Herald Tribune* European edition of May 10:

U.S. JAZZMAN, 3 HELD IN PARIS DOPE RAID

PARIS, May 9—An American Negro Jazzman, a Danish blonde and two other Americans have been arrested in a police crack-down on drug smuggling in the Left Bank student area, it was learned today.

Police said they were holding Dexter Gordon, 43, a tenor saxophonist from New York City, on charges of peddling drugs in the jazz cellars of the student quarter. Detained on similar charges were Lotte Nielsen, 27, of Copenhagen, and Roy Levelle, 24, and Donald Pallas, 33, of New York.

The notice in the *Tribune* was mistaken, as Dexter was arrested not for peddling drugs but for purchasing them. Dexter was surprised by the bust, because it was common in the States for the dealer to be arrested rather than the customers. He also noted, albeit years later, that getting busted in a country where the justice system is based on the Napoleonic

FIGURE 15. The booking photo taken on May 10, 1966, after Dexter's arrest in Paris. From the legal file of Dexter Gordon.

Code—in which an arrested suspect is considered guilty until proven innocent—was one of the dumbest things he had ever done. Immediately after the arrest, the police took him to the hospital at La Santé Prison where he was given a series of detoxification treatments. Then he was confined to the prison for nearly two months while he raised money to hire a lawyer and waited for Blue Note Records to help with his defense.

From his correspondence with Alfred Lion, we can feel Dexter's anguish and the bad memories that must have been stirred up from all of his troubles during the decade of the 1950s. He was never comfortable acknowledging his missteps as mistakes. He preferred to consider them as lessons. When he did talk about spending time in jails and prisons in the 1950s, he said that such experience saved him—presumably from an early death. But the 1966 Paris episode weighed heavily on him, and it made him determined to free himself from heroin once and for all.

The newspapers continued to pursue the story of the bust and its aftermath. And they seemed especially interested in exploiting the discovered relationship between the Black American jazz musician and "the Danish blonde." One Paris headline read, *"En jazz-tragedie."* An article in the Danish paper *Politiken* carried a photo of Lotte Nielsen under the headline (translated from Danish) "Jazz Star and Danish Girl Involved in Narco-Affair."

Dexter's first letter to Alfred Lion from Copenhagen in 1962 had listed his address as c/o L. D. Nielsen, Andreas Bjornsgade 22/5, Koben-havn. "L. D. Nielsen" was Lotte, and letters from Dexter with her home as his return address continued for four years, until a letter Dexter wrote to Lion on December 19, 1966, carried his new address as c/o Punja, Malakoff, Seine, just outside Paris. This was during a period when he was not allowed to reenter Denmark because of the Paris drug bust.

Although Dexter was always reluctant to talk about Lotte, and his friends from that time refused to share any knowledge they had about her, it would seem that Dexter and Lotte were a couple from 1962 through most of 1966. An article published in the Danish newspaper *Ekstra Bladet* a week after the drug bust seemed to confirm the relation-ship (translated from Danish):

LOTTE NIELSEN, WHO IS CHARGED IN A DRUG-CASE IN PARIS,
WANTS TO MARRY WORLD-FAMOUS DEXTER GORDON

"I will refuse to testify if asked and I would be able to avoid it if we were married." So says the 27-year-old Lotte Nielsen who is at a hotel in Paris while her fiancé, the world-famous jazz musician Dexter Gordon, is in hos-pital with a bad liver and nerves. Lotte Nielsen's name was yesterday in newspapers all over the world. According to an American news agency, Lotte Nielsen and Dexter Gordon were arrested and charged with drug deal-ing. "It was a mistake. We were not arrested," said Lotte Nielsen last night to *Ekstra Bladet*. "We were taken to the police station but allowed to leave again."

Are you going to marry Gordon? "Yes! But unfortunately not before he is able to divorce his American wife with whom he has two children and she does not want a divorce. But it will probably sort itself out."

On June 20 Dexter's friend Franca Jimenez wrote to Wolff in New York:

I guess you know by now that he was arrested here in Paris on a narcotic charge in the month of May. Mr. Gordon was supposed to be free on June 20th, but I have just spoken with his lawyer and the courts will not free him for another ten days. It is quite urgent that someone like you and your firm give a character reference for him saying that he is a top man in his field and that he has made recordings with your company. It is urgent that this information reach his lawyer this week, as the judges go on holiday in July. Without your kind help, it can be quite possible that they might hold him longer. Could you please be so kind as to ask Mr. Alfred Lion to do the same?

Lion and Blue Note obliged by sending letters and albums to the court, vouching for Dexter's status as a world-famous musician.

The drama took a further turn in June during a preliminary hearing in Paris. According to an article in the *Ekstra Bladet,* "Lotte Nielsen, engaged to jazz tenor saxophonist Dexter Gordon," admitted to the court that "she had smuggled opium from [Copenhagen] to her fiancé in Paris." Lotte claimed to not know the identities of the dealers—only that they were "two foreigners"—who sold her the drugs.

Dexter was released from prison on June 20, 1966, on two thousand dollars' bail while his case was still being adjudicated. According to his good friend, the jazz journalist Mike Hennessey, Dexter "walked into Jazz Land that night and told a jubilant Johnny Griffin and Art Taylor, 'I can hardly believe it!'" Hennessey spent a great deal of time with Dexter after his release and wrote a deeply moving and revealing piece about the arrest and Dexter's thoughts about his difficulties with hard drugs in the July 26, 1966, issue of *Melody Maker,* the British music periodical. Dexter:

> *I started using [heroin] around 1945 when just about all the big names were. But it was the most terrible mistake I ever made in my life. It destroys you eventually unless you fight it. It got to a stage where I told myself it just couldn't go on. I was spending up to two hundred dollars a day on junk, my kids were getting their father's addiction flung in their faces. So I fought it and went clean. But I was getting phone calls every day from pushers, and they were approaching me in the street. "Aw, come on, Dexter, let's swing . . ." I had to tell them over and over again that I was determined to kick it.*
>
> *They're building bigger and better prisons in the States and they're getting fuller and fuller. But I don't really see how that's helping the drug problem. How many convictions have I had? Too many.*
>
> *I have been off it twice for more than two years at a time and then it's no real fight. When you are working regularly, playing and rehearsing, it just doesn't come up. But when things are slow, you get bored and idle and depressed and the pushers start coming round—before you know you are back on it again. Boy, those pushers really made a believer out of me.*
>
> *I was a registered addict in Britain and they gradually ease you off. The same thing happened when I came to Denmark [in 1962]—a doctor helped me kick the habit. But when I went back to the States in '64 I guess I got mixed up in the scene again. Of course I want to beat it. I'm a perpetual optimist and I feel I can. I hope I can. But I just don't know whether I'll be able to. I've just got to try to kill the habit before it kills me.[2]*

Dexter remained in Paris after his release—the Danish government would not allow him back in Copenhagen—and awaited the outcome of his case. On October 16 he wrote to Frank Wolff from the Hotel Rotary in Paris:

I received the new album and many thanks—but the lawyer didn't receive any so I will have to give him mine I guess. As I told you the Judge's clerk is a jazz fan and also a woman who works for the Prefecture. Well, that's the luck of the Irish. And I go to court on the 19th of Nov. so I have to take care of this right away. So, maybe you can send me a few more copies, a selection!

The lawyer says everything is cool and that I'll probably get some of my money back. I'm still working at Jazzland until the 20 of Oct. Then we are off for a week and return on the 29th, if I get a raise. Business is very good. Also, I am going to Roma on the 22nd for the Radio—But just one day.

I just heard Montmartre in Copenhagen is closed—they really died without me this summer. Yusef Lateef was the only one who did any business for them. He did 2 two week stands. Anyway, that should be reason enough for them to bring me there . . . back-up. A.T. [Arthur Taylor] is working with me and two French players. But ce va.

It's 6 o'clock in the morning so please excuse this writing, hope you can read it. Anyway, I'm waiting on the new statement and the go ahead on the record date. So let me hear from you right away.

As always,
Very saxily yours
Dexter

On November 22 the case was finally resolved after Dexter's and Lotte's drug purchases were connected with several apprehended drug dealers, including a former actress named Huguette Le Metayer, also known as Heddy Miller. Dexter received a three-month suspended prison sentence and was ordered to pay a fine of three hundred francs, equivalent to about sixty-one dollars at the time.

From the arrest in May until the case was settled, Dexter lived under the shadow of uncertainty about his future in Europe. The news of a suspended sentence ended the seven-month ordeal, and as he said many times, this was the last time he would see the inside of a prison. He promised himself to get clean and he kept that promise. In his October letter to Wolff at Blue Note Records, Dexter asks about the next recording, but there was not to be one. As it turned out, *Gettin' Around* was the last album Dexter recorded for Blue Note. He would not make another studio recording until 1969. Many live recordings of his gigs at the Montmartre were released on SteepleChase Records.

Dexter's letters to Wolff and Lion not only allow us to trace his steps in Europe during his Blue Note years; they also show us that he was trying to settle into a good life and make a career for himself there while maintaining a relationship with his American record company. They prove that he was seriously involved in his recording career and thinking about his future as an artist. He was genuinely fond of Alfred and Frank who, after all, were the ones responsible for Dexter becoming known as "Our Man in Paris" after the 1963 Blue Note recording of the same name that is now a jazz classic.

By January 1967 Dexter had been able to get playing dates in Sweden, but his application for a work permit to return to Denmark was still being refused and a consortium of Danish writers and musicians as well as Dexter's friends and fans mounted a campaign in his support. Dexter was very moved by this protest and said often that living in Denmark gave him a feeling of confidence and security that he had never felt in the United States. He was accepted as an artist, and being a jazz musician was something to be proud of. He would say that in the States if he said he was a jazz musician he couldn't buy a car or open a bank account, but in Denmark he was applauded and respected. Of course, life off the bandstand was another story, but as an artist with a reputation and a history in jazz, doors would open for him. He made the effort to learn Danish, bought a house, rode a bicycle, became a resident. As Dexter put it, "I could breathe." And with the help of his doctor, H. Georg Stage, he was also able to get off heroin, for good.

Happy news came through on March 18, 1967, as reported by the newspaper *Politiken*:

DEXTER GORDON MAY PLAY IN DENMARK AGAIN

The Minister of Justice will not refuse the jazz musician because of drug abuse in France. A suspended jail sentence and a fine of 400 kr. for drug abuse is not enough to refuse the world famous jazz saxophonist Dexter Gordon a working permit in Denmark.

But sadly, more unhappy news came just three months later. Dexter and Lotte seem to have split up toward the end of 1966 when Dexter was still stuck in Paris. But we know that Dexter still cared for her in 1967, because on June 11 he visited her when she was a patient in the Rigshospitalet in Copenhagen. The following day Lotte died at the age of twenty-eight. The cause of death, according to the Danish National Archives, was a brain hemorrhage. Dexter must have been terribly distraught, but how much of the pain he shared with others cannot be known. I did learn from his friend Klaus Albrechtsen that on June 16, as Dexter was performing at Jazzhus Montmartre, Lotte's father stormed into the club brandishing a gun and threatened to kill Dexter, blaming him for Lotte's death. This episode must have devastated Dexter even further.

From the Danish Archives we know that early on the evening of June 18, officers responded to a call from the Hotel Stella that Dexter was discovered to be unresponsive in his room. An ambulance rushed him to Bispebjerg Hospital, where doctors determined that he had overdosed on a prescribed sleeping medication called Sovenal. The police report noted that "the doctor on duty was informed that the reason for Gordon's action probably was lovesickness." It is not clear who might have so informed the doctor. Dexter returned to work at the Montmartre the following night. He worked at Jazzhus Montmartre throughout all of June and July.

I only learned about this series of events when Danish television sent me a documentary about Dexter and Ben Webster living in Copenhagen called *Cool Cats*. In the film, Albrechtsen tells the story of the father pulling the gun at the club and Dexter's subsequent suicide attempt. I never heard Dexter mention this, as in fact he never mentioned Lotte Nielsen at all. I can speculate that it all was too painful for him and that he did not want to think about those very troubled times. I do know that Dexter once said that he had never considered suicide and that many drug users he knew died of accidental overdoses when they unknowingly took drugs that were stronger than those they were accustomed to. But we will never know exactly what happened to Dexter in his hotel room that night. I do know that he hated being humiliated in public and did not approve of any sort of public display in what he considered a private matter. He would often walk away from arguments or disagreements among musicians, so I can imagine that the scene in the Montmartre on June 16 was horrifying to him.

When I think about Dexter's experience of getting busted in Paris and going to prison there, I am reminded of James Baldwin's essay *Equal in Paris*. Baldwin had been accused of being in possession of a stolen sheet from a hotel. In fact, a friend had given him the sheet. He spent Christmas in prison in Paris but, like Dexter, took it as a lesson and a new way to think about himself and his life. Though the story of Dexter's life during this time was painful for him, I decided to include it in the book because it is another example of Dexter's life story as the phoenix rising. He rose from some very deep holes more than once. He conquered his demons and always ended up happy and contented, all the way to the very end of his life. When Skip Malone warned me to "walk away" from this story, he had a very sad expression on his face.

He suggested that I omit the negative parts of Dexter's life from the book and focus on the success of his career. But when we listen to Dexter, we know that he brought everything to his music, and the good, the bad, and the ugly were transformed when he played his horn.

For the rest of his life, Dexter carried a letter from the French minister of justice allowing him entry into France to work and then leave. Even after twenty years and all the accolades from *Round Midnight,* Dexter's name came up on a computer at the Charles de Gaulle Airport in Paris in 1987 because of the 1966 arrest, and we were detained. Of course, by then things had changed for Dexter. This time Dexter received an apology from Jack Lang, the French minister of culture, for the rough treatment at de Gaulle. Dexter had been disappointed when he was hassled at the airport until things could be straightened out. Then he said:

> *I had forgotten that the past never leaves you even if you fly First Class on Air France and are staying at the Hotel Crillon and have been nominated for an Oscar. They will always find a way to remind you that you were once arrested for using drugs.*

CHAPTER 15

The Khalif of Valby

Of all the musicians that I came to know during that period, Dexter was the one that showed the most solidarity with the radical revolutionary processes that had developed in America and was spreading all over Europe during the latter 1960s. He had a sound political perspective; he was definitely not into the Black mystique that some of the younger musicians fell into.

—Leonard "Skip" Malone[1]

Dexter's home at Dan Haven 6, in the Valby (pronounced *VAL-bu*) district of Copenhagen was removed far enough from the city center that you needed a car, a train, or a bicycle to get you there. Yes, Dexter Gordon owned a bicycle—and he rode it all over town. The image is hard to conjure for those who think of Dexter as the man in the iconic 1948 Herman Leonard photo with the curling cigarette smoke and the hat. When an ad agency wanted to use the "smoke" photo in a print ad for General Motors, I asked the director why they had chosen that particular photo of Dexter. He said, "Oh, we didn't know who it was. We just thought that was the perfect image of a jazz musician." Jazz musicians always seem to be thought of as being on the bandstand or in a recording studio with their instruments, clouds of smoke, and maybe a cocktail glass nearby. It was almost a joke to us that people would so often describe Dexter as "the son of one of the first Black doctors in Los Angeles, who joined the Lionel Hampton band in his senior year of high school . . ." Jazz history has tended to stereotype musicians into characters with little more substance to their lives beyond the bandstand and the road and the recording studio. But they all have histories that get them to the point of being musicians, and interesting lives off the bandstand as well as a culture around the music that is as complex as it is unique.

FIGURE 16. It did not take long for Dexter to adopt the Danish lifestyle of *hyggeligt*—a cozy contentment and harmony with one's self. Photograph © Jørgen Bo.

There were a number of stories about Dexter in the Danish newspapers when he moved to Valby. One journalist friend dubbed him the "Khalif of Valby," which he loved. The title derived from a slight misinterpretation of language. Dexter has a tune called "Soy Califa," which means "I am from California" in a kind of Los Angeles Spanish. He would always announce the tune in a dramatic manner. So, "Soy Califa" came to be understood in Denmark as "I am the Khalif" (Khalif being a Muslim spiritual leader), and when he moved to Valby, he became the "Khalif of Valby."

When he first moved to the house at Dan Haven 6, it was to rent a studio from the owner. He could practice there. It was quiet and just what he wanted in the period of his life following the major drama that began with the Paris drug bust, the tragic death of Lotte, and her father threatening Dexter with a gun at the Jazzhus Montmartre. Here was yet another example of Dexter's lifetime of dramatic ups and downs, and his remarkable way of recovering and coming back even stronger after his ordeals. His albums sometimes made the statements. In 1960 in Los Angeles there was *The Resurgence of Dexter Gordon,* and then in New York in 1976 there was *Homecoming.* He often said, "My life will have a happy ending because all of the unhappiness has already taken place. It must be in the genes, because I should have died young. But that wasn't my fate."

As Dizzy Gillespie once said about Dexter, "He did everything wrong and it all turned out right."

After a few years, the elderly owner of the Valby house told her son that after her death he could sell the house "to that nice Mister Gordon" if he wanted it—and he did. It was the first home Dexter ever owned. He settled in and had a family with his Danish wife, Fenja, and their son, Benjamin Dexter Gordon, called Benjie, born in 1975 and named after Ben Webster. When I first met Dexter that year as a tour manager for bands traveling in Europe, he invited the musicians to his house and cooked black-eyed peas and rice for them. I was very impressed and remember sitting in the backyard and thinking how nice to see a jazz musician living well. He said that he had seen a red fox in the backyard and laughed out loud thinking about the other "Redd Foxx" (the American comedian and actor best remembered for his comedy records and his starring role on the 1970s sitcom *Sanford and Son*). I asked Dexter about living in a place with so few Black people and he said, "We had the Copenhagen branch of the Black Panthers here. Bobby Seale came to town and my friend Skip Malone has people out there picketing the U.S. Embassy and reminding us what is going on in the States." But it wasn't easy being away in the 1960s. Dexter said that he would not have survived to return in the 1970s if he hadn't lived in Copenhagen and gotten himself together. He always dreamed of coming home and playing his music, and he wanted to play well enough so that the audience would take notice and he could show them that bebop was here to stay.

Dexter's good friend Leonard "Skip" Malone chose to live in Copenhagen when he finished his U.S. Army service in Germany. He married a beautiful and talented photographer named Kirsten and they had two daughters. Skip and Dexter took Danish classes together. Dexter said that proper Danish pronunciation was almost impossible to learn, but when we took a trip together to the countryside, he was perfectly understood by people who spoke not a word of English. In Copenhagen, English was spoken commonly by jazz fans and people on the Montmartre scene. It was, and still is, a kind of hip English that often sounds like another language. I have noticed that people on the jazz scene don't like to say "no" to a direct question or proposal but instead signal a kind of negative response by repeating "yeh yeh." Dexter said that one thing he liked about the Danes was how they avoided confrontation and never said no. They liked everything to be *hyggeligt* (hew-glit), which fit right in with Dexter's idea of how life should be. Dexter loved to use the Danish word *hyggeligt,* a word not easy to define in English but is said to mean cozy or comfortable, content, at peace, and in harmony with one's self and the environment. According to his good friend Torben Ulrich, "in Denmark being *hyggeligt* is a way of life and perhaps a sort of Danish religion." For a New York girl, the idea of *hyggeligt* was a bit disconcerting, but I started to understand how Dexter felt about living there.

Of course his time in Copenhagen wasn't all *hyggeligt.* Since his arrival in October 1962 he worked at the Montmartre so often that it became his second or maybe first home. The record producer Michael Cuscuna, who became his very good friend, always said that Dexter was the most optimistic person he had ever met. Dexter would say that if Bird had been busted and spent time in jail, he would have lived longer because he would have had time away from the constant hustle and a break from drugs. Leave it to Dexter to consider time in jail as a positive experience.

In 1968 he applied for residency in Denmark. His doctor, H. Georg Stage, wrote an impassioned statement detailing part of Dexter's long struggle against the allure of drugs and his several successes in getting clean, and emphasizing that Dexter had never harmed or endangered anyone but himself. The doctor even invoked scripture in asking the authorities to approve Dexter's application. Here is Stage's letter, translated from Danish:

March 4, 1968

Statement by Dr. H. Georg Stage
Dexter Gordon b. 27/2–1923 in USA has asked me, as his doctor in Denmark since 1962, to accompany his application for residence permit in Denmark with a statement.

In autumn 1962 he by incident came to me, wanting himself supplied with great amounts of injection medicine with cocaine and morphine.

Through the city medical officer and the national health administration I was given permission to try ambulant cure. It succeeded in the course of a little more than 4 months. Detailed report sent to the health administration.

In 1965, after a journey to the USA and especially after great family disappointments, came a relapse. Once more I took him (with permission) in ambulant cure treatment. It went slowly yet finally came through.

He had certain conflicts with the police in Sweden regarding purchase of "black" morphine for his own use. In France too he came in conflict with the police for the same reason. This latter incident however and its consequences seems to have frightened him so much that he by now apparently has held himself free of morphine for 1½ years.

As far as I can see, and my wife also agrees (he has been a private guest to our house a number of times), he is now free of "dope."

Since 1962 Denmark has been his Paradise. Here he feels secure and the morphine temptation became lesser, became practicable, so that he wanted to break his habit and this on top was manageable ambulantly, an extremely rare thing.

The big world, especially the USA, makes him insecure, afraid, and resistance weakened—and then he relapses.

Thus I believe that without any morphica risk for Denmark he can be given a residence permit for a certain period of time; then when he behaves well the permission can be prolonged almost unlimited, particularly if he at the same time knows that any morphica consumption (little or great) will result in immediate expulsion.

When I use the term morphica risk I especially have in mind that to my knowledge he never has led others astray, probably on the contrary, since he knows it is a downward path. (This circumstance probably was his greatest asset in the Swedish and later in the French case as well, that he had only purchased for his personal use.)

Once I wrote the health administration that [if] he could continuously stay in Denmark he could stay free of narcotics (morphine), but not so out in the world. Now the world has turned its back on him. England and France do not want to see him. And the USA prefers he stay away. Race discrimination alone makes him sick and scared. He is allowed to work in Sweden, Denmark, and Germany. This builds a very powerful reason for him to stay "clean" now, not to spoil the last possibilities in Europe.

Because as it is written in very old scripts: "Holy fear is the beginning of much wisdom"—then I believe and hope that the fear Dexter Gordon now houses will reject many temptations, in particular if he can be allowed to live in his beloved Denmark.

Signed Doctor H. G. Stage

The application was approved and Dexter was welcomed as a resident of Denmark. He began to refer to himself as a *musiklærer* (music teacher) when he found out that going into the Danish high schools with Kenny Drew to give workshops had helped him get his residency papers. But he still entered his occupation as "jazz musician" on any documents he needed to sign. He began to settle into a *hyggeligt* Danish life, with his bicycle, his long engagements at the Montmartre, his friends, and a routine that allowed him time to practice, write music, read, and reflect.

Soon after Dexter was granted his Danish residency, on April 4, 1968, Dr. Martin Luther King Jr. was gunned down on the balcony of the Lorraine Motel in Memphis, Tennessee. Demonstrations and protests broke out in a hundred cities across America. Dexter watched it all on television with Malone, and Dexter said they were horrified by what was going on in the States. Dexter said living in Europe at the time made him feel very helpless and sad.

Even living in Denmark, Dexter was fully aware of the crises at home, and when the Danish police attacked a huge peaceful demonstration against the Vietnam War on April 27, 1968, Dexter joined pickets at the American embassy. This was another thing that Dexter and I had in common. In later years he would often say to me, "Are you going to the parade?" when I was going to a demonstration. In early 1968 Dexter worked in Paris, Rome, and Germany. In April he was back in Copenhagen doing school concerts. On April 20 he performed "Requiem for Martin Luther King" at Vallekilde High School with the Danish Radio Jazz Group featuring Idrees Sulieman.

In October at the 1968 Summer Olympics in Mexico City, two American sprint medalists, Tommie Smith and John Carlos, raised black-gloved fists in the Black power salute on the victory stand as "The Star-Spangled Banner" was played. Seen on television throughout the world, the gesture enraged America's political establishment, and the International Olympic Committee banned Smith and Carlos from the Olympic Games for life. Dexter took a cue from them in designing his Christmas card for 1968 (next page).

Malone, Dexter's closest friend in Copenhagen, wrote about Dexter's politics in 1969:

> Of all the musicians that I came to know during that period, Dexter was the one that showed the most solidarity with the radical revolutionary processes that had developed in America and was spreading all over Europe during the latter 1960s. He had a sound political perspective; he was definitely not into the Black mystique that some of the younger musicians fell into. When the Black Panthers Bobby Seale and Masai Hewitt visited Copenhagen in 1969

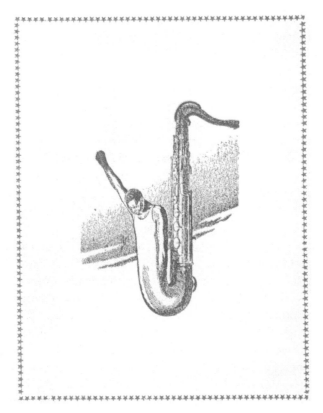

FIGURE 17. Dexter's Christmas card for 1968. Drawing © Klaus Albrechtsen.

and held their speech at Gruntvigs Hus, I saw Dexter's tall frame at the back of the audience, soaking in every bit of the Panther rhetoric. Later that evening Bobby Seale, Dexter, Art Taylor, Johnny Griffin, and Sam Jackson were all invited for drinks at the home of one of the arrangers. And the Panthers were familiar with Dexter's music, and of course they all had a lot of stories to exchange about their California background.

Later he titled one of his recordings *The Panther.* During those political days, there were many benefits arranged to raise money for the Black radical and anti-Vietnam movement in the USA, and also to focus interest on the current situation.[2]

In early 1969 Dexter worked in Holland and then traveled to New York to record an album for Prestige Records with James Moody, Barry Harris, Buster Williams, and Tootie Heath. The album was *Tower of Power* and it included his new original compositions "Montmartre" and "The Rainbow People," written in Copenhagen. He returned to

New York again in July 1970 to record *The Panther* for Prestige with Tommy Flanagan, Larry Ridley, and Alan Dawson. The album includes his compositions "The Panther" and "Valse Robin," in honor of his daughter, Robin. On July 12 he played at the Newport Jazz Festival, then had a gig in Chicago, after which he returned to Europe to perform with the George Gruntz Dream Group in Zurich, Switzerland.

He worked steadily in the Montmartre through most of the second half of 1970, with a few side trips to Germany. He also played steadily at his home club from May through the end of 1971. It was almost unheard of for a jazz musician to have that kind of steady gig in his hometown for such a long stretch. In 1972, he performed at Randy Weston's Pan-African Jazz Festival in Tangier, Morocco. Then he came to New York to record once more for Prestige. He played a jam session at Radio City Music Hall with Harry "Sweets" Edison, a gig with the Lionel Hampton Reunion Band, and another concert at the Newport Jazz Festival.

As mentioned earlier, living in Copenhagen made it easy for Dexter to accept work in nearby France, Germany, Italy, Spain, Portugal, Switzerland, Luxembourg, Belgium, Austria, Sweden, Norway, Finland, and very often Holland. Wim Wigt, his Dutch booking agent, found gigs for Dexter in venues and towns big and small throughout Holland and neighboring countries as well. Normally when Dexter toured in Europe it was as a solo musician picking up local rhythm sections in each city along the way. But in Holland he had a "working band." In 1972 he went on tour with the Dutch rhythm section of Rein de Graaff (piano), Henk Haverhoek (bass), and Eric Ineke (drums). On October 12 Dexter wrote to friends in Copenhagen from Liège, Belgium. In his sign-off he refers to the name he gave himself for the amusement of his Danish friends: "Bent Gordonsen."[3] He wrote:

> Dear Folks,
> This is "den gamle rejsemusiker" [the old traveling musician] letting the folks back home know that I'm O.K and am defending the colors! This tour is quite fantastic; we are traveling through Holland, Germany, Luxembourg, Belge and France! It's six weeks, no 7 weeks, and I'm getting rich! Anyway, it's very well organized and seems to be a success. For the most part I'm working with the same group . . . Hope everything is in order.
>   Love, Absalon[4] (Gordonsen)

When Dexter would recite the names of the towns he had played in during his time in Holland, people were incredulous. Wigt found him gigs in Hilversum, Leiden, Veendam, Venlo, Zwolle, Den Haag, Heemskerk, Amsterdam, De Woude, Rotterdam, and Eschede. Dexter would tell friends that there were jazz lovers in all these places in a country the size of the state of Maryland. When a band travels together and has meals together and works this often, they get to know each other in a very special way. They learn each other's habits and moods, and how to play together. The music improves every night, and with Dexter we can be sure that he found a way to communicate what he expected from the rhythm section. Dexter always had a particular idea of what he wanted to hear, and if he wasn't comfortable with the band, he would definitely let them know. He had very kind words about how serious his "Dutch band" was and how much they cared about the musicians from the States who came to play in Europe.

In a 2014 interview in Amsterdam, drummer Eric Ineke told me:

> With Dexter, I had communication right away. Dexter had a way of telling you things in a very nice way. In the car, when we were driving, he'd say, "Eric, can you . . . ?" He thought that if he told me some things to do in the music, it would get even better. I remember all of one thing that happened right on stage. It was in Germany and we were playing a ballad. I got out the brushes, but I used to have my brushes a little smaller for fast playing. It was easier than the other way. So I played a ballad. And Dexter was doing this thing with his ear like he couldn't hear me! And he was looking at my brushes, and he said, on stage, "Eric! Open up those motherfuckers!"

The pianist Rein de Graaff recalled the tour with Dexter fondly and remembered the first time he ever heard Dexter:

> I was in the Army and I found out at midnight that Dexter Gordon was on the radio, a live broadcast from Utrecht from a jazz club with a Dutch rhythm section. Everybody was asleep in the barracks so I went in this place where the showers were. I had a little portable radio and I heard him, and it was the most unbelievable stuff that I had ever heard. I was always telling people about this radio show. That was 1963 and I said, "I want to play with this man." About ten years later, I got to go on tour with him. I will never forget that.
>
> One day in 1972, Wim Wigt called me and said, "Do you want to go on tour with Dexter Gordon? It's going to last about three months, not every day, mostly Holland and Belgium and a little bit of Germany near the border, but actually every weekend, maybe one gig in a week, two gigs in the week." We were playing, playing, playing, playing . . . We learned a lot from him because he knew all the tools; he knew all the dramatic things about balance. He taught me that it's a balance of sweet and bittersweet. He taught me the lyrics to "You've Changed." Most of the time when we played with him, Dexter stayed at my house. My wife and I had been married for maybe two years then. We lived in Veendam. Everybody in the town knew Dexter and he knew them. The kids would say, "Hi, Dex" when he walked in town.

While researching Dexter's years in Europe, I met Jan-Eric and Mari-Anne Askenstrom, serious and longtime jazz fans from Gothenburg, Sweden. Jan-Eric reminded me that Dexter may have lived in Denmark, but he worked often in Sweden and was very important to the jazz history there. He made sure I did not leave this important part of Dexter's European sojourn out of the book by compiling research on Dexter's gigs there, finding photos and recordings, translating articles about Dexter, and finding literary references to him that he translated and sent to me over the years of my research. From 1962 through 1981 there are references to 173 gigs in Sweden compiled and handwritten by Folke Andersson, the connoisseur and expert on all things Dexter in Sweden. In Stockholm, Dexter appeared at the Golden Circle (Gyllene Cirkeln) eight times beginning in 1962 and also at the Golden Hat. He also played the Pawnshop in Mosebacke and in many more clubs in the provinces. In the 1960s Swedish Public Service Radio hired Dexter to give a series of lunch concerts at high schools all over the country that were broadcast live nationwide. Until he began traveling with his own band in 1978, Dexter would play with local musicians, including Lars Sjosten (piano), Bjorn Alke (bass), and Sune Spangberg (drums). Dexter's gigs in Sweden were well covered by the jazz journal *Orkester Journalen,* and the jazz authority Lars Westin supplied us with invaluable information. "I first heard and met Dexter in October 1964, when I was sixteen," Westin wrote,

> but I didn't get to know him personally until a few years later when I was attending the College of Journalism in Stockholm. I listened to him whenever he was in Stockholm and even went to other cities to catch his performances. He was very friendly and even passed me a joint occasionally. In January 1969, I took the opportunity to go with him on a tour, standing on my knees in an already over-crowded car. The last time I met him was at one of his last visits to Stockholm in the 1980s and he greeted me [with] "Lars! How are your knees?"

In the documentary film *Main Thing Sunshine* (named for a remark Dexter made after a long road trip in Sweden one summer), Gunnar Lindgren, tenor saxophonist and owner of the ArtDur Jazzclub in Gothenburg, says:

> Sometimes when Dexter was short of money he called from Copenhagen and said, "Gunnar, I need a gig." Then I tried to the best of my ability to rearrange my bookings to make room for Dexter. He never asked what I would pay him. He knew that I was fair. So he showed me his train ticket and I counted out the bills for the fare and for the gig. But I remember once when

the place was packed and I wasn't quite aware of that. When I had finished counting out the bills, Dexter kept standing there—"Come on, Gunnar"—like when training a dog to jump over a hurdle. I counted out a few more bills and Dexter was fine with that.

There is a brilliant and insightful passage about Dexter in the novel *Klasskämpen* (The working-class warrior) by Svante Foerster:[5] "Dexter Gordon tastes like coarse rye bread, parsley and cellar-chilled vodka. The basic tastes, pure and strong. He is elementary but with power. When you have listened to him you tell nothing but the truth for a long while. You board planes and carry coal sacks and burst out laughing and don't tell a single false word. He is a moral tenorist . . . I played the whole of [the album] *Go* and the whole of *Dexter Calling*. Then I was blessed, clear-headed and strong."

Dexter celebrated his fiftieth birthday with a big party in Copenhagen on February 27, 1973, and worked at the Montmartre through most of the year. In July 1973 he played the Montreux Jazz Festival with his boyhood friend, pianist Hampton Hawes. Like Dexter, Hampton was targeted in Los Angeles as a drug user. He was arrested on heroin charges and sentenced to ten years in a federal prison hospital, which was twice the mandatory minimum. On January 20, 1961, after serving three years at the Fort Worth (Texas) Federal Medical Facility, Hawes was watching President John F. Kennedy's inaugural speech on television, when he became convinced that Kennedy would pardon him. Hawes wrote to Kennedy asking for a pardon, and in 1963 Kennedy granted him executive clemency. Hawes's was the forty-second of only forty-three such pardons given by Kennedy in what turned out to be the final year of his presidency. Hawes went on to have a successful jazz career until his death in 1977 at the age of forty-eight. Also on the bill at Montreux were Dexter's good friends Gene Ammons and Kenny Clarke. Dexter was deeply saddened when Gene died in 1974 from cancer at the age of forty-nine.

One of the things Dexter liked best about performing at large jazz festivals was seeing the other musicians and having rousing reunions that went on until the early morning hours with lots of laughter, back-slapping, storytelling, and copious amounts of drinks and reefer. After Montreux, Ammons came to Copenhagen and played at the Montmartre with Dexter and Horace Parlan. It was a very festive reunion for them.

In July 1973 Dexter recorded with his friend Jackie McLean on Steeple Chase Records. The album was named *The Meeting* and featured Kenny Drew, Niels-Henning Ørsted Pedersen, and Alex Riel.

Dexter was back in his hometown club from January through July 1974 and from February through October 1975. That month Dexter made his first trip to Japan, with Kenny Drew, Niels-Henning Ørsted Pedersen, and Tootie Heath. The trip did not work out very well. The flight on the Russian airline Aeroflot was very cramped and hot, and the vodka was all too free-flowing. Dexter found out he was too tall for the hotel rooms in Japan; he never felt comfortable there, and he didn't think the audiences appreciated his style. In July 1976 Dexter went to Macerata, Italy, with Johnny Griffin, Parlan, and drummer Tony Inzalaco. Tony was one of Dexter's favorite drummers and they played together often in Germany, France, and Italy. One favorite stop for Dexter:

> In Milano, Italy, on the main piazza near a gigantic cathedral and La Scala, on a corner over a large bookstore was a jazz club. Quite classy and plush. Working with Italian musicians, one of many gigs in the country and having fun. What made this gig so outstanding in my mind was "Spaghetti Time." Every night at the stroke of midnight, the doors of the kitchen would open and Le Chef and a couple of waiters would roll out a portable hot wagon of pasta and proceed to pass plates to everyone, free! The music stops in mid-tune and the chef shouts, "SPAGHETTI TIME!"

During this long period of stability, with Dexter enjoying his European travels, and even more so the long stands playing before adoring fans and visitors to Copenhagen at the Montmartre, he had settled into a comfortable home life in Valby with Fenja and Benjie. Toward the end of 1975, when Dexter would begin to think about making his permanent return to the States, Fenja and Benjie would be a major consideration. And there would be many others.

CHAPTER 16

Homecoming

> What was it about Dexter? Well, besides his music, he was
> sort of the bridge between Charlie Parker on the alto and
> what became possible on the tenor saxophone. Dexter's
> playing was always an amalgam, to me, of everything that
> came before, of course. But he was also that bridge—so a
> lot of the guys that were getting into bebop at that time,
> they all liked Dexter. He wasn't doing what Charlie Parker
> was doing, no. You know, he didn't play Charlie Parker
> on tenor; he played Dexter Gordon on tenor. But he was
> playing music that had the same qualities, really.
>
> —Sonny Rollins[1]

In 1975 I was working in Holland for the booking agent Wim Wigt and
touring with bands that traveled mostly by train using Eurail passes to
save money, when I received an urgent call for me to go to Nancy,
France. I was to meet Dexter Gordon and his group and get them to
Copenhagen by train. There was a warning of a rail strike in France and
so the band needed to be rerouted. I had a huge book that contained all
the European railroad timetables. Dexter asked me if that was the only
book I read, when he saw me poring over it all the time. When I arrived
at the concert hall in Nancy, the band was on stage. I remember it so
vividly because my life changed at that moment. Dexter was playing
"Tenor Madness," the tune we all knew from Sonny Rollins and John
Coltrane. That I had chills and felt I had been transported to another
planet is an understatement. (I am not the only person to have had what
we call the "Dexter Gordon moment." In many of my interviews people
told me that the first time they heard Dexter was also an indelible
moment for them. One person literally fainted at the Montmartre in
Copenhagen on the first night that Dexter arrived there.) This was 1975

and I couldn't believe what I was hearing. He had Kenny Drew on piano, Jimmy Woode on bass, and Tony Inzalaco on drums, and they were swinging so hard the audience kept jumping up and screaming, which was not all that common in Europe at the time. Dexter had to play two encores to get the crowd to leave the hall. I of course had heard Dexter on records, but this was the first time I had heard him in person and his sound and presence was staggering in its power and beauty. Why hadn't we heard him in New York, and how could he have been away all these years, I wondered.

After the set, I went backstage and met Dexter. I told him that Wim Wigt had sent me to guide the band to Copenhagen. He said, "That's the nicest thing Wim has ever done for me." He then proceeded to drop what I thought was just another jazz musician's pick-up line. He said, "Didn't we meet in an earlier lifetime? I've been waiting for you." I suggested that he had been in Europe a bit long if he thought that line was new or would work with the girls. He laughed his raucous laugh and that, as they say, was the beginning of a beautiful friendship. The next day we went to Strasbourg, which is only about an hour from Nancy. We took the night train to Copenhagen that went through Germany— Hannover to Hamburg and then a train-ferry between Puttgarten and Rødby, Denmark. The train goes onto the ferry and the passengers go upstairs to the lounge during the crossing. Dexter called this "Ben's train," because Ben Webster did not like to fly and he always traveled to Paris from Copenhagen and back by train and ferry. All the stewards on the ferry knew Ben and were especially hospitable to him.

Dexter remembered this trip a bit differently from my memory of it, as he set it down in a poem he wrote to me on Christmas Day, 1989:

TO MAXINE
I'M YOURS FOR THE TOUCHING

Jean-Henri e les garcons
were off on a tear,
a railroad strike all
over France
Nothing was moving, not
even a truffle.
Strasbourg, Austria, where
I worked that night,
I met a girl ever so slight
who offered to show me the
way to Milano, not Chicago!
We got a vogne ready & made,

Lower berths, side by side,
to make it safe
then to the Buffet car for
ginger and spice, every thing nice
back in our car she said:
"I'm yours for the touching."
From Vingtnemille we crossed
the border to France where
that night I performed
the Marseillaise, also,
après le concert.
Fin By Dextér

In Dexter's version of the story, there was a train strike in France and then he worked in Strasbourg. He refers to it as Austria, but Strasbourg is actually in France and I'm pretty sure that the gig was in Nancy, France. This brings us to a brief discussion of memory. There is not one "right" story here. I remember things one way and he remembered them another. In jazz history, lots of stories that become accepted as facts are memories that change over the years. Life is improvised as well as memory, so no one story has more weight than another. The line about the girl "ever so slight" is definitely me. The "vogne" is, I think, a reference to the "vagone," or sleeping car, in French. Dexter moved between languages with ease—French, Danish, English, Spanish—and sometimes combined them all in one sentence. The reference to "Vingt-nemille" (Ventimiglia), I think, is from another trip we took years later, but perhaps he liked the word and wanted to put something about performing "La Marseillaise," the French national anthem, in the poem. I have not changed any of the spelling in the poem as it reflects the way he worked things out on paper.

After that concert in Nancy, we went to a restaurant, where I said, "Why don't you come to New York to play? People need to hear you. No one is playing like you there. They would love you."

"I want to come home but haven't been able to figure out how to do it," he said. "Everyone is discouraging me from even thinking about it."

Since I knew nothing about management or booking and was completely oblivious to how complicated it might be, I said, "I'll call Max Gordon at the Vanguard and tell him to book you. I've known him since I was fifteen. He will give you a gig." I waited until it was about 10 p.m. in New York, which was 4 a.m. in Nancy, and called Max. "Max, I'm in France and I heard Dexter Gordon tonight. You must book him. He sounds so great."

"Forget it. No one will come. He has been gone too long."

"No, no, no. You must give him a gig. He's great. *If you don't give him a date, I will never speak to you again.*"

This threat did not do much good, as Max replied, "I don't care if you never speak to me again." And then he hung up the phone on me.

So much for my first attempt at getting Dexter a gig. Dexter and I started discussing what it would take for him to come back to the States. He had saved money for his return and we figured out how much it would cost to pay his airfare, pay a band, rehearse, rent a hotel room, do publicity, and pay my phone bill. We thought if we worked on it for six months and then announced his return that it would be worth a shot. The next night I called Max again and made him an offer. "Okay, Max. Dexter wants to come home. What if you give him a gig at the club for no guarantee and he covers the band? If it works and people come, we can talk about his working there more regularly and you can pay him. If it doesn't work, you don't lose anything."

"That's not a very good deal for Dexter," Max said. "Are you sure you want to try to be a manager? Okay. I'll give him a week."

We spent the rest of the trip to Copenhagen plotting out the next six months. Dexter was going to begin to take Antabuse (a medication that can help people stop drinking by causing unpleasant side effects if alcohol is consumed while taking it). He said he wanted to practice and write some new music and get in shape for the return. He even wrote a tune called "Antabus," which he said helped reinforce his resolve to abstain.

By the time we got to Copenhagen, we had decided to try to do this together. We shook hands and agreed to work on his return for one year and see if it could work out. If it did, we would renew the handshake every year at midnight on New Year's Eve. The rest is history. It worked out even better than we had hoped it would. Yet contrary to some of the jazz myths, Dexter's return after fourteen years in Europe didn't just happen overnight.

Woody Shaw was the one who got the interest in Dexter's return going. He kept telling people how good Dexter sounded, how modern he was, and how it would boost the scene to have him back. Woody always went to all the clubs in New York to listen and sit in, and of course people listened when he said someone was playing great. Word began to spread. When I got home from Europe, I began to work on Dexter's return. He gave me a list of the people he knew who might give him a gig and the places he worked when he would come back to Los Angeles at Christmastime for many years to visit his mother and daughters. I started making calls, but the response was not as positive as we had hoped. Most club owners didn't think he could or should have his own band. They would book him with a local rhythm section but not hire him with his own musicians. I kept a list of those who didn't believe in his return and those who were enthusiastic and positive about the idea. Joe Segal in Chicago was one of the people who said he knew Dexter would be a huge success if he came back. "There's a space missing that he can fill," Joe said. The other person who believed in Dexter was Todd Barkan of the Keystone Korner in San Francisco. He and Dexter were good friends, and Todd booked Dexter right away and continued to book him for years to come. One of the things that Dexter insisted upon was having a working band. He had been playing in Europe with pickup bands for too long. Of course, in Copenhagen he had an excellent rhythm section with Kenny Drew, Niels-Henning Ørsted Pedersen, and either Tootie Heath, Alex Riel, or Makaya Ntshoko on drums. But many times on the road he didn't feel able to play what he wanted to play because the band just wasn't up to it.

I started calling, and calling back, and then calling people again. When I got my first phone bill, I almost fainted. Those were the days before cellphones and the internet, and the bill was huge. I went to Jack Whittemore, the best jazz agent in the business, for advice and he said, "You must be doing something right. Keep making those calls." He paid the bill, checked my call list, and made some suggestions about others I should call and how to make a deal. Jack, so very kind and generous, represented Ahmad Jamal, Art Blakey, Stan Getz, Horace Silver, and more. He was the biggest and the best and he was a beautiful person who drank Jack Daniel's and grew orchids. His office was in his apartment on Park Avenue near Grand Central Station. When I first called and asked him to book Dexter, he said, "No! I don't have time. It will take too much work. You can do it. I will teach you to be a booking agent. It's all in the timbre of the voice, and you have the right timbre to sell anything." Well, this was another case of not knowing what I was doing but being bold enough to think I could learn. I would go to Jack's office, where he showed me how to write a contract, let me look at his notes, and listen to him on the phone. He even showed me how he kept some contracts in a secret drawer that he kept locked.

Jack Whittemore did his work in a kind of code he had developed at Shaw Artists, where the agents sat in open cubicles and didn't want other agents to see their contacts and phone numbers. They each cooked up their own code. Jack's was something like, "Add four to each number, subtract two." For names, it was reversing the first and middle, or something like that. It was like something you read about in spy novels, but in this case it was about how much the gig paid and what the percentage was and who the promoter was. I never did manage to work in code, but I did keep my little bit of contact information with me at all times. When Michael Cuscuna and I shared an office, I would put away my Rolodex at night.

Now that I have had a chance to reflect on his lessons, Jack was right about a lot of things. I still have my Rolodex. Jack encouraged me and introduced me to Helen Keane, who managed Bill Evans. She was very supportive and kept reminding me not to worry about who didn't like me, or who said I was too pushy or aggressive. She said the business was a men's club and they would resent me trying to come in from the outside: "Who is that girl? Who does she think she is? She doesn't know anything about this business." I was just trying to help out some great jazz artists. I never did want to compete with the big guys or be at the center of the music business.

I kept making the calls and getting some small gigs for Dexter. We started doing publicity that said Dexter Gordon was coming back after fourteen years in Europe. Well, that wasn't exactly the case—he had made several return trips during that span—but it sounded good. Only Ira Gitler commented on the slight overstatement about his return. Ira had known Dexter since the 1940s and had heard him on Fifty-Second Street. He remained one of Dexter's greatest champions and wrote about him in many jazz publications over the years. Dexter had come back to play in Chicago and Los Angeles once a year in most years, but he didn't seem to make much of a splash.

Now that Dexter believed he could come back to the States and have his own band and a career performing and recording, he began to make plans to return permanently. This got quite complicated. When Dexter told his Danish wife, Fenja, and his friends in Copenhagen that he was considering a return to the States, they all discouraged him, and they blamed me for suggesting that he leave. Kenny Drew, in particular, thought it was a big mistake. He said that Americans didn't care about bebop anymore, had forgotten him, and that it was too much pressure. But Dexter was determined to give it a try. He kept saying to me: "We will do this together. If it doesn't work, no regrets, but I want to give it my best shot." In our many conversations then, and more over the years, I agreed to take the brunt of many unpleasant situations for Dexter so that he could continue to do what he wanted to do with his life:

play the tenor saxophone and be a jazz musician. I agreed to stand between him and the business, and although he made all of the final decisions, he did not want to be included in the negotiations and politics of the music industry. He especially wanted to avoid any confrontations. I made an office out of the extra bedroom in the apartment Woody Shaw and I shared on East Thirty-First Street. Every month, Dexter would send me an American Express money order to cover my expenses and I would call him every week with a report of how things were going.

He started practicing intensely and got himself together, and we made a plan for the big return in September 1976. The first gig would be in Baltimore for the Left Bank Jazz Society at the Famous Ballroom, something of a warm-up before the New York dates. I put together a band of good New York players and Dexter flew in and checked into an apartment hotel. A few days later we took the train to Baltimore for the Sunday afternoon gig. During the weeks of those first gigs back in the States, we would speak on the phone at least once a day. That would continue for all of the seven years that I was his manager. The fans went wild in Baltimore, but Dexter didn't like the band. It wasn't what he wanted. Not modern enough. Not strong enough. So I fired the band. I knew all the musicians, especially the piano player, who was an old friend. They brought me up on charges at Local 802 for firing them. I also knew the union delegates and when I answered the charges, one of them said, "Maxine, why did you fire the band after one gig?"

"Dexter didn't like the band," I said. "He said they sounded sad."

"You can't fire a band because they sound sad. That is not a good enough reason." We settled on payments to each musician of two hundred dollars spread over ten weeks at twenty dollars a week. The piano player called me all kinds of names and said that twenty dollars a week for all those weeks was so sad. We did remain friends, but he would tell everyone how cheap I was.

That was when Woody Shaw stepped in. He told Dexter not to worry; he would get a band for him. Woody brought the players he had been working with: Louis Hayes, Ronnie Mathews, Stafford James, and himself. That band had toured for months in Europe with Junior Cook as the tenor player and Louis Hayes as the co-leader. I was the road manager for that band and Woody and I started a relationship during one of those tours and were living together by the time Dexter came back in 1976. The first gig with Dexter was at Storyville, a club on New York City's East Side that George Wein was running. It had a short life and was managed by Rigmor Newman, who was married to trumpeter Joe

Newman, Dexter's good friend from the Lionel Hampton band. Dexter would play two nights there in October before he went into the Village Vanguard. We thought it would be a good idea to showcase the band at Storyville, invite the press, and see how many Dexter fans would show up. The event turned into one of those legendary jazz moments that have taken on mythical proportions. Some writers claimed that Dexter had just magically reappeared in New York, that a line stretched around the block, that it rained but no one left, that he played until three in the morning and had standing ovation after standing ovation.

No one thought to ask about how long it took to plan for that first night, how much Dexter had invested in the possibilities for his own future, how hard the band rehearsed, how nervous we were about the outcome. Well, some of the myth is based on fact. There was a standing-room-only crowd, it did rain, and he did get ovation after ovation. He was so grateful to Woody and the band for setting things up so he could play anything he wanted to play. Their set included "Tivoli," a beautiful waltz written by Dexter and inspired by the famous Copenhagen amusement park, as well as Jimmy Heath's "Gingerbread Boy," "Body and Soul," "It's You or No One," and "Round Midnight." Dexter said he had the same feeling that night that he had gotten with the rhythm section of Sonny Clark, Butch Warren, and Billy Higgins when he recorded *Go* in 1962. He could just float on top and not have to worry about pulling anyone along. Woody was thrilled with Dexter's playing, and he was touched a short time later when Dexter told him that he'd like to play Woody's composition "The Moontrane." Dexter said that although he had never gotten to play with John Coltrane, he knew where Trane had come from, and that playing Woody's tune was very meaningful to him. Woody had played with Dexter in Europe in George Gruntz's big band and remembered one night when he was warming up in the dressing room. Dexter came in and listened and then said to him, "It sounded like Fats Navarro warming up." Woody loved that and it became one of those stories that was repeated many times.

The rhythm section was tight and happy to be playing with Dexter. On the second night at Storyville, Bruce Lundvall left guitarist John McLaughlin's wedding reception to come over to the club to hear Dexter. Bruce had been a fan since his college days and still had his Savoy 78s and all of Dexter's Blue Note albums. Bruce was president of Columbia Records at the time, and when he came into the dressing room after the gig to introduce himself, he asked Dexter if he would like to sign a recording contract with Columbia. Dexter looked at me and I looked at

Cuscuna and we all started thinking about how things seemed to be working out the way we had dreamed them. Michael was to become Dexter's producer and one of his closest friends. Woody had selected him, and Dexter knew that Woody gave very good advice. It was one of those moments when you see your wildest thoughts start to become real. We had invited several record executives, and some of them wanted to set up meetings to discuss deals. But when Bruce came up to Dexter and they shook hands, Dexter was convinced that he was dealing with a man of his word. In this case, Dexter turned out to be right and he and Bruce remained friends for the rest of Dexter's life.

Robert Palmer, the *New York Times'* popular music critic, wrote about Dexter's return in his liner notes for *Homecoming—Live at the Village Vanguard:* "The excitement Dexter Gordon created in New York in 1976 surprised almost everyone who was a part of it"; and that is another example of myth. Dexter and I were *not* surprised. We were happy and pleased, but not surprised. We had spent six months preparing for his return. We had spent his hard-earned money, and I had spent twenty hours a day talking and writing press releases to spread the word. We had called in all the favors we could, and when October arrived, Dexter was ready.

Palmer's notes continue: "The hard-core jazz fans were startled when overflow crowds showed up for his engagements and cheered and pounded tables, serving notice that the saxophonist's greatness would never again be the secret of a handful of connoisseurs."

The truth is that Dexter had never lost his original fans—the ones who still had those Dial and Savoy 78s, the ones who had all the Blue Note releases, the ones who were waiting for him to come home. One of his favorite gigs in New York was on the Jazzmobile in the summer of 1977 at Dewey Square, around the corner from Minton's Playhouse in Harlem. When he arrived, fans were already there waiting and they wanted to hear those tunes from the 1940s. They called out for "Dexter's Deck," "Dexter Digs In," and "Dexter Leaps Out." He hadn't played those tunes in years, but he dug deep and played them for the crowd that had remained loyal to him since they first heard him three decades earlier.

After the initial two nights at Storyville, the band got ready for the weeklong gig at the Village Vanguard. When they began to rehearse on Monday, Charles Mingus came by the club. Robert Palmer describes Mingus "looming over a table close to the bandstand and urging the saxophonist on with shouts and laughter. 'Yeah, yeah,' he would exclaim whenever Gordon played a particularly felicitous phrase, 'you're gonna be teaching New York some stuff, man. Some lessons.'"

Max Gordon was elated in his especially cool manner, even admitting that perhaps he was wrong when he hung up the phone on me that night I first called him with the idea of Dexter's return. *Perhaps* he was wrong. To describe Max Gordon is a daunting task. (He was, of course, not related to Dexter, but when I married Dexter and became Maxine Gordon, he said that I did that so I would have the same name as his.) He was a man who opened a small basement club in his home neighborhood of Greenwich Village in 1935, which is still going strong decades after his death in 1989. He was a man who loved music, art, and poetry, who sat every night in the kitchen of the club as the boss of a world that he had created. He was a loyal and true supporter of Dexter and many other musicians. After the week at the Village Vanguard, the band went out on the road. When they returned in December for another week at the club, the word was out. Now there *were* lines of people down the block and around the corner on Seventh Avenue, and all the sets were sold out. (Dexter said "sold" and "out" were his two favorite words.) The fans waited and waited because Dexter's sets were very, very long. He did not time them in the standard sense. An hour was way too short for him. That could be just two or three tunes. But the audience waited and they never seemed to be disappointed.

During the second week of the December gig, the recording contract with Columbia Records was finally worked out. Before he could sign, Dexter had to endure a somewhat acrimonious negotiation to get out of an earlier contract with SteepleChase Records, a label started in 1972 by a Copenhagen college student named Nils Winther. Dexter had no record contract when Winther offered him a deal to record his Jazzhus Montmartre performances that were broadcast on radio. "I trusted this young Danish guy," Dexter said. "The Danes seemed so much more trustworthy than the Americans." He signed a one-page contract on March 12, 1974, without the advice of a lawyer or manager, because he considered it to be a simple gentleman's agreement. The contract granted SteepleChase all rights to all of Dexter's Montmartre broadcasts "forever" and forbade him from recording for other companies during the term of the deal. The following year, Dexter signed another contract with SteepleChase that extended through July 14, 1977.

When Lundvall offered the deal with Columbia, I asked Dexter if there would be any conflict in his signing. He said there would be no problem since his deal with SteepleChase was friendly and he was sure that Winther would let him out of the contract and be pleased that he had this new opportunity. As it turned out, he was mistaken. Dexter wanted to record at the Village Vanguard on December 11–12, 1976, and that meant that he was still under contract to SteepleChase. All was not settled until March 31, 1977. In the final amendment to the contract, SteepleChase allowed Dexter to record one double and one single LP for Columbia and released him from the exclusivity clause. The 1974 contract required him to make two LP records for SteepleChase, but as part of the settlement Dexter agreed to allow tapes from Swedish radio programs or parts of takes to be used instead of him recording new albums. He also paid four thousand dollars to SteepleChase. Dexter's lawyer was the formidable Frank Harding, who was relentless and patient and in the end was able to secure the release that allowed Columbia to release the double album *Homecoming—Live at the Village Vanguard.*

Dexter was very disappointed by Winther's combativeness. He felt that he had only tried to help a young jazz fan build an independent label in Copenhagen by agreeing to record for his label. Dexter was very pleased with one SteepleChase album, *More Than You Know,* recorded in 1975 with a string orchestra and arrangements by Palle Mikkelborg. He had always wanted to record with strings and the album included "Tivoli," which was later recorded by McCoy Tyner. It also included "Girl with the Purple Eyes," written for Elizabeth Taylor, who shared a birthday with Dexter. In 1982 Dexter expressed his displeasure with SteepleChase in an interview for the BBC. He said that SteepleChase issued records after he had signed with Columbia, which he considered illegal. A letter from Winther to Dexter's Danish lawyer stated that "instead of taking immediate legal steps against Dexter, SteepleChase would rather try to excuse what had happened as Dexter might have forgotten all about the contractual situation between the two parties." In the end, Dexter refused to ever discuss anything concerning SteepleChase Records again.

The Columbia deal was the first major recording contract that I worked on, and Marvin Cohen, the head of business affairs at Columbia, was very helpful and patient throughout the whole ordeal. I asked for certain things in the contract that were not standard, such as a customized foreign royalty structure, and he suggested that I might be wrong. Nevertheless, we got what we asked for. After the first year and the first royalties, Marvin said that I had made the perfect deal for Dexter. It wasn't like any other deal that he had approved, but it did make sense for this particular jazz artist. I have always been proud of winning those arguments with Columbia.

Dexter and Cuscuna went to Columbia's offices and signed the contract on December 11, just a few hours before the first live recording session. Then they took a cab to the Vanguard, where the recording equipment was all set up and Malcolm Addey was ready to do his magic as recording engineer. The results (and the next night's) are the double album *Homecoming—Live at the Village Vanguard*. I remember that night because when it was all over and we were listening to the playback, Dexter looked at me, smiled, and said, "Okay, kid, we did it."

When I looked out at the audiences during that time, I saw Cecil Taylor, Charles Mingus, Art Blakey, Jimmy and Percy Heath, Yusef Lateef, Horace Silver, Cedar Walton, Julius Hemphill, Billy Higgins, and many other musicians who came to welcome Dexter back. One afternoon we were standing on a corner at 141st Street in Harlem and Cecil Payne, the great baritone saxophone player, walked by. He said, "Hey Dex, thanks for coming home and bringing bebop with you. I've been working ever since you got here." Dexter thought that was the greatest compliment he had ever heard. He smiled and said, "Thanks, man. Glad I could help."

From the beginning of our time working together in 1976, on every New Year's Eve Dexter would call or I would be at his gig and he would say, "Let's keep it going for another year." I would agree and that was our annual contract. No paper, no commitment beyond a mutual agreement to go on for one more year and see how it goes. If either one of us didn't like the way things were going, we would end it. I had been part of a company some years earlier called MsManagement. I kept the name and Dexter liked to call it "MisManagement." He would say: "Oh yeah, please mismanage me. I have been doing that all these years on my own." I asked him once why he thought that he and Wardell Gray didn't have greater success after "The Chase" was such a big hit in 1947. He said, "You weren't old enough to work on it. Nobody wanted to come near two wild tenor players with habits."

CHAPTER 17

Bebop at Work

So much of Dexter Gordon's enduring greatness as an artist
involved his unsurpassed abilities as an eloquent speaker
and singer on his instrument. His inimitable introductions to
songs—"suddenly . . . I saw . . . polka dots and moonbeams
. . . all around a pug-nosed . . . dream . . ."—taught me so
much about the magical dance of poetry and melody that is
at the core of the music that moves us most deeply.

—Todd Barkan[1]

After the release of *Homecoming—Live at the Village Vanguard*, we
were off and running. Michael Cuscuna stepped in as Dexter's producer
and they would discuss personnel and repertoire, spending many hours
organizing ideas that would become future recording sessions. I worked
very long hours in the office Michael and I rented together on West
Fifty-Third Street across from the Museum of Modern Art and down
the block from Columbia Records.

Woody Shaw recommended Hattie Gossett as the person to run the
office. Hattie is an acclaimed poet, performance artist, scholar, and
fierce warrior for the rights of so many whose voices are not heard. She
is also someone who came up at the same time as I did, listening to
bands at the Five Spot, particularly Monk and Mingus. She is the author,
in my opinion, of one of the greatest jazz poems ever written—"in the
window/monk"—which captures those great days of the 1960s on the
Lower East Side. Hattie sat in the front room of our brownstone office
and answered the phone, made appointments, kept the accounts,
designed fliers, defended me from the press and their less-than-positive
inquiries, answered the mail, organized my life, and basically kept everything going so I could concentrate on bookings, travel, and plans for
the future. We liked to think that we had a five-year plan, but since this

was the business of jazz, things changed daily or sometimes hourly. Dexter would often stop by the office, but I would talk to him by phone every day, especially to see how things were going when he was on the road. I sometimes had to make rapid road trips to fix a crisis, but mainly I worked from the office. When we needed to make long-distance or overseas calls, Michael and I used the phones in one of Columbia Records' conference rooms. They had something called a WATS (Wide Area Telephone Service) line and Bruce Lundvall allowed us to use it. This was a very big help with the expenses of running an office. When Woody Shaw signed with Columbia, we expanded our work and Hattie even toured with Woody's band when they did a southern college tour. I am not sure that she ever forgave me for asking her to do that, although she did write about it in *presenting . . . Sister NoBlues,* a fearless and brilliant book. Bruce Lundvall had an assistant named Diane Nixon who was a genius at getting things done, organizing him, giving advice, and finding documents and phone numbers way before e-mail and the internet. Diane is as responsible for Dexter's and Woody's success at Columbia Records as anyone. She died young, and life was never the same without her.

The person we called the "brains behind the operation" was Jim Harrison—promoter, publicist, publisher, and the man with his finger on the pulse of the jazz scene then and for many years thereafter. Jim is a legendary jazz figure who spent many hours putting up posters and fliers all over town, including at the Port Authority bus terminal where he could catch the eyes of jazz fans traveling to and from the city. In those pre-internet days, much of Dexter's audience knew where he was appearing by word of mouth, or what we referred to as the Jim Harrison technique. When Dexter played on a touring Jazzmobile in Harlem, crowds filled the streets thanks to Jim and his team. When he played Grant's Tomb, the police were amazed at the throngs of fans. One police officer asked me: "How did they know about this? Who is this guy playing saxophone?" Jim knew how to reach the hardcore jazz fans and they knew how to spread the word. When he saw that Black musicians were not getting enough press coverage in the 1970s, he started *Jazz Spotlite News* and hired jazz musicians like Frank Foster and others to write articles. He promoted gigs and supported artists; he founded the Jackie McLean fan club because he wanted to hear Jackie play and thought that promoting gigs for him would be the best way to do that. When I had a problem at the office or an issue at a club, Jim would be at my side. He was my "backup," and it was years before I realized why

I never really had a problem stepping into the jazz scene and was not considered an outsider. It was Jim. He and his beautiful wife, Fannie, had their special seats at the bar at the Vanguard and never missed a Dexter appearance. They stayed for every set and would always remain after the gig to hang out with the musicians. By 1986, when *Round Midnight* premiered, Fannie had been ill for quite a while, but she was determined to be there and she was, in all her elegant glory. To the end of his life, Dexter could count on Jim Harrison to support him and the music they loved. I always say that I would never have made it without Jim's help.

Sometimes people would drop by our office to make suggestions or just to see what we were doing. In those days, it was easy to hang out with musicians and friends without having a formal appointment. One such person was Frank Weston, father of the pianist Randy Weston. Frank would often bring us lunch. He was a distinguished gentleman, an admirer of Marcus Garvey's Pan-Africanism movement, and a great cook. He would sit on the office couch and say: "I want my boy to come home. Can't you help him get some gigs here?" Randy had been living in Annecy, France, and when Frank saw that Dexter had returned, he thought it was a good time for Randy as well.

The office grew to include working on Johnny Griffin's return to the States from Europe and tours with his own band, which included Ronnie Mathews, Ray Drummond, and Kenny Washington. Dexter funded Johnny's return and they appeared together at Carnegie Hall. We also did bookings for concerts in Martinique and Guadeloupe, where I was able to book Dizzy Gillespie after he called and said he wanted to go there. That was a great day for the former teenage jazz fan who loved the music and wanted to find a way to be around it and its creators.

In the winter of 1977, Dexter made a brief return to Denmark for a tour that took him into the "Danish hinterlands." The group included Kenny Drew (piano), Hugo Rasmussen (bass), and Alex Riel (drums). Dexter and Kenny had known each other since the 1940s. Skip Malone wrote of their trip together:

> During the drive over to Jylland, Dexter and Kenny were constantly teasing each other. Dexter jokingly referred to Kenny as "my Jewish mother" because Kenny never fails to chastise Dexter when he is drinking too much or whenever he is late for a job. Then Dex gets on Kenny about his driving, "Why are you wearing those gloves—you think you're Nicky Lauda?" "Man, get off my back about driving," answers Kenny. "I haven't had an accident in 30 years of driving. And stop spilling all those ashes over the

floor of my car!" "Car? You call this plastic bubble a car. This sad-ass car . . . why don't you get a real car like me?" During the whole drive they both carry on like this. I call it their Laurel & Hardy routine.

Malone also wrote about a scene at a restaurant called Wulff's Bodega, late after a gig at the Creole Jazz Club in Horsens: "After we finished eating, Dexter took out his soprano sax. He said, 'The soprano is a helluva difficult instrument. It requires more air than the tenor. It is similar to the oboe. It offers the same kind of resistance. That's why I like it. I have to practice on it every day to perfect my tone, my sound. Have you ever heard of anyone playing soprano with a good solid tone?' Then he stood up and started playing 'All the Things You Are.'"

Back in New York, an invitation arrived one day for a jazz party to be held on the South Lawn at the White House on June 18, 1978. Dexter could not contain his usual ultracool self. President Jimmy Carter was throwing the party to honor the twenty-fifth anniversary of the Newport Jazz Festival. Dexter said that he never expected, in all his dreams, to be invited to the White House. Yes, he had played for Queen Margrethe II of Denmark and had met many dignitaries in Europe, but an invitation to the White House represented something much deeper to him. It made him think of the years in and out of jail when he wondered if he would ever make it anywhere again. When he picked up the invitation at the office and opened it, he turned to me with a big Dexter smile and said, "Well kid, coming back to the States was a very good idea. I think we have proved that."

When we got to the hotel in Washington and the other musicians started arriving, it was one great reunion. Hugs and laughs and stories were told and retold. Dexter had always been a jazz fan first and loved musicians, so being in their company for this event made for an especially great day. He was especially pleased to be with Dizzy Gillespie, whom he called John, and his old bandleader Lionel Hampton and bandmate Illinois Jacquet. He was thrilled to see Mary Lou Williams and Eubie Blake and Benny Carter and Clark Terry. Max Gordon and his wife, Lorraine, were there. Max was very pleased about Dexter's invitation to the White House and liked to take credit for his successful return from Europe. Max does deserve much of the credit, after all.

They served jambalaya and pecan pie, and there was a band from New Orleans; it was a very festive atmosphere. The program went overtime and then President Carter, channeling his former life as a Georgia peanut farmer, sang "Salt Peanuts" with Dizzy. It was something that I could never have imagined in my wildest dreams: yes, we went to the White House and the musicians played their best for the audience, but it was mostly that they were together. There are lots of great days in a life filled with memorable moments, but this June day always ranked at the top of them all for Dexter.

After the success of the *Homecoming* album, Dexter told Lundvall and Cuscuna that he wanted to do an album with arrangements by Slide Hampton and he also wanted to bring Benny Bailey over from Europe to play trumpet on the album. When we worked out the budget, we didn't think we could pull it off, but Bruce somehow managed to get the budget approved. Slide wrote some of the most beautiful arrangements we had ever heard for Woody's "The Moontrane," "Laura," "Red Top," "Fried Bananas," "You're Blasé," and "How Insensitive." Benny Bailey came for the date and so did Bobby Hutcherson. Frank Wess played flute, and Woody Shaw, George Cables, Rufus Reid, Victor Lewis, Wayne Andre, and Howard Johnson were all featured. Dexter was thrilled with the recording, and Michael remembers all the drama involved and last-minute hysteria, but I can only remember the result and Dexter's expression when he heard it. The album was *Sophisticated Giant* and he considered this recording among his best.

By this time, Dexter had his dream band—his working band. He first played with the pianist George Cables at the Keystone Korner, on the recommendation of Todd Barkan, and George agreed to join the band. Rufus Reid had worked with Dexter in Chicago and was his first choice for the bass position. Woody chose Eddie Gladden, whom he had known for many years in Newark, as the drummer, and that was the best choice for Dexter. Gladden was one of a kind—he swung so hard and was able to fit into any situation without blinking. Whenever chaos broke out, Eddie would just take out his sketch pad and start drawing until the rest of us figured out a solution to the problem at hand. He would not take foreign currency for payment when abroad; he always carried his own hot sauce on the road, and he could find the best weed anywhere. He loved to work in Holland, where weed was legal. He said that Holland was the sanest country in the world but he loved Newark and was proud of his hometown. When he died in 2003, George Cables and I went to his funeral in Newark and couldn't find words to describe our time with him. To this day we say his name and smile because we share so many great memories of this remarkable drummer and friend. Dexter loved this quartet and although it didn't stay together long enough, he always talked about "the band" and how they lifted him up.

FIGURE 18. Dexter's "dream band" in 1978 (left to right): Rufus Reid, George Cables, Dexter, Eddie Gladden. Photograph by Art Maillett. Courtesy of Sony Music Archives.

In 1978 Dexter recorded *Manhattan Symphonie* with the band. He especially liked his version of "As Time Goes By" and George's composition "I Told You So." It was Dexter who named that tune after a phrase he often found himself using in his many "discussions" with George.

Max Gordon rallied again to produce a concert for Dexter at Carnegie Hall on September 23, 1978, which was John Coltrane's birthday and the due date for Woody III. (He wasn't born until almost three weeks later, so I was able to still be there and run up and down the stairs, with people yelling at me to sit down.) Max was very pleased about the sold-out concert and congratulated me again for calling him back that night from Nancy, France, and insisting that he give Dexter a gig at his club. By the time of the Carnegie Hall concert, Dexter had a driver, Chuck, who would help with anything that might come up and could also sell signed LPs at gigs. If Dexter had a performance within four hours' drive from New York, Chuck would drive him. They became good friends. We also had security with the help of Jimmy Bland, a retired police officer who could scan the scene and move Dexter into the car in the blink of an eye. We laughed about how many people it took to make a jazz musician's life easier. Dexter became so recognizable because of his height and presence, and so the staff grew, the office grew, and the concerts and club dates piled up back to back. We had come a long way from what had been just an idea when we first met in 1975. The tempo of our lives was very rapid indeed.

In October 1978 everything changed for the better in my life and the life of Woody Shaw. Woody Louis Armstrong Shaw III was born on October 12. I worked up until the time that his godmother and midwife, Helen Swallow, said we had to go to the hospital. I went home with him the next day, and one month later we had his christening at St. Peter's Church and his party at the Village Vanguard. Max Gordon agreed to be his godfather, and as he held the baby in the church while Reverend Gensel put holy water on Woody's forehead, Max turned to me and said, "Kid, this doesn't look right. A Jew in a church holding a baby at a christening."

"Max, you knew it was a christening," I said.

Max started a college fund for his godson and bought a rosewood crib, and we kept a Mexican baby basket in the kitchen of his club for the baby. When I first went to the Village Vanguard as a fifteen-year-old and sat at the back next to the bar with the other teenagers in the listening section, I never dreamed that I would grow up to have Max Gordon be the godfather to my son. Something about it, though, made it feel predestined. Max hosted the party that afternoon at the Vanguard and Grandma Rose Shaw cooked all the delicious food for the party with her friends and served it from the fabled kitchen, which also served as the band room. Woody's band played and the room was packed with people celebrating the birth of this "jazz baby." Horace Silver never forgot the food, and any time he saw me he would say: "Those barbecue beans were the best I ever had. Please let me know when Rose is making them again." We also had ribs, fried chicken, potato salad, greens, candied sweet potatoes, coconut cake, sweet potato pie, and more. Hattie Gossett took care of all the arrangements—the invitations, planning, cleanup, and thank-you notes. When I look back at how this new baby was raised on the road and in the kitchen of the Village Vanguard, and on many nights slept next to the drums, I marvel at who he has become. He has survived good and bad babysitters (Becky was the best); Tiny House nursery school; road trips; napping in Count Basie's lap; squirting ketchup on Willie Bobo's head; karate lessons; bilingual school in Cuernavaca; jazz festivals in Brazil, Europe, and all over the States; and French-speaking day camp in Paris during the filming of *Round Midnight*. He went on to be an honor student in boarding school and a graduate of Hobart College; he studied in Hanoi and India, received a BFA in Jazz Performance from the New School, was David Baker's associate instructor at Indiana University, received a master's degree in Arts Administration from Columbia University, and was a Du Bois Fellow at Harvard working on a documentary and book about his father, Woody Shaw. He is a producer, writer, artist, web developer, the CEO of Dex Music LLC, and founder and director of the Dexter Gordon Society and Moontrane Media Group. To me, it is his grandparents in Newark who gave him the rock on which to build this phenomenal life. They were always there, Grandma especially, who watched and listened and would meet me at the train station in Newark on weekends to take him to the house and make sure he had her food to eat and way too many new clothes to wear. This baby is on the cover of the iconic album *Woody III* with his father and grandfather, and he is my guiding light and inspiration for everything.

In 1978 and 1980 Dexter was *Down Beat*'s Musician of the Year, and he was inducted into the magazine's Hall of Fame in 1980. He received a Congressional Commendation, was feted with a Dexter Gordon Day in Washington, D.C., and a National Endowment for the Arts Jazz Masters Award in 1986. The awards and accolades kept coming and the concerts got bigger and bigger. With the CBS All-Stars he went to the Montreux Jazz Festival and on the legendary trip to Havana in 1979 with Woody Shaw, Stan Getz, Jimmy Heath, Percy Heath, Bobby Hutcherson, Cedar Walton, Tony Williams, Willie Bobo, and more. Also in 1979 he went to Jamaica to visit his friend Melba Liston, whom he had known since junior high school and who was living in Jamaica and directing the popular music studies program at the Jamaica Institute of Music. They shared many laughs and memories of their lives on Los Angeles' Eastside and then played a concert together with some of Melba's students. When Dexter made a real friend, it was a friend for life, and Melba was certainly one of those.

In 1980 he went into the studio with Art Blakey, Cedar Walton, George Benson, Percy Heath, and Woody Shaw. The album was *Gotham City* and included a beautiful version of "A Nightingale Sang in Berkeley Square" and a cover shot by the celebrated photographer Richard Avedon. The musicians had a very good time with lots of laughs and stories about the Eckstine band, the road, and their many fellow musicians. They were a group of players who all loved what they did and loved each other and the lives they had chosen to live. Cedar Walton was his sardonic self and Art Blakey was the elder statesman. Dexter

FIGURE 19. Dexter and Woody Shaw in a recording session for the album *Gotham City* at CBS Studios, 1980. Photograph by Art Maillett. Courtesy of Sony Music Archives.

always loved the company of his fellow musicians and considered himself a fan who was lucky enough to become a jazz musician. He could not imagine a life for himself that would be better than being with "the cats."

Our goal was to get gigs in all fifty states for Dexter and his band. I never did manage to get Wyoming, North Dakota, or Hawaii, but I did help a serious Dexter fan in Mississippi who had dreamed of bringing Dexter to Jackson, and it was one of Dexter's most memorable concerts. Dexter was spending months at a time on the road in the States and Europe. One of his favorite spots was the iconic San Francisco jazz club the Keystone Korner. Todd Barkan, the musical mind behind that club's fame and success, first brought Dexter there as a single in 1973, teaming up with some great local musicians, including Eddie Moore on drums. It became a kind of ritual for Dexter to play at the Keystone Korner over the Christmas holidays. Todd programmed holiday festivals with Bobby Hutcherson, Max Roach, and countless other great artists, and Dexter worked at the club until it closed in 1983. Dexter and Todd had a special friendship that continued until the end of Dexter's life. He often sent postcards to the young jazz club owner, written in their own secret code, when he traveled in Europe. Todd Barkan:

He used his saxophone and his bands as an extension of his physical heart and soul. He created a universal language that touched our hearts through his music. I never had a better or dearer friend, and neither has our music. I feel he's with me every day, in my own life, and in my relationship with jazz and with life. He was an invaluable gift to us all.[2]

When George Cables and Rufus Reid left the band to pursue their own careers, they were replaced by Kirk Lightsey on piano and David Eubanks on bass. This group traveled widely in the United States and Europe and to Dakar (Senegal), the Caribbean, and Brazil. Eddie Gladden remained in the band until the end of this very intense and productive time. Dexter became a headliner at festivals where he had not even been invited to appear as a guest when he was living in Europe. He was now the international jazz star and he would shake his head and marvel at what was happening. He had an apartment in New York City with a terrace and a view of the Hudson River and the George Washington Bridge, and his saxophone repairman, Saul Fromkin—referred to as the Saxophone Doctor—made house calls. He had Norman Annenberg as his lawyer, Sidney Greenberg as his doctor (who had been the doctor for the Dorsey brothers and Frank Sinatra), an office, a driver, a security person, a band, an accountant, and lots of decisions to be made every Friday morning at our weekly meeting.

Then we planned his sixtieth birthday party at the Village Vanguard for the afternoon of February 23, 1983. His band played and lots of musicians and friends were invited. His daughters came from Los Angeles. On that day he said to me, "It's over. Let's close the office and take a break. I'm tired." There was nothing for me to say back to him except, "Okay, let's do it." Of course, it wasn't easy and people were not happy with the decision, but Dexter was right. We had a good run but we had worn ourselves out and it was time for a break. He wanted to live a "normal life," if there really is such a thing.

On his sixtieth birthday he told me that he didn't want me to be his manager anymore. He wanted to live his idea of a "normal life" off the road and try to be a family with the three of us. Looking back, it seems so simple, but this was not an easy decision. It was fraught with drama, anger, and jazz gossip. But to Dexter it was simple, and we needed to live a simpler life. Woody went to public school within walking distance of our apartment. I cooked three meals a day and found out what it took to stay home rather than work long hours and never have time to rest, think, and read those books that pile up on the side of the bed.

Staying home was the hardest job I ever had in my life: making the meals, including the three-minute soft-boiled eggs in the egg cups with the toast points, walking to and from school with Woody, after-school activities, housekeeping, laundry, trying not to think about the music business, trying to sleep more than four hours a night. Both of us would often wake up and think it was time to catch a plane or go to a gig. It took time to regroup but slowly I realized what Dexter meant about a "normal life." By most standards it wasn't "normal," but it was a life off the road and for that I am eternally grateful.

We began to go to Cuernavaca, where Dexter started natural health and acupuncture treatments, ate regular meals at the same time every day, and rested, read, and reflected on his life. Our trips to Cuernavaca would last for months at a time. We had a beautiful house, Villa Verde, with a view of the volcano Popocatépetl and a cook named Maria de Los Angeles to make us delicious meals. I did the shopping in the fabulous Cuernavaca Mercado, buying all kinds of fruits and chili peppers, along with fresh vegetables, herbs, and blue tortillas. Dexter walked to the *zócalo* and sat in the café with a few of the other people who had come to this beautiful place to live a more relaxed life. The renowned artists Elizabeth Catlett and her husband Francisco Mora were there and our good friends Nadine Markova and Larry Russell had a house in Cuernavaca and visited often.

We built a life there, and Dexter found a sister, which was something he had always wanted. One day some friends brought a woman from Philadelphia to the house to meet us. Her name was Shakmah (born Anna Layton in Chester, Pennsylvania) and she was a spiritual healer and teacher. When she and Dexter looked at each other, they began to speak in Danish. I made a joke about them definitely being the only Black people in Cuernavaca who could have a conversation in Danish. Shakmah had been to Denmark in her youth and loved the country and the language. They went off to the garden and started a conversation that continued way into the evening. After that they met every day and I never did know what they were discussing, but it was serious and in hushed tones. Then one day Dexter said, "I have a sister. Shakmah and I were brother and sister in an earlier life and we have found each other." He laughed, but he was serious. They were bonded and spoke on the phone almost every day. She worked with him using her spiritual gifts to help guide his health.

Our "normal" life was about to change once again, with a phone call, not unlike the way Dexter's life changed with the call from Marshal

Royal asking him to join the Lionel Hampton band when he was seventeen years old. Dexter didn't expect that call, but it turned out that he had prepared himself for the opportunity it presented. This call would come from Bruce Lundvall, and in many ways it would seem that Dexter had begun preparing for it when he made the decision to exit the road on his sixtieth birthday.

CHAPTER 18

Round Midnight

When the film was released in America, [Marlon] Brando
sent a letter to Dexter in which he said that for the first
time in fifteen years he learned something about acting.
Dexter's comment was, "Lady Bertrand, after this, who
needs an Oscar?"

—Bertrand Tavernier[1]

Dexter:

*When Bertrand Tavernier first came to the apartment in New York with the
original script for* Round Midnight, *I told him I couldn't do it. The script
wasn't real and the dialogue was not happening. He promised to let me work
on every aspect of the film with him and he kept his promise. I owed it to all
the jazz musicians who could have been actors but never got the chance to
make a movie.*

*When I was a boy growing up on the Eastside in Los Angeles, all the kids
wanted to grow up to be movie stars. After all, we were living in the movie
capital, and some of my father's patients were movie stars. I remember going
with him in the 1930s in his Model A Ford to make house calls after dinner
to the big houses of famous people where a maid would offer me lemonade
as I waited for him.*

*Sometimes, a big open-back truck would come to the neighborhood and
my friends would get to pile in and go to the movie set in Toluca Lake where
they filmed the Tarzan movies. They would come home with money in their
pockets for candy and ice cream. I wasn't chosen because they said "you're
too light." Well, everyone thought that was very funny and I told them,
"You watch. One day I will star in a movie and win an Oscar. Just you
watch." Well, Paul Newman won the Oscar the year I was nominated with
him, but I came closer than many people ever imagined I would.*

For Dexter, the making of *Round Midnight* began with a phone call
early in 1985. It was from Bruce Lundvall, who as president of Columbia Records had signed Dexter to a recording contract in 1976 and had
become his very good friend. Though Bruce had a big job and a big

FIGURE 20. That's me with Dexter on the set of *Round Midnight* in front of the *boulangerie*. Dexter's mother's family name was Boulanger, which became Baker in English. Photograph © Irene Kubota Neves.

office, Dexter felt the need to protect the handsome and debonair record executive whenever he came to hear Dexter play. In clubs Bruce would always be hounded by musicians who would push their demo tapes at him, filling his pockets with cassettes by the end of the night. Dexter would tell the guys to back off and let the man just listen and hang out.

I asked Bruce in 2013 to describe the events that led up to his call to Dexter about making the movie. Bruce Lundvall:

> I got a call in 1985 from my good friend Henri Renaud, the French pianist and record executive. He said, "The director Bertrand Tavernier wants to have real jazz musicians, not actors, in a movie based on Bud Powell and his relationship with Francis Paudras, the French artist and designer."
>
> I said, "Dexter Gordon."
>
> He said, "Exactly. Seriously, Bertrand really wants to do this. He is coming to the States. Can you arrange a meeting with Dexter and Bertrand and the producer Irwin Winkler?"
>
> I called Dexter and arranged to pick the two of you up at your home and go to the Pierre Hotel on Fifth Avenue. Dexter was late, as he often was, and the meeting was like three people from three different planets—Dexter, Winkler, and Tavernier. Dexter the bebopper, Tavernier the French poetic director, and Winkler the businessman from Hollywood with dark glasses and a Cuban cigar.

Dexter said, "May I have a little mild restorative please?"

That meant he wanted a glass of wine, so we opened a bottle and the first question Winkler asked was, "Dexter, how come jazz doesn't sell?"

Dexter took a long pause then said, "Art form."

Tavernier was beside himself. Winkler mentioned that in *Rocky,* the 1976 blockbuster movie that he produced, the theme song was a hit. "I need someone to write the theme song," he said.

I said that Benny Golson or Horace Silver would be good. It would be in keeping with the time period. If not them, then either Quincy Jones or Herbie Hancock. Quincy was working on *The Color Purple* at the time and so Herbie got the job. We left the meeting and were in the limo going back to the apartment and Dexter said, "I'll believe it when it happens."

I went back to the office and that same afternoon I got phone calls from Tavernier and Winkler. They were saying, "He's perfect! He's perfect for the part." Tavernier said, "He even walks bebop. Will he do a screen test?"

I called Dexter and said, "Looks like you're going to be a movie star."

Dexter said one word. I'll never forget it: "Hollywood."

Dexter was a bit skeptical about the idea of being in a jazz film because there had been other times when projects were discussed that never quite happened. In 1962 a Hollywood agent named Bob Leonard sent a letter to Alfred Lion at Blue Note Records saying, "I am very happy to announce that a film production company in New York is flying Dexter Gordon to New York, arriving March 15th, to consummate a picture deal entitled 'The Horn' and starring Dexter Gordon."

Lion replied, "Dear Bob: Thank you for your kind letter . . . Frank [Wolff] and I also heard about the film production where Dexter is supposed to be engaged. Of course, you never know how these things really turn out in practice, because it seems the producer is really fishing a little bit in the dark so far."

Obviously, *The Horn* was never made, and it was always Dexter's way to not get overly optimistic about a big offer or the suggestion of big money easily made. He would often say to me: "Don't get too excited about this. Let's just keep on doing what we do. I will practice and play the tenor, and you will keep everyone together." But the *Round Midnight* offer turned into reality, and the release of the film became an important event for Dexter and for all jazz musicians. "My life has a happy ending," he often said, always certain of the statement's future truth. "Why do most jazz stories dwell on the negative side of this life? We are people who get to play music for a living. What could be better?"

Dexter agreed to the meeting Lundvall arranged with Winkler and Tavernier at Winkler's apartment in the Pierre, one of the famous old New York hotels with an elite address, a view of Central Park, an elegant lobby, and a doorman in an impeccable uniform. As we entered the elevator Dexter smiled, turned to me, and said, "Don't get too excited. I have been through this before. When the discussion gets around to money, something usually goes wrong with the idea of making a jazz film."

The fact that Winkler had produced the *Rocky* films and was a very successful Hollywood mogul made Dexter even more skeptical. The entry hall and sitting room of the apartment were painted in a dark green enamel, with extraordinary paintings hung on the walls. I said, "Wow, this guy has really good taste." Right away I had a very good feeling about meeting Irwin. But Dexter and Bruce remained very casual. They both adopted a kind of ultracool manner, which is a way of pretending that you're not particularly impressed; that no matter what happens, you've seen or heard all this before and it's all just routine.

Irwin Winkler was nothing at all like the stereotypical Hollywood producer that Dexter was expecting. He was from Brooklyn and his mother still lived there in Sea Gate, a private gated community of mostly Jewish residents at the far western end of Coney Island, at the southern tip of Brooklyn. When a New Yorker like myself asks someone of a certain age where they grew up, their answer usually suggests certain things about them: the kind of money their family had, what their early education was like, and what kinds of people they grew up among. When people would ask me where I came from, I would say, "My grandmother lived on 102nd Street and West End Avenue." A New Yorker would nod, having gleaned much of what they needed to know about me. That Irwin still maintained his Brooklyn ties though he lived in grand style in Hollywood made me like him even more. When he said to me, "If you need anything, just let me know," Dexter looked at him and said, "She will be calling you day and night, and I hope you mean what you say, because when she gets angry or is lied to, she becomes impossible to live with." Irwin laughed and told Dexter not to worry because he was a man of his word. That was a rare quality indeed, since our years in the music business had left us with a very skeptical ear for truth. Sure enough, every single promise Irwin made to Dexter was kept.

As negotiations got under way with Warner Bros., the studio that was bankrolling the project, some executives got a bit nervous, just as Dexter had predicted. Most of the concern was about casting a jazz musician in the leading role of a movie. All of Dexter's business dealings were handled by the brilliant Norman Annenberg, a Harvard Law School graduate who was also a violinist with an office above Carnegie

Hall. He and Dexter had a special relationship and Dexter trusted Norman's advice completely. The part Dexter would play in the film, as the saxophonist Dale Turner, was growing larger, and he would appear in most of the scenes. To the studio executives this seemed very risky, and their view was quite understandable. It took a lot of cajoling by Bertrand and Winkler, with some help from the very influential Clint Eastwood, to get the studio on board. The unsung hero was Warren Lieberfarb, president of Warner Home video, who came up with the last two million dollars needed to make the film.

Dexter's screen test was shot in a studio not far from our apartment, and we walked there as I recall. He was very relaxed about the whole idea and felt confident about acting. He loved movies and actors, and always thought he had a talent for the craft, especially after his experience acting in the 1960 play *The Connection*. He felt that there were so many great musicians who never had a chance to act in a film or to tell the story of the life of a jazz musician in a realistic manner. Even though Louis Armstrong, Billie Holiday, Duke Ellington, and Billy Eckstine did appear on screen, always in a musical context, Dexter said they could have acted in any dramatic film—and without the standard practice in their time of Black musical actors being confined to scenes that could be edited out when the films were shown in the South. Dexter admired Paul Robeson, of course, and Canada Lee and Marlon Brando. For the screen test, Dexter was given some dialogue, which he read smoothly. Bertrand loved the sound of Dexter's voice and the way he spoke, the way he moved, the way he took direction, and of course he loved his playing. Bertrand was convinced that Dexter was the one and only person to play Dale Turner, whose character is based on a combination of the brilliant pianist Bud Powell and the tenor saxophone legend Lester Young. The next step was for Annenberg to work out all the details with Warner Bros.

While negotiations went on, Dexter and I stepped out of the picture for the next few months until all was settled. We went to our house in Cuernavaca, where Dexter could relax, work on his health, and practice. Dexter had not been playing a great deal since 1983 when he took a break from the road. His genius doctor and beloved friend there, Saul Martinez, wished there could be more time for Dexter to get ready for the grueling work schedule that lay ahead, but there was no choice in the matter. Dexter had been saying all along that he considered this film an obligation. He began to practice every day to begin the process of getting himself back into playing shape.

One afternoon when he was taking a nap, he had a dream that would make a serious impact on his preparation. He said that his old friend Ben Webster—who had died in 1973 and whose tenor sax, a Selmer Mark VI, Dexter would play for the rest of his life—walked into the bedroom and sat down on the side of the bed. Dexter said he felt the bed sink down quite a bit under Ben's weight. Dexter greeted him and Ben said, "Hey Dex, I heard you can't play anymore."

Dexter became quite frightened and replied, "That's not true, Ben."

"Well, if it's not true, prove it," Ben said. "Get up and start practicing."

The very next day Dexter seriously turned up the intensity of his practicing for the first time in years. He called his friend, the saxophonist Larry Russell, who was living nearby, to come over and practice with him. Dexter would wake up, have his breakfast, walk barefoot around the garden, and then start playing long tones followed by scales, chords, melodies, and vigorous lines of improvisation. Our garden had beautiful bird of paradise and hibiscus plants, and Dexter would walk around and check out the trees and plants. Sometimes he would sit by the pool thinking and practicing.

He got out some books and wrote out musical exercises for himself. One day he said to me, "The tenor saxophone is not giving me an easy time. I should have known that I couldn't put her down and then just start playing when I felt like it." He even went to some of Larry's gigs in Cuernavaca and sat in to work on getting his chops back. He enjoyed those gigs since most of the audience didn't know who he was and they weren't expecting anything great. And there certainly weren't any jazz critics filing stories for their newspapers or magazines. There were some very good musicians in Mexico City and Cuernavaca, and Dexter enjoyed playing with them. He was very grateful to Larry for helping him get ready for the movie. Larry's wife, Nadine, was a very good friend of mine and a renowned photographer, and she and their daughter Marissa were central to our life in Cuernavaca.

Dexter was never worried about the acting. He felt that most jazz musicians could act if need be. They had to act their way out of a lot of situations in their lives on the road, and they had to act in front of an audience most nights. At heart, Dexter was a very quiet man who liked to stay home and read a book or watch a baseball game on television. We had a satellite dish installed on the roof for just that reason. Dexter was a big fan of the New York Mets, and they, like Dexter, were in the midst of a very good run. After *Round Midnight* premiered in October 1986, we got back to New York in time to watch the Mets defeat the

Boston Red Sox and win the World Series. Dexter loved the Mets players so much that he imagined them as members of a hard-swinging big
band and gave each primary Met an instrument or role to play:

THE ORCHESTRAL NEW YORK METROPOLITAN BASEBALL CLUB

Lead Alto: Keith Hernandez

Baritone Sax: Gary Carter

3rd Alto: Ray Knight

Tenor Sax: Darryl Strawberry

4th Tenor: Dwight Gooden

1st Trombone: Ron Darling

2nd Trombone: Kevin Mitchell

3rd Trombone: Danny Heep

1st Trumpet: Len Dykstra

2nd Trumpet: Jesse Orosco

3rd Trumpet: Howard Johnson

Piano: Bill Robinson

Guitar: Wally Backman

Bass: Sid Fernandez

Drums: Mookie Wilson

Percussion: Rafael Santana

*Vocalists: Tim Tuefel, Lee Mazzilli, Roger McDowell—"The
Amazettes"*

Conductor: Davey Johnson

Preparing his playing chops for *Round Midnight* by going out to perform and relate to an audience took a lot out of Dexter. He liked to refer
to his performing self as "Society Red," his alter ego. Red was the one
who had to put on the special custom-made clothes for the gig, have his
shoes shined, get his mind together, practice, and be ready to play—and
then socialize with the fans after the gig. Dexter at home was very different. He believed that being prepared was the secret behind a good performance. He considered the most important part of the day to be his
afternoon nap. Without that, he said, disaster loomed. That was why he
enjoyed playing at clubs that booked him for long stands, like the Jazzhus Montmartre in Copenhagen or the Village Vanguard in New York.

In Cuernavaca, Dexter practiced, exercised in the pool, had regular massages, and drank horrible-tasting herbal teas. He also thought a great deal about what *Round Midnight* would mean to all the jazz musicians who were still struggling for acceptance, and for all those who had died young, before ever getting the opportunities that Dexter had. He was always talking about the "what-ifs." *What if* Ben had been beloved at home the way he was in Copenhagen? *What if* Coleman Hawkins had made a movie and had a career as an actor? *What if* Louis Armstrong had been secretary of state? *What if* Dizzy Gillespie had been elected president? *What if* Billie Holiday had not been arrested and handcuffed to her bed in the hospital?

The phone calls and conversations about the film began in earnest when the negotiations with Warner's started to look promising, and Bertrand and his screenwriter, David Rayfiel, had started serious work on the script. After Dexter read the first draft, he asked Rayfiel if he had ever been around bebop musicians. The early working title was *Paris/ Jazz,* and Dexter was not at all pleased with the use of a kind of slang that would never be spoken by real beboppers. He said the musicians' dialogue made them sound like they all had southern accents, not like they were cats who had come up through Pittsburgh, Detroit, New York, or Los Angeles. He told David that beboppers were very urbane and sophisticated, and as an example cited the elegant speech patterns of Duke Ellington.

When we got back to New York in May, Dexter told Bertrand that he might be better off with a more experienced actor to play Dale—perhaps Carl Lee would be a good choice. Dexter said he could not do the part unless it was written to be truer to the musicians of the late 1950s. Things did not look good when Rayfiel left our apartment in a hurry, forgetting his raincoat, and Dexter said, "If I made that movie the way it is written, I would have to give back my lifetime membership in the NAACP."

The original script had dialogue such as this:

Buttercup: What y'all waitin' for, time t'fly, baby?

Leo (later to become Dale): Ain' goin' . . . not in no aeroplane's got a Johnny Deathbed on it.

Buttercup: You an' your dam voodoo shit!—Get your jive ass through that gate!

There was an exchange in the original script that Dexter liked, especially with the character played by Bobby Hutcherson, who was named

Red in the original script and later became Ace in the film. Unfortunately, Dexter did not like the way the script had them speaking to each other. In the script, Red is holding a bowl of food for Leo to try:

Leo (Dale): Needs somethin', Lady Red.

Red (Ace): Okra, I expec'.

Leo: Y'burn but you don' eat. Turner loves Paris.

Red: It be the most beautiful city in the worl'—if y'could find okra in it.

In the final version of the film, Ace speaks that last line with the kind of articulation Duke Ellington might employ:

It is the most beautiful city in the world. It would be perfect if you could find okra in it.

In the film, Dale refers to several of the male characters as "Lady." This is a reference to Lester Young, who famously gave Billie Holiday the nickname "Lady Day" and often honored both male and female friends with the affectionate term of "Lady."

Tavernier based the story of *Round Midnight* on many conversations he had with Francis Paudras, a French commercial artist and draftsman, about his relationship with Bud Powell in Paris in the late 1950s. Powell thrived as a genius and was one of the originators of bebop in the 1940s despite his many years of terrible suffering with mental illness. In 1952, at the age of twenty-nine, he was released from Creedmoor Psychiatric Hospital in Queens Village, New York, into the custody of Oscar Goodstein, one of the owners and the manager of the jazz club Birdland. Goodstein became Powell's agent, manager, and legal guardian. He was the inspiration for the character Goodley, played in *Round Midnight* by Martin Scorsese. The hotel in which Dale stays when he comes to New York to play at Birdland is meant to suggest the Alvin Hotel, which was on Broadway and Fifty-Second Street, right across from the club. This is the same location where Lester Young died in 1959. During another one of Powell's stays in the hospital, a woman named Altevia Edwards (called Buttercup) took over as his manager and caretaker. Her character appears in the film played by the extraordinary Sandra Reaves-Phillips. Powell and Buttercup went together to Paris where Bud played extended engagements at the Blue Note with Pierre Michelot (who plays himself in the film) and Kenny Clarke (played by Billy Higgins).

When Bud went to Paris in 1959, he met Paudras, a great admirer who became what he referred to as Bud's protector. He is portrayed in the movie as the character Francis Borler, played by François Cluzet (whom Dexter predicted would go on to become one of the most important film actors in France. "You will be rich and famous," he said). Bud lived in the Hotel Louisiane in the Saint-Germain-des-Prés section of Paris and the hotel is shown in detail in the film. The drummer Kansas Fields also lived in the hotel, and the character of Ace in the film, played by Bobby Hutcherson, is loosely based on him.

The hotel was also home at times to Jean-Paul Sartre and Simone de Beauvoir, and its guest register has included Charlie Parker and Miles Davis. Some scenes in *Round Midnight* were shot in the hotel, but the room interiors were built in Studio Eclair in the Paris suburb of Épinay-sur-Seine. Paudras was an avid collector of Bud Powell recordings, and just as in the movie, he spent all his money going to the Blue Note and the underground club Le Chat Qui Peche. As in the film, too, he often crouched on the sidewalk to hear the music coming up through the ventilation grates of the club. Many of the characters in the movie and many of the scenes came from stories that Paudras told to Tavernier about Bud and his life in Paris. But as the script took shape and the film progressed, the story became less literally about Bud and more about the fictional saxophonist Dale Turner.

Dexter knew that there would be no way of avoiding a tragic ending in the film, despite his certainty that his own jazz life would end happily. But the story ends when Francis receives a telegram carrying the news of Dale's death in New York, followed by a memorial concert. That's it. There is no dead body, and Dexter was glad. The portrayal of jazz musicians as tragic figures was something that always bothered him. He said that if people would just think about the contributions of these great musicians and the lives they were forced to live in order to make music, jazz history would hew more closely to the real story. He also said that he wished the work they did wasn't called "playing" since that makes it difficult to be taken seriously. "Oh, he's not busy, he's just playing," Dexter would say mockingly.

As the days and weeks went by, decisions were made about the cast and the music. Bertrand insisted that all the music would be recorded live as the musicians were filmed, and that put additional pressure on Dexter to get himself together. He felt that Dale would not be in very good shape when he first arrived in Paris but that he would get stronger as the plot develops. That scenario would fit conveniently with Dexter's own plan. Dexter would also play Dale as being a few years older than himself (Dexter was sixty-two in 1985), and I was a bit worried that people would think the movie was the story of Dexter's life. But he wasn't concerned about that. To understand Dale, Dexter was thinking about Bud Powell and Lester Young and about what Paris was like when Dexter first arrived there in 1962, and when he played in the Blue Note and recorded there with Bud. He thought a lot about the terrible experiences Lester had in the army in 1944 when unlike many other drafted musicians who were placed in military bands, he was assigned to a regular unit, deprived of his saxophone, and was court-martialed and imprisoned for possession of marijuana and alcohol. Dexter believed that the experience changed Lester forever, just as Bud's spirit and soul were so damaged by the electric shock treatments he was forced to endure in mental hospitals. Dexter also spent time thinking about Buttercup and her relationship with Bud. He did not want her to come off as she was originally portrayed in the script, as the villainess that Francis Paudras's stories made her out to be. The relationship between Francis, Buttercup, and Bud had been a complicated one, and Dexter didn't like to see her portrayed in such a negative manner. "Taking care of Bud was not an easy job," he said. "She is not to be taken lightly. Think of what she went through to try to help him." Dexter made sure that Sandra Reaves-Phillips, as Buttercup, would have a scene in which she would sing and be happy, rather than be just a negative counterpart to Lonette McKee, who played the beautiful and saintly singer Darcey Leigh. Dexter said, "I know it's a movie, but it wasn't all that simple."

Dexter certainly came to know this character, Dale Turner. But Dale is not Dexter. To this day, however, some people believe that the character of Dale and the story of *Round Midnight* are based on Dexter's life. There is even a Danish documentary about Dexter and Ben Webster, *Cool Cats,* that shows a Danish musician weeping at the end because he believes that Dexter's life was tragic. It is important to remember that the film is fiction, that Dexter always considered his life to be anything but tragic, and that he was acting. And that is why he was nominated for an Oscar.

In June we packed up our suitcases, our duffel bags full of books— Dexter's was red and mine was turquoise—and the rest of our household, including Woody's babysitter Martine, and moved to Paris. We made arrangements for Woody, then seven years old, to go to day camp in our new neighborhood. We had a beautiful three-story house in Saint-Mandé, a lovely area about three miles east of Central Paris near the Bois de Vincennes and on the Metro 1 line. I was worried because

Woody didn't speak French and I thought he would have a hard time adjusting. I could not have been more wrong. His first French words were *pain au chocolat* and *escargots*. He would walk to the *boulangerie* in the morning for croissants and baguettes, and Dexter would watch him from our third-floor bedroom window. I was a wreck at first because this city kid had never gone to the store by himself in New York and didn't walk home from school alone. But he made friends right away and reported about the delicious lunches in the park. The father of one of the kids in camp had the charcuterie in Saint-Mandé and lunch was served on real plates with real food, as Woody often pointed out when we would bring out the plastic or paper plates at a picnic.

Woody came to the set on some days and he even got into a scene with Dexter at the airport, which did not make the film's final cut. The days on the set were very long and there were long periods of waiting between takes. Dexter had an air-conditioned trailer which helped immensely, and he had the fabulous Monique Dury as his dresser. In the credits she is listed as Wardrobe Assistant, but she was much more than that. In one photo, you see Monique wiping the sweat from Dexter's brow. She looked after him in a way that was so caring and kind, and she would know what was coming before anyone else did. She had worked with some of the best directors, including François Truffaut, and was a costume designer with many credits to her name. Dexter and Monique were a formidable force to be reckoned with. If someone came to the door of the trailer and Dexter was resting or was not ready, she would tell them to wait. If they persisted, she would tell them in a way that made them turn and not come back. She protected Dexter and knew all the secrets of making a movie. She gave him hints about who was in charge of what, whom he should listen to and whom he should ignore, and what to expect next. When the cast went to New York to shoot exterior scenes, Dexter insisted that Monique go along.

Every morning Dexter and Bertrand would discuss the scene to be filmed that day and its dialogue. Dexter often suggested drastic revisions, contributed new ideas, and told Bertrand what life was really like for musicians of the period. Bertrand would very often agree with Dexter's suggestions because his goal was to make the film realistic and respectful of jazz and the musicians who had created the music. One memorable scene came directly from Dexter. Francis has brought Dale back to his apartment where they are chatting and listening to records. In the background we hear Lester Young playing clarinet on "They

Can't Take That Away from Me." Dexter has Dale speak in a language that every jazz musician will understand and appreciate:

> *Dale:* Y'hear that, Francis? Used to be all straight tonics and seventh chords ... Then Lester played the sixth and ninth and he kind of stretched it out—same colors Debussy and Ravel had, y'dig? Those real soft tones. Then Bird went on to elevenths and thirteenths. I was going there already ... And all the cats began jamming that way, was ... evolution, man! You don't just go out and pick a style off of a tree one day ... The tree's inside you, growing naturally.

Another bit of dialogue that Dexter changed to reflect his own experience came in a scene between Dale and Darcey Leigh—their relationship loosely resembles that of Lester Young and Billie Holiday. The original dialogue read:

> *Darcey:* Have you any regrets?
>
> *Dale:* Regrets? One, yeah. I never should have recorded "Sophisticated Lady" in B-flat. Should have done it in plain old F.

A pretty good line, but in the film Dexter changed it to:

> *Dale:* Regrets? One, yeah. I wish I could have played in the Basie band.

These were both actual answers that Dexter would repeat many times, whenever he was asked the same question in real life. He did not believe in regrets or wishing that things had gone differently. To him, the past was what it was and couldn't be changed, so what was the use of regretting? In reality, it was "The Chase," one of his most famous tunes, that he regretted recording in B-flat, instead of "plain old F."[2] And Dexter really did wish that he had gotten a chance to play with the Basie band. Once in his later years when he was on the road with his own group and they crossed paths with a Basie band reunion tour (which included Marshal Royal, who had given Dexter his first gig with Lionel Hampton), Dexter asked Basie if he could sign up for a gig. "Bill, I will go on the road with the band and you don't have to pay me anything extra or give me billing," Dexter said. "Just let me sit in Lester's chair and play that music." Basie laughed and said, "It's too late, Dexter. You are too famous and there is only one bandleader in this band."

Dexter added another classic ad lib in the film that scores with every saxophone or clarinet player who sees it, provided they are old enough to recognize the name of a certain musical brand. As he is getting ready to practice in Francis's apartment, he removes a reed from his mouth and, mounting it onto his mouthpiece says, "Happiness is a nice wet Rico reed."

One of Dexter's favorite scenes in the movie was shot on the beach in Normandy, when Dale is wearing his long tweed overcoat and sitting on the sand with Francis and his daughter Bérengère.

> *Dale:* Funny how the world's inside nothing. I mean, your soul and your heart is inside you and babies are inside their mamas, and if you are a fish you are inside water . . . But the world is inside of nothing. I don't know if I like that or not.

The line was in the script, but after he delivered it, Dexter as Dale turned to Francis and ad libbed: "Did you write that down?"

That was pure Dexter. Just when you thought he was saying something profound, serious, and world changing, he would turn, crack a joke, laugh, or smile. He was not one to take himself too seriously. He always put an ironic twist on things and had that impish smile when events were becoming too grim.

For the sake of authenticity, Bertrand had decided that all the music in the film would be recorded live as the cameras rolled, and that they would never use the kind of playback system that is usually employed in filming musical scenes. This would be the first time that an entire score would be produced this way in a fictional feature film. (Only Dexter's tune "Tivoli" was played by additional personnel and was overdubbed into the final cut.) Herbie Hancock was concerned about this idea, but in his first meeting on the set with Bertrand, they suddenly heard the soft and heavily accented voice of master set designer Alexandre Trauner (who created the sets of so many classics of the French and American cinema, including *Quai de Brumes, The Children of Paradise, The Apartment,* and *The Man Who Would Be King*). "I am well aware of the dynamics of sound," Trauner said, according to Tavernier. "I did the first talking picture with René Clair back in 1930." There was a weighty pause. After such a statement, no one dared express even the slightest doubt about Trauner's ability to make good on Bertrand's promise.

When the first dailies came in, Herbie was enchanted. The sound quality was so extraordinary that he marveled, "If only every jazz club could have such good acoustics! Filming the music live was a real challenge for the musicians, the crew, and myself. We never really knew where we were going and there could be enormous differences between two takes. This made the shooting a deeply moving and stimulating adventure."

At the studio in Épinay-sur-Seine, Trauner meticulously recreated the Blue Note club, the Hotel Louisiane, and Birdland for the film. On the set of the Blue Note, there was a dressing room right off the stage. Dexter would sit in there between scenes and it became a meeting place for the musicians—all except Herbie. When I asked Dexter why Herbie didn't hang out in the dressing room with the band, he explained that it was just like Billy Eckstine's band or Lionel Hampton's band. There is always one musician who stays aloof from the "cats." That would be Herbie.

Bertrand would come into the dressing room with Bruno de Keyser, the director of photography, and Frédéric Bourboulon, the first assistant director, to talk over the next scene. I often hung out in the dressing room and it was exactly like being in a club. There were many times when I forgot they were making a movie, and Dexter said he felt the same way. He got so accustomed to the lights and cameras that he said he was transported back to the original Blue Note where he had played when he first came to Paris in 1962.

Since I had spent many nights in New York's original Birdland, I watched the carpenters build the set and then helped make sure the details, down to the triangular shape of the ashtrays, exactly matched those in the club, or at least the way I remembered them from when we were teenagers. At times, the set designers would ask me questions about the audience and the dressing room and the atmosphere. I was so thrilled to have had a hand in that work, and whenever I watch the film I am always looking in the background at all those small details. When you see *Round Midnight,* you know that the set has everything to do with the atmosphere and authenticity of the story.

Being in the company of an artist like Alexandre Trauner is something unforgettable. He was seventy-nine years old in 1985, and his assistants would circle him and hang on every word he said. They studied photos, built miniature sets and replicas, making sure the colors were right and that the lighting always created exactly the mood Bertrand required for each moment. Though the film was shot in color, it almost looks like it's black and white. The costumes are all in muted shades, and it has the feeling of an older film. I cannot look at any movie in the same way after having spent those many weeks on the set of *Round Midnight.* So many people working together, so many hours, so much tension—and then in the end, this beautiful product emerged. Bertrand saw what he wanted even before he began to work on the film. It is Bertrand's film, and Dexter always said that he was just lucky to be in the right place at the right time. Of course, Dexter had a way of being modest about how luck came into play for him. There is always more to the story than luck.

When Freddie Hubbard was hired to come to Paris to play the tune "Society Red" in the Birdland scene along with Cedar Walton, Ron Carter, and Tony Williams, the musical part of the film started to come together. The scenes in the Blue Note in Paris were made even more authentic than they would have been with just American jazz musicians by having Pierre Michelot play bass. He had played with Bud Powell and Kenny Clarke in Paris and worked with Dexter many times. Dexter said from the beginning that Michelot was the right person for the part. For the recording session scene, bassist Mads Vinding and trumpeter-composer Palle Mikkelborg came from Copenhagen, which was a pleasant reunion for Dexter. The atmosphere was very lively and there were those special jazz musician moments where one word sets them off laughing and pounding each other on the back as they recall certain shared stories.

Dexter was particularly pleased that Wayne Shorter would be in the film. When Wayne showed up with his soprano saxophone, Dexter said, "I want to hear you play the tenor." Wayne explained that he hadn't been playing much tenor since he started working with Weather Report in 1970. Dexter suggested that he start practicing. The managers of the hotel where the band was staying in Paris mentioned to Bertrand that Wayne was heard practicing at all hours of the day and night. When Dexter heard that, he smiled and said, "I had better be ready for him."

When the scenes with Dexter and Wayne were filmed, Wayne came to the set and played "Dex's Deck" and "Blow Mr. Dexter." Those were tunes from Dexter's Savoy recordings from the 1940s. Dexter hadn't heard them in a very long time and hardly ever played them. He never forgot that and told the story over and over. He thought Wayne was one of the best "young" tenor players, along with Joe Henderson. He referred to them as his children.

Many of the script changes that were suggested by Dexter or Michael Cuscuna, or others on the set, Bertrand accepted with grace and interest. There were a few difficult moments but they passed quickly. Nothing negative ever lingered into the next day.

As the weeks passed, though, Francis Paudras had some issues with the script as it grew more and more fictional and less bound to the facts of Francis's relationship with Powell. Dexter would say: "It's a movie, after all. It's not a documentary. We are telling a story based on Bud, not Bud's life story."

When I discussed the making of *Round Midnight* with Cuscuna in 2012, I realized that I only remembered the good parts and he remembered the very bad parts. Michael and I worked together for many years in that office we shared on Fifty-Third Street when he was the producer for Dexter and Woody Shaw on Columbia Records. He and Dexter had a very special and close friendship. Michael Cuscuna:

> I remember being pretty appalled by the script, and so were you and Dexter. But then I guess you addressed that grievance with Bertrand before anything was signed. And he said, "No problem, I want to make it real, I want it to be what it is." And he lived up to that word, from that day forward to the end of the film. I really admired the fact that he wanted to get it right. We had a lot of meetings at your apartment. I remember we had meetings with Herbie and his manager at your apartment, we had meetings with Bertrand, and we did a lot of early stuff before shooting began.[3]

When there were problems in Paris with the music or the musicians, Dexter and I would say, "You need to get Michael." So Bertrand would call him. Michael was not technically the music coordinator because the soundtrack had gone to Herbie's label rather than Blue Note Records, and that meant that Herbie's manager was the official music coordinator. But Cuscuna was the problem solver. When Cedar Walton, Freddie Hubbard, and Billy Higgins were called to fly in from Los Angeles for the Birdland scene, Michael was brought in and put up at the same hotel as the musicians. He remembers this situation with typical Cuscuna clarity:

> I just commuted back and forth between New York and Paris for those weeks of filming. But the one good thing I remember is that when they built the Birdland set, they did such an amazing job. I took Cedar and Billy to show them the set, and their fucking jaws dropped. They were like, speechless. Literally speechless.

Having all the music recorded live was no easy task for the musicians, but the results were good and made the film so much more realistic. Dexter did not often listen to his own recordings, but he did during the filming and he was satisfied that his playing sounded appropriate to the character, improving as time went on. By the time he played in the Birdland scenes, he thought the music was just right.

One day on the set there was a knock on the trailer door and Cedar Walton came in. He had just arrived to play in the Birdland scene. He said, "Dexter, is it true that I have flown all the way to Paris to play the blues?"

Dexter replied, "Why not? Who else could I have gotten?"

Cedar had been shocked when he saw the set for Birdland, as Cuscuna observed. And when he saw the rushes, he laughed heartily at the people from Senegal and Martinique posing as the audience in New York City. Cedar had a special way of taking in an entire situation and then making some kind of philosophical statement about what was happening. Sometimes he just chortled. You don't find all that many jazz musicians who chortle. Cedar brought something to that scene in Birdland aside from the authenticity of his having played there so often. He brought his unique way of seeing the irony in a situation and his sense of swing that Dexter knew he, and the film, needed. Dexter loved the Birdland scene in the movie. It was one of his favorites. When we watched it together, he would often start talking about the Royal Roost on Forty-Eighth Street and other clubs in his old Los Angeles neighborhood as if he had forgotten that the Birdland he was seeing was really a set built in a movie studio outside Paris. Cuscuna:

> Some of those music sequences were good, but the things I remember more were the problems, and I guess that's when I would come over.

One particular problem—and its solution—stands out.

> It was a Monday morning, and Freddie's not due on the set until six that night. So I go to the studio in Épinay-sur-Seine and we're doing whatever we're doing all day, and then Bertrand says, "You know, we sent the car to the hotel for Freddie but he won't come down." You and Dexter and I are talking about it, and little Woody, who was seven years old, says, "Why don't you send another car for him, have it wait there, and when he's ready to come down, he'll come down." It worked! I'll never forget that it worked. I mean, he's two hours late, but Freddie finally got there, and he was all chipper and sane and spruced up and did the Birdland stage scene. So this little kid said, "Well, just tell the car to wait and he'll be there." How do you think he knew that? From Dexter? I don't know, I don't know, I think probably from the way his mother thinks.

The best part of the story is that Freddie Hubbard did not realize that he had come to Paris to be in a movie. He thought he had flown in for a gig with Herbie Hancock. He said to me, "Max, it looks like Birdland."

"It's a movie set," I said.

"Why does it look like Birdland?"

"You are making a movie."

He said, "No one told me it was a movie. What kind of movie? Are we playing 'Society Red' like on the record, in a movie? Is it about Blue Note Records?"

"No, it's a fictional story based on Bud Powell in Paris."

"Oh shit, no one told me that."

I told him he needed to talk to Herbie and Herbie's manager about that. Years later, Freddie said to me, "Hey Max, remember when we flew first class to Paris to play the blues? I'll never forget that. Dexter should have won the Oscar!" Freddie Hubbard was one of a kind. So much beauty came out of that trumpet, and even on a bad day he could move everyone with his sound. I am so glad he got a chance to be in that film and got to fly to Paris to play the blues. Those of us who knew him since we were teenagers in New York look at that scene in *Round Midnight* and remember how remarkable and special Freddie Hubbard was.

Cuscuna remembers being driven to the Épinay-sur-Seine set in the mornings before shooting:

> You guys came separately 'cause you were in a separate house—and, you know, we'd get the call sheet that they'd sent us at the hotel, and we'd look up the pages that were being shot that day. Bobby and Billy and I would read the pages and we'd start to talk about what didn't sound good, what sounded unrealistic, and by the time we got to the lot, we'd go over to Bertrand, and make our suggestions. He was so appreciative, he just sucked it all up.
>
> My one great contribution to the movie was when Dexter's character is coming into the hotel room in New York and saying, "Cozy, like Cozy Cole," and I said, "Bertrand, no fucking musician in the world would say that. But, Martin Scorsese is playing a scumbag. Have him say it, and he'll seem even more scumbaggy." And then Dexter just rolls his eyes.
>
> When they were recording sound in Studio Davout, there was lots of waiting time. Hurry up and wait is always the name of the game. I asked the musicians to play a blues and then I wrote "Call Sheet Blues" on it as the title. I put Herbie and Wayne and Ron [Carter] and Billy's name on it 'cause they were the four guys playing. It won a Grammy for best original composition of the year! One of the big disappointments for me was that Blue Note did not get the soundtrack. I don't think it's the best Dexter, and I hope that he is not remembered for his playing in the movie. He has so many other great recordings for people to hear him on.

Cuscuna got to play the producer in the studio scenes, and one of them made it into the movie:

> These scenes are improvised more or less, so in one of the scenes François, who is playing Francis Paudras, says to me, "You know, why don't you ask me this or this or this?" So, on camera I say to François's character: "You know, I don't know what you've done with Dale, but I mean he sounds better than ever, his whole outlook on life is better—you've really worked miracles," and blah blah blah . . . we have a whole conversation like that. So, at about this time, the real Francis Paudras comes in, and he's standing in the

back, watching. By now we're about finished shooting, and everything else after that is going to be just audio recording. Everyone takes a long break, and all of a sudden Paudras comes up to François, and says, all in French—I'm just picking up little bits of this—"Dirty motherfucker! You are not me! That's not me! You're not me!" and lunges at him. They start to throw punches. I don't know most of what they are saying because it was all in French. A couple of guys from the crew pulled them apart. After that, Francis didn't show up on the set again.

One of the remarkable things about *Round Midnight* is how much improvisation went into the development of the characters and the story line. Bertrand was able to see that the original idea and original script were taking on a life of their own, and that this life was being driven by the way real jazz musicians think and live. He did not resist the changes, and he was able to follow and appreciate the story as it went its own way. Had he resisted, he would have had a disaster on his hands, and he knew it.

Dexter was always a very kind and quiet person unless he felt that he was being asked to do something he absolutely could not do. Then he would become the most stubborn and defiant person I have ever met. He said that he always had to fight his way out of situations that were wrong for him and that he would not be doing that anymore. After all, he was in his sixties and he knew what worked for him and what did not. He knew which musicians he could play with and which ones did not have the same feeling for the rhythm or the compositions that he needed to hear. He could not and would not play a tune that he didn't feel right about. Bertrand came to understand Dexter after a very short period of working together, and they maintained their friendship throughout the filming and for the rest of Dexter's life. Cuscuna:

> After the scenes in Studio Davout, we went to dinner with Bruce Lundvall at Le Dôme on Boulevard du Montparnasse. I remember it was August because La Coupole was closed. We had a delicious dinner with *fruits de mer* piled high on many trays. Dexter was telling early Paris stories, and he tells about how he had brought in this tune, "Valse Robin," that he had written for his daughter: "Yeah, I handed out the music, and Rene Urtreger says, 'Excuse me, Dexter, but I do not play waltzes.'" Everyone laughed. Dexter loved to tell that story.
>
> So then we leave Le Dôme to go to a particular club, and when we get out of the cab we have to walk along an alley maybe a block long. Along the way we pass by another small club and I notice a sign in the window that says "Rene Urtreger." I say, "Dexter! Look, come here!" Dex and Bruce come over and Bruce says, "Oh, we gotta go inside." So we do, and Bruce and Dexter go up to the bandstand and, at the end of a tune, Dexter moves over

to the piano, leans into his hands, and says, in his deepest, slowest Dexter voice, "Rene, do you still not play waltzes?" Rene laughed so loud. That was just so fucking bizarre, a story told by Dexter at dinner about Paris in the early sixties, and now he's in a movie about that time and place, and the story he was telling comes back around to us an hour later as we walk down this alley.

When the long night finally ended and the sky was beginning to lighten, Dexter, Bruce, and I walked in the middle of Rue des Lombards toward Boulevard de Sébastopol. Dexter stopped, looked around, and said, "I am very glad that you are both here because I had the distinct feeling that I was dreaming that I was in Paris and that I was making a movie about a jazz musician in Paris." He smiled that huge smile of his, turned to me, and said, "Don't ever forget this moment. It goes in the book. Do you promise?" Well, all these years later, I have kept my promise and it's here in his book. There is a photograph of Dexter and me and Bruce Lundvall walking on that street that Bruce had hanging in his office at the Blue Note. He said that night was one of the greatest of his life. It was one of those times when you are there, but you definitely feel that you had already been there before.

Being in Paris for the months of shooting the film brought back so many memories for Dexter. He didn't have too many free days, but when he did we would go to Saint-Germain-des-Prés to eat and walk around the streets and visit the sites of the old clubs, like Le Chat Qui Peche. He said it was like living his life inside a dream about a tenor player going to Paris. Only this time he was there to make a movie about a jazz musician, so it was layer upon layer of life told and retold. So much of what was not good for Dexter he filed away in a place where he preferred to leave it. Not all his memories of Paris were good, but during the making of the film he only thought about the good things he had done and learned, and how many oysters a person could eat in Pigalle.

Many mornings a wonderful Cambodian doctor who was also an acupuncturist hired by Bertrand would come to the house and give us treatments together. We would both be lying in bed with needles all over and the doctor would be telling us how much French people needed acupuncture for their livers, and about his life in Cambodia. He was a very lovely and comforting presence. Dexter had been having acupuncture treatments since we first went to Cuernavaca. In Paris he felt that they gave him the energy he needed to get up and go to the set, to be the leading actor as well as the leading player in the live music scenes.

Dexter had a saying that went something like, "Well, at least we are in Paris." This meant that no matter how bad things were looking or whatever bad news arrived on a particular day, we should be grateful that we were in Paris. We had been there many times together and would be there after the release of the film, but this time we had a house and a housekeeper; Woody had a babysitter; all the bills at home were paid; and our attorney, Norman Annenberg, got the mail and took care of the calls. It was hard work for Dexter, but it was also like entering another part of the universe where there was one and only one thing to think about, and that was the making of the movie. Dexter liked the idea of being able to concentrate on the project without the realities of daily life interfering. He said, "Just think about the movie. If I do the best job possible and put all my energy into this, everything else will fall into place." I usually had the job of worrying about what was next and it was not easy for me to get in line with the program, but Dexter was right, as he most often was, and I eventually calmed down and tried to follow the flow.

Martin Scorsese, whose scenes came only at the end of the film, would come to the set to see how things were going and to visit with his good friend Bertrand. They would speak in whispers with their heads very close together and then burst out laughing. Scorsese would stand behind the camera, out of the way, and watch with a very serious expression on his face. I would try to stand next to him whenever I could, just trying to see what he was seeing. This was impossible, of course.

One day Martin turned to me and said, "Pack your bags."

"What are you saying?" I said.

"Pack your bags. You are going to the Oscars."

I laughed and said, "Oh, please don't say that to Dexter. I hate to see him disappointed."

"I know what I'm saying," he said. "In this picture he is just like De Niro in *Raging Bull*. Bertrand will have to cut any scenes that he is not in. This is *his* movie. Everything about him is perfect. He has become Dale Turner and that is what Hollywood loves in an actor. He will definitely get nominated. Trust me on this."

I didn't mention any of this to Dexter, but Scorsese did tell him that he should be ready for the reaction to the movie. Dexter said he was always ready, and they had a good laugh about that. When they screened the rough cut of the film in Paris, Bruce Lundvall flew over to see it. He remembers his conversation with Bertrand at the time:

> Tavernier said that Dexter was the best actor he had ever worked with. Some people think he's playing Dexter, but not at all; he's playing the part. I was

sitting next to Pierre Michelot. The ending was so long and so sad and eve-ryone was crying and Pierre was crying uncontrollably and I was too. They had to keep the lights off for about ten minutes until people settled down. I thought Dexter did an amazing job. I watched it recently after a long time not seeing it. I sat there until one in the morning, alone, watching it. It was just phenomenal. I couldn't sleep after that.[4]

The experience of making a film seemed to be something that Dexter had prepared himself for since his childhood in Los Angeles. He had seen many, many movies and he did not find it particularly shocking that he should have the leading role in a film about a jazz musician in Paris. "After all, who else could do it?" he said. We were so sad to leave the beautiful house in Saint-Mandé, but Dexter assured me that we would have plenty of time to be back in Paris.

He loved working with François Cluzet, the way he adapted the character of Francis and their ability to communicate through and past the language difference. In 2011 I went to the premiere in New York of *Les Intouchables*. François, who starred in the film, was so happy to talk about Dexter and how much he loved being with him in the filming of *Round Midnight*. It was so very nice to see that Dexter's prediction had come true. Well, at least the part about François being famous. Dexter also predicted that the film would withstand time; that it would be the best film ever made about jazz and jazz musicians because the music was recorded live and people would be able to hear what was really happening on the bandstand. After more than thirty years, that prediction holds true.

To Bertrand Tavernier, who has directed more than twenty films and received many awards and citations, the experience of making *Round Midnight* was also supremely profound. Tavernier:

The actual making of this film was much more than a shoot. It was a fourteen-week labor of love that could not have happened without Dexter's considerable contributions. He is an exceptional acting talent. A well-known film director told me that Dexter looked as if he'd made three hundred films, because his work seemed so controlled. And yet, no other actor could have done what he did, because he is a jazzman. His musical interpretations sounded so bebop and so fresh at the same time. I would also like to pay tribute to Billy Higgins, the exceptional drummer who radiates so much light, and to Bobby Hutcherson. Both of them helped me on many occasions to solve the numerous problems engendered by this type of shoot. They are truly rare beings.

The last word, which naturally belongs to Dexter, sums up the whole spirit of the production. At the end of the last day of shooting, he asked me, "Lady Bertrand, how long will it take me to get over this movie?"[5]

CHAPTER 19

A Night at the Oscars

Dizzy made the best expression I ever heard in my
lifetime. Dizzy said, "You have to have one foot in the
past, and one foot in the future."

—Jimmy Heath[1]

Dexter laughed when Martin Scorsese told him that he would get an
Oscar nomination for his performance as the saxophonist Dale Turner
in *Round Midnight*. Scorsese, who played the role of Goodley, the Birdland club owner, insisted that Dexter would be nominated because his
performance was like that of Robert De Niro's in *Raging Bull,* which
Scorsese directed. By the time *Round Midnight* was nearing completion,
Dexter let it be known that he thought Scorsese was right. I had my
doubts. After all, this was Dexter's first acting role in a film (he had
acted in the play *The Connection* in Los Angeles in 1960); he was a jazz
musician and only three Black men before him had ever been nominated
by the Academy of Motion Picture Arts and Sciences for Best Leading
Actor in a film. Sidney Poitier was the first to be nominated, the first to
win, and the first to receive two Best Actor nominations. He was a
runner-up in 1958 for *The Defiant Ones* and won in 1963 for *Lilies of
the Field.* James Earl Jones was nominated in 1970 for *The Great White
Hope,* and Paul Winfield was nominated in 1972 for his role in *Sounder.*
With a gap of fifteen years between Best Actor nominees for a Black
actor, the thought that Dexter, in 1987, would be the fourth Black actor
to be nominated seemed impossible to me. He would be the fifth nomi-
nee because Poitier was nominated twice.

Of course Dexter thought differently. He would laugh and say, "Start
thinking about what you want to wear to the Oscars." Not long after
the film was finished, he and Arthur McGee, the first Black designer on

214

FIGURE 21. Dexter on the set of *Round Midnight*. His portrayal of Dale Turner earned him a 1987 Oscar nomination for Best Leading Actor in a motion picture. From the private collection of Dexter Gordon.

New York's Seventh Avenue and a legend in the fashion world, began talking about satin bowties and other extravagant Oscar-worthy apparel. I thought they were going to be very disappointed and kept saying that it was a bit premature to be discussing fancy cravats. But Dexter was undeterred, talking up the Oscars and anticipating what such a measure of recognition would do for jazz musicians and the way people would think about the music in the future.

When the film premiered at the Venice Film Festival and then opened in New York on October 3, 1986, the reaction was tremendous and Dexter got rave reviews. Still, I did not think he should believe he was going to be nominated for an Oscar. As 1987 began, we went about our lives, flying down to Mexico to our house in Cuernavaca with its view of the volcano Popocatépetl and the bougainvillea-filled garden where Dexter would practice. Woody, who was then eight years old, went to the Colegio Internacional, and studied karate, and I supervised the staff in what Dexter would refer to as "Maxine's queendom." We had a satellite dish installed so Dexter could watch television from the States. He was a very serious baseball fan, a New York Mets fan as we already noted, and he had to be able to follow them in the spring; otherwise, we would be leaving Mexico too soon to suit me.

On the morning of Wednesday, February 11, 1987, Dexter was watching the *Today Show* with Bryant Gumbel as host when he yelled for me to come in from the garden and watch because they were about to announce the Oscar nominations. I stayed outside, yelling back that he shouldn't feel disappointed if his name wasn't called. But he remained certain that I was wrong. All of a sudden, I heard Dexter howling with raucous laughter and the phone began to ring. I ran into the front room and he said, "I told you so!" I screamed and cried, and he laughed and nodded his head. Then he said, "So, what are you wearing to the Oscars?"

He had never doubted that he would be nominated and he began to work on his acceptance speech, trying out phrases: "This is a great day for jazz . . . A great day for all jazz musicians . . . A great day for Louis Armstrong, for Billie Holiday, for Billy Eckstine, for Duke Ellington, for Count Basie, for Marshal Royal." We invited friends to the house for lunch and had a party into the night sitting outside on the terrace. Dexter had fully believed the word of Martin Scorsese, and now he knew that his performance proved he was an actor after all.

The other announced nominees in the Best Actor category were Bob Hoskins for *Mona Lisa,* William Hurt for *Children of a Lesser God,* Paul Newman for *Color of Money,* and James Woods for *Salvador.* Herbie Hancock was nominated for best original score for *Round Midnight,* which was very exciting for Dexter and Bertrand Tavernier as they had worked very hard in selecting the right compositions that would tell the bittersweet story and fit properly with the setting and period of the film, Paris in the early 1960s.

The Oscars ceremony would be held on March 30, 1987, at the Dorothy Chandler Pavilion in Los Angeles. We flew up from Mexico City, but our clothes were coming with Arthur McGee and my old friend Irene Neves from New York. Arthur knew what Dexter would be wearing and he had prepared the outfit after many meetings and conversations with Dexter. My outfit, on the other hand, had to be discussed by phone. Arthur knew my size, so that wasn't a problem. He made me a long skirt and a jacket made of gray pinstripe suiting material with a white satin lining and pearls and rhinestones on it. He wanted the jacket to look as if the beads had been thrown onto it, and he said that he had ordered the beading to be redone after the first attempt had looked too orderly to him.

But the Oscars ceremony was not to be the only big event on our trip. Shortly after the nominations were announced, Dexter received a letter from Albert Nellum, an influential and highly respected Black business and cultural leader, and Eugene Jackson, a longtime film actor, about an event to be held before the Oscars, honoring both Dexter and Herbie Hancock as Oscar nominees. The letter read, "For the past several years, we have joined some of your colleagues in the industry in honoring the Oscar Nominees at a gathering the night before the actual ceremony. This recognition has become our way of reinforcing for the honorees and perhaps even more important for their peers, our recognition of the talent, the special efforts and the tremendous perseverance such achievement represents in the industry."

We had never before heard of what became known as the Black Oscars,[2] but Dexter was very excited to be invited. On Sunday, March 29, one hundred of Dexter's and Herbie's friends and admirers, mostly from the Hollywood community, gathered for cocktails and dinner followed by a brief program that included the presentations of the Black Oscars—ebony sculptures of the Tree of Life—and plenty of time to socialize. Dexter invited Marshal Royal and his wife, Evelyn, who had been a singer with the Lionel Hampton Orchestra, and other Los Angeles friends as well as Norman Annenberg, his lawyer, and Arthur McGee, who dressed both of us for both black-tie Oscar events. Dexter wore a beautiful black satin jacket with his satin cravat, and I had a soft blue silk outfit. In his speech, Dexter had an opportunity to thank Marshal Royal for letting him join the Lionel Hampton band when he was just seventeen years old, and for not sending him home when he sounded like a kid right out of high school. Marshal and Evelyn were very touched by the public gratitude, and the crowd gave Marshal a standing ovation.

Dexter also acknowledged Tom Bradley, the mayor of Los Angeles at the time, who first inspired Dexter when he was a record-breaking track star and team captain at UCLA, and a classmate of Jackie Robinson. The event's host, the comedian and social activist Dick Gregory, made trenchant comments about how few Black actors had been nominated by the Motion Picture Academy. Quincy Jones presented the Black Oscar to Herbie Hancock and was his charming and generous self.

Later on, during the socializing, Dexter told the actress Cicely Tyson to be sure to tell "Dave" (as he called his friend Miles Davis) that he brought his designer with him, to make sure he looked sharp for the Black Oscars. The sly remark referred back to 1948 when Dexter first started telling Miles that he needed to get himself a hipper dress style, because his "Brooks Brothers look" just wasn't making it. Years later, while on tour in France, Dexter ran into Miles in a hotel lobby. Miles ran over and literally jumped up into Dexter's arms. They laughed and started talking and were so happy to see each other. Dexter looked at Miles's white leather outfit with fringe hanging from the arms and his white boots with rather high heels and said, "Miles. What is that shit you are wearing?" I was worried that there was going to be some trouble brewing but I was completely wrong about that.

"Oh Dex, this is the style now," Miles said.

"It's okay on stage if you like it, but not walking around. It's just not hip," Dexter replied.

Miles nodded his head and they walked away laughing and talking. Forty years later, and they had almost the same conversation that they had in 1948.

The Oscars and Black Oscars of 1987 made for quite a celebration and a kind of avenging moment for Dexter because he had suffered so much in Los Angeles in the 1950s and was always reluctant to return, even though he had been born there and his mother and daughters still lived there. He had skipped the Los Angeles premiere of *Round Midnight*, though I had strongly suggested that he go. I lost that argument. He said that the thought of going to Los Angeles gave him nightmares. But he was so proud to be nominated for the Oscar that he started preparing himself for the trip as soon as he heard the announcement.

We certainly had the appropriate suite in Los Angeles—the movie star suite at the Beverly Hills Hotel. The Motion Picture Academy assigned a woman to take special care of us during our stay, and when she said that we could dine at any restaurant or go to any show or nightclub of our choice, Dexter said he wanted to go to a Lakers game and watch Kareem Abdul-Jabbar play. We got tickets in the VIP section at the Forum and sat next to Kareem's father, Ferdinand Lewis Alcindor Sr., whom Dexter knew from his years as a jazz trombonist in New York. Dexter called him Al, and they had many musician friends in common. As they watched Kareem and the Lakers beat the Houston Rockets, they reminisced and laughed about the "good old days." After the game, they visited Kareem in the locker room and then headed for the bar. Kareem recalls that he had to go find them when the bar was closing and get them back to the hotel. I had left them there knowing that it was going to be a long night.

Because the Oscars ceremony began in the afternoon to accommodate East Coast television viewers, it was still daylight when the limousine picked us up and took us to the theater. We walked on the red carpet wondering whether we were in the same dream at the same time. The hostess who showed us to our seats said that if we needed to get up for any reason we should just signal, and some lovely young aspiring actors dressed in formal attire would come to take our places. They would look much better on television than empty seats. A few hours into the interminable ceremony, Dexter became restless so we signaled for the seat fillers and went to the bar. There Dexter found three of his fellow nominees, Bob Hoskins, James Woods, and William Hurt, throwing down the free drinks and having a great time. They all figured that Paul Newman was a lock so they might as well enjoy themselves, and Dexter went along. After a while the hostess came over to me and asked if I could help get the men back to their seats because the Best Actor category was coming up soon. I told her that it was too late. From my experience as a road manager for musicians and jazz festivals, I knew when it was too late to get someone to do something they weren't interested in doing. She looked very upset, so I went over to Bob Hoskins and implored him to get everyone upstairs to their seats. After some grumbling they agreed, but Hoskins said to Dexter, "Please go back to playing the saxophone. The competition out here is tough enough." They all roared with laughter and got back to their seats just in time to hear Bette Davis announce Paul Newman as the winner. The Best Picture that year was *Platoon*. Herbie Hancock did win for Best Original Score for *Round Midnight*. That was a thrilling moment for everyone who had worked so hard on the film.

When it was all finally over, we filed out and went back to the hotel. Dexter didn't want to go to any parties. He just invited some friends to our suite for room service snacks and champagne. He was pleased but exhausted from all the interviews and attention. My job as movie star wife included makeup, two hair salon appointments, the fitting of clothes, very high heels, and lots of smiling and acting the part. Dexter continued to remind me that soon we would be getting back to our regular life and he was looking forward to it.

From Los Angeles we flew back to Mexico and returned to our life with Woody in Cuernavaca. Of course things were never really the same. The Oscars changed so much for us, but Dexter still worked at having a calm and peaceful life.

CHAPTER 20

Cadenza

These days people will say to me, "Oh, gee, you're out
here alone now. All these people are gone." Well, I don't
really know what they're talking about. They're all still
here. They haven't gone. Not to me, because hearing them
in my head all the time, thinking about my times with
them, I even have dreams sometimes about hanging out
with different guys . . . And I'm still with them, which is
good for me, 'cause those are the people I want to be with,
not the people that are left out here.

Dexter? Well, you know, I mean I love him. I don't know
what else to say about him. He's there, he's one of a kind,
you know. And he's really a very beautiful person, he's a
kind person. A lot of people don't understand, wouldn't
know anything about that. But Dexter was really a kind,
kind person. And I admire that. He's an example for me.

Sonny Rollins[1]

Dexter should leave his karma to science.

—Dizzy Gillespie[2]

Things did not quiet down as we had planned after the Oscars and the
"movie star year." When we returned to New York, Dexter got a call
asking him to perform with the New York Philharmonic. He said he
had dreamed of being on stage with the Philharmonic since his childhood, when he first began listening to the orchestra on their Sunday
afternoon radio broadcasts. The acclaimed musician, composer, and
educator David Baker was commissioned by the Philharmonic to write
a concerto based on the compositions and themes of Duke Ellington.

The conductor was James de Priest, one of the first African American maestros on the world stage, director emeritus of conducting and orchestral studies at the Juilliard School, and laureate music director of the Oregon Symphony. *Ellingtones: A Fantasy for Saxophone and Orchestra* in three movements—Moderato, Waltz, and Passacaglia—was performed at Avery Fisher Hall on June 4, 5, and 6, 1987, with Tommy Flanagan as the pianist, Ron Carter as the bassist, and Dexter Gordon as the tenor saxophonist.

In July Dexter went on tour with the Round Midnight Band, including Cedar Walton, Bobby Hutcherson, Pierre Michelot, and Billy Higgins. They performed ten concerts, including the jazz festivals at Montreux, Switzerland; Umbria, Italy; and San Sebastián, Spain. Everything about the tour was very different from any pre-movie tours he had done. Limousines were waiting at the airports, the hotel suites were first class, the crowds were huge, and Dexter had top billing. When we arrived with the band in Montreux, the driver stopped at the Montreux Palace, a very luxurious hotel overlooking Lake Geneva where we had once stayed with the Columbia Records All-Star group. The band started getting out of the van and the driver said, "No, Monsieur Gordon. You and Madame are not staying here." I was very disappointed and insisted that we wanted to stay there with the band. The driver said he was asked to take us to another location. I was preparing to complain to George Wein, the tour impresario, when we arrived at a magnificent villa facing Lake Geneva. We entered the palatial home with a terrace overlooking the lake, several bedrooms, a sitting room, a valet, a cook, and a private driver to take Dexter to the festival. Dexter laughed so loud and repeated the story to everyone he met: "She was about to complain to George Wein until she saw where we were staying!" We had half the villa and Stan Getz had the other half, with a private entrance as well. Dexter asked Stan if he always got this kind of treatment and Stan just laughed.

When we went to Perugia for the Umbria Jazz Festival, Dexter needed bodyguards because he had been awarded the David di Donatello award as best actor in a foreign film. This is Italy's version of the Oscar, and fans flocked to see and hear him, and get his autograph. People asked if he was really playing saxophone in the film. He was a movie star in Italy, not a jazz musician who made a movie. Our friend, the legendary promoter Alberto Alberti, made all the arrangements, and Dexter said that it was the first time he had a police car driving in front of the car instead of behind him with a siren blaring. The bodyguards joined us of course for many delicious meals at Dexter's insistence—but they always watched the door while they ate. Alberto Alberti, who was from Bologna, was one of the great champions of this music. He played drums and booked bands in Italy, and he made sure they had the best meals and the best audiences. Any chance to work with Alberto was something Dexter looked forward to. I worked with many producers and promoters in Europe but nobody came near Alberto for the love of the music and for his love and respect for the musicians who created it. When things got difficult on the road, Alberto would turn to me and say, "Don't worry." That's when I knew we really had a problem, but I also knew that he would find a way to solve the problem.

In Strasbourg, France, Dexter opened for Dizzy Gillespie's band. He played "Round Midnight" as he did every night on that tour. During intermission, Dizzy said to him, "Come into the rehearsal room. I want to show you and Cedar something." They went into the room and Dizzy told him he had been playing "Round Midnight" wrong. "You are playing it the way Miles recorded it," Dizzy said. "I wrote the introduction and ending to that tune for Monk. You aren't playing it right." Dexter was stunned and asked Dizzy why he had never mentioned this before. Dizzy said, "I was waiting until I saw you to tell you." Dexter and Cedar worked out what Dizzy told them and then called Bobby and Pierre to the room. From that day on, Dexter played the composition the way Dizzy showed him. He called Dizzy "John" and said he was the "Albert Einstein of modern music."

In San Sebastián Dexter was elated to receive a visit from his son Mikael, then twenty-two. Dexter had not seen him in many years and in fact had seen him rarely since his birth. Dexter's friends Skip and Kirsten Malone also came from Copenhagen, and Skip did some interviews with Dexter for the film *More Than You Know* that Malone and Don McGlynn made about Dexter. We had a fabulous lunch outdoors on a terrace with a jazz fan who was a Basque separatist and who explained for us the political conflict that had been going on in Spain for many years. When Dexter went into the house to look for the bathroom, he opened a door and found a room full of weapons. He told Skip and shortly after that we excused ourselves and returned to the hotel.

Dexter loved being with his fellow musicians who had performed in *Round Midnight*. He was especially happy to be with Bobby Hutcherson, whose brother Teddy had been Dexter's close boyhood friend. Billy Higgins, one of Dexter's all-time favorite drummers, was another old friend. When Billy was a small boy, Dexter would come over to sit on the porch with Billy's older sister.

In September the Round Midnight Band, with Buster Williams, performed at the Hollywood Bowl on a bill with Miles Davis in a concert that turned out to be less than sparkling. Then they went to Chicago for a free outdoor concert at the Petrillo Band Shell in Grant Park. Dexter played very well and was delighted with the band and the audience, which was said to be the largest ever assembled at the venue. They gave Dexter ovation after ovation. The city had to send in extra police because of the enormous crowd. I said to the organizer, "Well, it's a free concert, what did you expect?" He said, "It was free last night"—he meant with a different band—"and we only had five thousand people. We have a hundred thousand tonight." The size of the audience was never confirmed but of course it lives on in jazz mythology as an unforgettable event.

Just before Christmas 1987 Dexter made a video in New York with Tony Bennett singing "White Christmas." It was a very special occasion for Dexter, as he greatly admired Tony and was very happy for the chance to spend time with him. Then it was time to pack up Woody and the duffel bags full of books and head once again to Cuernavaca. I began to talk with Dexter about the idea of a sixty-fifth birthday party in Cuernavaca, since he really hadn't had a big party since his sixtieth, in 1983. At first he wasn't very enthusiastic about the idea but after some mild coaxing and reasoning, he agreed. We made a guest list and he said he wanted a Veracruz band and a mariachi band to play. We had quite a large group of friends in Cuernavaca by this time. My friend Cathleen and I began to make endless lists of what to buy, whom to hire, how to get the ice, where to find the bands, where to get the servers and people to clean up. We had lists about the decorations, the tables and chairs, the tortillas, the party favors, and more. Maria de los Angeles was our cook, and one of the best. She took charge of the menu and hired her helpers, including her husband (our gardener) and her daughters. The menu included *taquitos, tamalitos,* various salsas, *mole verde* and *mole poblano, ensalada de nopales, barbacoa,* blue corn tortillas made by hand outside over a charcoal fire, *tres leches* birthday cake, and also beer, rum, champagne, *horchata,* and *agua de limón.*

One group of musicians from Veracruz played the traditional music of the region called Son Jarocho; the other band was a local mariachi band. There was an interlude during which Dexter played "Bésame Mucho" on the soprano saxophone for Gil Evans, who had come to Cuernavaca with his son Noah for natural health treatments. As the party wound down, Dexter thanked the guests for coming and said, "If

FIGURE 22. Lunch with friends in the garden of our home in Cuernavaca, Mexico. That's me, standing. Photograph © Irene Kubota Neves.

you had told me that I would be at my own sixty-fifth birthday party, I would not have believed it. This is a jazz miracle. So many great friends and musicians died young. I salute them and pledge that they will not be forgotten."

When we returned to New York in 1988, Dexter was offered a part in the television series *Crime Story,* produced by Michael Mann. The episode was "Moulin Rouge," about a Black nightclub in Las Vegas, the actual club where Wardell Gray was working when he died in 1955 under unexplained circumstances. In the episode, Pam Grier played a reporter investigating attacks on the club and Dexter played Rollie, who is there to look after the club owner's interests. Dexter's character ends up being shot and killed. In *Round Midnight* Dexter had refused to die on screen, but for *Crime Story* he agreed to the dramatic moment. Dexter received offers for other television and film work but his health began to fail and he was not able to accept.

That fall we went to Japan where Dexter performed *Ellingtones* with the Tokyo Symphony Orchestra at Muza Kawasaki Symphony Hall. David Baker conducted his own concerto and it was a spectacular triumph for both of them. The performance was recorded but never released commercially. Maybe someday it will be. This trip to Japan was much better than his first trip years earlier, which had many short-comings and made him feel that he was not welcome. He joked that it had to do with his height, but this time everything was arranged perfectly; the host could not have been kinder and the orchestra was excellent. There were many large meals with endless toasts, trips to shrines, acupuncture, massages, and a press conference. As the movie star treatment continued, Dexter would turn to me and say, "Don't get used to this. I am still just a tenor player."

In October 1988 Dexter was invited to be a fashion model for Italian *Vogue* aboard the Jazz Cruise on the *SS Norway*. Arthur Elgort, the acclaimed fashion photographer who would do the shoot, wrote in a memoir, "To me, Dexter Gordon is larger than life. We met for the first time in 1987. I was doing a shoot for French *Vogue* and Dexter was one of the musicians I was to photograph. I was very excited. When Dexter stood in my studio and played, 'If You Could See Me Now,' I was mesmerized." (Dexter loved that Tadd Dameron composition written for Sarah Vaughan in 1946.) "I was so happy when the opportunity arose for me to go on the floating jazz festival aboard the *SS Norway* in 1988. It was there that I was invited to photograph and film Dexter on vacation. In the moments that we spent together I made so many photographs that were important to me. You can't miss with Dexter. Photographing him was just a matter of me trying to keep up with him. Everything he did was great in my eyes."

We left from Miami on the *SS Norway*, a luxurious cruise ship built in 1960 as the *SS France*. It was one thousand feet long, held two thousand passengers, and had a crew of nine hundred. The ship had twelve decks and our penthouse suite came with a balcony, a sitting room, and a personal valet. When the valet came into the suite, offered to unpack our bags, and said that if I would choose what I was wearing to dinner at the captain's table that evening he would have it pressed for me, I had another "movie star wife" moment, and Dexter and I laughed out loud. He smiled and said to the valet, "Oh please don't do that. She will expect that kind of service when we get home. Just bring an iron and an ironing board to the room please." He then turned to me and said what he had been saying since *Round Midnight* created all the commotion: "Don't get used to this. We are going back to our regular life very soon." Then he would laugh.

When we walked the long promenade deck, I felt as if I were cruising somewhere in the past. It was all very much like a movie I had seen over and over. There were art deco murals, mosaics, teak handrails, and antique nautical art everywhere. The best thing about the cruise, as

Dexter kept repeating, was that we were "on vacation." He did not come on the ship to perform. Even though he had his horn with him, he had no intention of playing in public. He swam in the pool, unwound in the sauna and steam room, and hung out with old friends who *were* there to perform. Dizzy was on the ship, Clark Terry was there, Benny Carter, Cedar Walton, Milt Hinton, Tommy Flanagan, Illinois Jacquet, and many more of Dexter's old friends. For me, it was that jazz-fan-grows-up dream that kept recurring. Was I really having an endless and delicious dinner with Dizzy Gillespie? And did he really know who I was when he saw me? How lucky could a girl be?

When the ship would dock at islands along the way and everyone got off to shop and see sights, Dexter would stay on the ship to swim, lie in the sun, and practice. I went with Dizzy when he would go into town to shop and look around. In St. John, he took me to a store and bought me a camera. He told the salesman, "Give her the best, smallest, and easiest-to-use camera you have." I still have that camera among my most treasured possessions. We had a few parties in our suite that went long into the night. We ate some sumptuous meals in the formal dining room, had formal afternoon tea, and late-night buffet dinners from endless tables of food on the deck. There was an informal afternoon discussion with some of the musicians hosted by Milt Hinton. This scene and others were filmed by Arthur Elgort and can be seen in his lovely twelve-minute film, *Dexter on Vacation*. In that film, Dexter says to the camera, "The most amazing thing about this trip is 'I'm on vacation!' It has taken years for this to happen."

Of course, Dexter practiced every day, as he always did. He would take his horn out on the balcony and warm up, play his way through scales, and then play whatever song came into his mind. I could always tell what kind of mood he was in and who he was thinking about by the tune he chose to play. On this trip, he kept it light and seemed to have Lester Young in mind, though that's just a guess. One day when we were in the suite, Clark Terry came by for a visit. He and Dexter sat out on the balcony and reminisced and laughed that way that jazz musicians do when one word reminds them of something or someone and they just howl. Then they say another few words and howl even louder. Then Clark said, "Hey Dex, they are saying you can't play anymore. They are talking about you."

Dexter replied, "Oh man, I'm on vacation."

They laughed and then Clark said, "Why don't you come down and play one tune with the band? We've got Tommy Flanagan on piano."

There was a long silence and Dexter said, "But Clark, I'm on vacation."

Clark looked at Dexter and after a long pause, he said, "Dex, they are saying you can't play anymore."

Dexter stood up, looked out at the sea, turned to Clark, and said, "What time do we hit?"

Then they opened the minibar and talked and laughed about Duke Ellington and Ben Webster, and I left them there and went to the spa.

For the next few days Dexter stayed in the suite with room service food, and he practiced and practiced. He didn't go to the pool and he didn't want to have dinner with the captain or the other musicians. He got very serious and took naps between practicing sessions. When he got like this, he grew very silent and I knew to leave him be. Arthur Elgort did come to the suite a few times to film him, but Dexter kept at it. On the night of the gig we went to the theater and Clark introduced him, and then he walked over to Tommy and leaned over. I had no idea what they were going to play, and I was a bit nervous because he hadn't been playing in public and he had said he wasn't going to play on this trip. I remember sitting in the wings, and then they began to play "Stardust." I was very surprised because that wasn't a composition that was in his regular repertoire and I didn't remember ever hearing him play it. I had seen him listen to the Coleman Hawkins version of the beautiful Hoagy Carmichael ballad from 1935 with Django Reinhardt, and the Ben Webster version on his 1964 Impulse album, *See You at the Fair,* but I didn't expect to hear him play it that night on the ship.

The performance on the ship—and preserved on Arthur's film—let everyone know that Dexter could still play and that he had lots more left to say with his horn. He played sweetly and magnificently, with plenty of Dexter power when he needed it. When they got to the ending, he began to play a closing cadenza, and it went on for a very long time. He kept inserting quotes from other tunes, like "Mona Lisa" (for Nat King Cole) and "Con Alma" (for Dizzy), and other melodies kept creeping into the ending. He had once told me that these quotes came naturally from the musicians he was thinking about as he played. There were so many memories on that ship that he just kept playing. I worried that he might not be able to get out of the maze of melody he was creating, and then finally he floated down to the ending. The ovation went on longer than the cadenza had. Later he told me, "I did have a little problem getting out of the tune."

FIGURE 23. Dexter warming up for the 1988 performance of *Ellingtones* with the Tokyo Symphony as I look on. © K. Abe/CTSIMAGES.

That was Dexter's last public appearance and he was grateful to Clark Terry for pushing him to play that evening. We talked about that trip many times and he loved every minute of it.

In 1989 Dexter had a role in the film *Awakenings* with Robert De Niro and Robin Williams, directed by Penny Marshall. The film tells the true story of the late British neurologist Dr. Oliver Sacks, who in 1969 discovered beneficial effects of the drug L-DOPA. He administered it to patients who were awakened after decades of catatonia and now faced having to deal with a new life in a new time. Dexter portrayed one of the patients, Rolando, who played piano but did not speak. The irony was that Dexter was undergoing treatments for throat cancer at the time and was not permitted to speak for several months. When he saw that *Awakenings* included a nonspeaking character, he wanted to do it. He always admired Robert De Niro, and he made the film against doctor's orders.

On my birthday, January 4, 1990, we celebrated at home and I reflected on the time since that first meeting in 1975 and how many lifetimes we had lived in the years we were together. A journalist once asked Dexter when he and I first met and he replied, "The first time was around 1490, but it took us many lifetimes to work things out to find each other again." It was a very romantic and poetic thought with just the right touch of Dexter Gordon irony. My birthday gift was this poem:

TO THE
BIRTHDAY CHILD

To live under pressure,
Problems you handle with pleasure,
And after, still have time for leisure
Sweet Birthday Child of Mine

You feed your wild and hungry family with ease
While maneuvering the telephone with one hand
The other hand rattles the pots and pans
All the while spreading glee

After the tired and the wounded
We thought a little smile
And a big cheer from your fans might help
After all, you are the
Sweet Birthday Child of Mine

BY DEXTER
(4TH JANUARY 1990)

In March 1990 Dexter entered Thomas Jefferson Hospital in Philadelphia. His chosen sister, Shakmah, arranged for private nurses and a private suite. His doctors were considered the best in the field. Because his father had been a doctor and because he had faith in the medical profession, he opted for chemotherapy over surgery because it was an option that would have allowed him to continue to play the saxophone. He was registered under a fictitious name and did not want visitors to see him in bad shape. Bruce Lundvall was an exception and Dexter wanted a chance to thank him for all he had done for him. He listened to Lester Young playing "Lester Leaps In" with the Count Basie band, and on April 25, 1990, Dexter died of kidney failure.

He had written out all his instructions and we followed them exactly. He was cremated, and his ashes were scattered in the Hudson River from a yacht as a memorial service was being held at Oberia Dempsey Community Center in Harlem.[3] Dexter's friend Judge Bruce Wright presided over the memorial, and the trombonist Slide Hampton led the musicians, including saxophonists Junior Cook, Cecil Payne, and Ralph Moore; drummer Ben Riley; bassist Santi Debriano; pianist Patti Bown; and trumpeter Terence Blanchard. Lou Rawls sang "Willow Weep for Me." Dexter left his copy of *Les Misérables* to Bruce Wright, who was among many other things a poet and defender of the legal rights of many jazz musicians.

An exception to the no-eulogy request in Dexter's instructions was granted to Wesley Brown, the novelist and playwright who had worked with Dexter on his original memoir manuscript. Brown recalled that night in 1943 when the "cocky twenty-year-old sax man" climbed the bandstand and took a solo on "Sweet Georgia Brown," making an impression on the two masters, Lester Young and Ben Webster, and sending the crowd at Minton's Playhouse into furious debate. "By dawn the verdict was not in," Brown said, "but the word was out."

At the very same time that musicians played for Dexter in Harlem, jam sessions were breaking out in Los Angeles, Paris, and Copenhagen.

As Dexter had insisted so often, "My life has a happy ending."

For the Love of Dex: The Matriarch and the Messenger

There really are no words to express the powerful feelings of love, pride, and personal vindication that well up within me upon realizing what a monumental feat my mother has accomplished after so many years (twenty-eight to be exact). The journey that I have witnessed her travel, and have been fortunate enough to have shared *with* her, has truly been a remarkable if not epic one. It is a journey rooted in the ardor of unwavering sacrifice, dedication, and unrelenting commitment to the cause and legacy of someone whom we love deeply and will always honor and cherish for the everlasting beauty that he gave to the world—namely, Maxine's late husband and my late, great stepfather Dexter Keith Gordon (1923–90), one of the foremost progenitors of twentieth-century music.

I write this with a mix of powerful feelings: feelings of deep admiration, of awe, remembrance, gratitude, and a deep sense of long-awaited justice and redemption. If only there was a more adequate way to express how I have witnessed my mother continuously push her capacity for personal growth and triumph past virtually every psychological and practical limitation that life has to offer—daily standing upright in the face of inconceivable odds while carrying countless others with her across the finish line and beyond their known potential—then perhaps I might feel more at ease in trying to express the significance this colossal undertaking has for me as a proud son and lifelong student of this precious heritage of ours—known to us as *jazz*.

Jazz, that is, the way of *life,* is the way of interpreting the world through the humanizing lens of aesthetic experience rooted in musical tradition, family, history, community, and the development of the creative intellect and imagination, faculties by which those of us indigenous to this heritage remain ever in synch and viscerally responsive to the ongoing rhythms and challenges of everyday life.

In the completion of *Sophisticated Giant: The Life and Legacy of Dexter Gordon,* I am all too aware of the profound level of effort and sheer persistence that this vitally important work of cultural and historical revelation took to bring into fruition. I am very inspired by how deeply the soul of a woman on a mission to close the arc of her beloved husband's autobiographical narrative was able to probe into the historical underworld of long-forgotten human memory, in order to excavate every last bit of truth-bearing authenticity and detail of what jazz truly is, and what it *means* at its deepest spiritual core—not just to us, but to those who actually created it, lived it, and died for it.

Notwithstanding the often seemingly insurmountable odds that confront those of us whose lives are so intimately interwoven with this music and its history, I have learned to value and even cherish what my mother and I, and so many other families bound to jazz as a still misrepresented and largely misunderstood cultural tradition, have had to go through across many decades of uncertainty and hardship. Of continuous strivings down long, often vacant paths that bear scars of loss and the brutality of neglect, greed, and social indifference, and that often echo the pain of many fallen heroes, sometimes leaving that path almost completely void of any foreseeable light.

This is a unique path, though, a righteous one imbued with unimaginable richness and dynamic personal power as its intrinsic rewards; its specific challenges are untrodden and there are few preexisting shortcuts. The path requires countless tests of will, wit, strength, and survival in the mist of a landscape in which struggle against inequality and perpetual fortitude against injustice and deception are the very basis of survival amid the complex landscapes of its human terrain.

This is a path that demands constant engagement with subject matter and intimate relations of family members, close friends, loved ones, and communities often beset by the most grave conditions of human frailty and spiritual and social plight. And yet, throughout even the most trying of times along this journey never once have I seen or heard Maxine falter or acquiesce to self-exempting clichés of forfeiture. Never once have I seen her question the valor and integrity of being among the very few willing to walk the path, and among the even fewer to have actually completed it so victoriously.

Never have I seen Maxine give in to the forces of popular thought and conventional "wisdom" that throughout the history of jazz have so consistently and peculiarly projected narratives of self-defeat, retreat, and foregone conclusions of futility as the inevitable "fate" of the strong Black minds and irrepressible voices of our music's history. Voices that, like Dexter's, by the very nature of what they expressed and how they expressed it, challenged systematic social injustice and indifference to human suffering with sounds and expressive tales of human truth and triumph—of joy, pain, pride, and courage—through the transcendent, healing mysticism of musical storytelling that defines jazz *itself,* and that, through its creation, so clearly defied the very odds that purportedly determined the fate of our heroes.

But this is her ilk, you see. Our ilk. We *live* this music. We have survived through it, breathed it, pained and fought for it and its people because we know that anything as powerful in its capacity to uplift and heal as this music is, is to be sacrificed for and defended vigorously on behalf of those who originated it—and for whom this book has been so beautifully and lovingly written. *This* is what Maxine has taught us through the example of her work as an uncompromising defender and protector of the dignities of great women and men, and through the unwavering historical preservation of otherwise lost stories of precious human life, hope, and imagination against unimaginable odds.

Since as early as I can remember, Maxine has been a go-to source of inspiration and leadership in the jazz community. And this no doubt precedes my birth by many years. She has helped, defended, and represented countless musicians, often in times of the greatest depths of desperation and vulnerability in their lives. But never once did I see Maxine openly take credit for these acts of kindness. Jazz has always been her mission in life: to support the music and its musicians under any and all circumstances. Well, under *most* circumstances.

Whether it was when we were living in Mexico, Paris, or New York City or throughout her many travels and activities around the world, Maxine's outgoing charisma and congeniality have always opened new routes of possibility and opportunity for those fortunate enough to cross her path. It's as if she has always been driven to give back to the world in some profound measure, to reinvigorate a sense of humanity wherever she goes, particularly in communities lacking in love, vision, or opportunity. Always with a bright light of generosity and spiritual strength, Maxine demands that people see the possibilities that lie ahead for themselves, even if it means obliterating the obstacles, and the opposition, that stand before her or in front of those she loves. Even if it means pushing you (or me) to near breaking points of frustration, moments that on the surface can feel like the emergence of an earthquake or the eruption of a mammoth volcano (funny enough, we lived not too far from a volcano in Cuernavaca, Mexico) but that actually turn out to be a revitalizing catharsis of personal growth, empowerment, and revelation. Maxine demands not only that you try your best, but that you aspire to achieve even more than what you think you are capable of. This is the way of her people, of Legends, and of the thousands of cultural and intellectual masters whom she has studied and whose countless books, stories, and ideas she has either read or heard firsthand.

Maxine, you see, is one of our leaders, an ingenious organizer, administrator, and manager of often irreconcilable and inconsolable minds and moods, a patron of unforgiving truths and hard-won justice, a lover and believer in human dignity and the power and beauty of Spirit. But don't just take it from me, the proud son. Take it from any one of the many giants she has worked with over the decades, whose perhaps otherwise unrealized dreams she helped nurture, protect, and bring into fruition through the most epic twists and turns of triumphant fanfare.

Lest we forget, our Sophisticated Giant, Dexter Gordon, was himself miraculously led to the fulfillment of his final promise out from the shadows cast upon his legend by those whose limited imaginations were capable of envisioning little more than the future memory of a name once lauded but ("like most of those jazz musicians") doomed to obscurity in the wake of unsalvageable anonymity—or perhaps more precisely, negligence. Or so they thought! Just when they said it was over, and just as she has been known to do time and time again, Maxine proved them all wrong, every last one of them, leading yet another giant down the path to victory.

It was Maxine who brought Dexter back to the world at large through his much celebrated re-inauguration and the revival of the long-lost bebop mission, rekindling the flame of a once-valiant musical culture in need of new hope and revitalization, leading Dexter back to a renowned homecoming of grand events and canonical recordings, films, first-time awards, and legendary performances with his many beloved peers and compadres. And because of this extraordinary feat of leadership and vision, Dexter, as we all know by now, became the first and only jazz musician ever to be nominated for an Oscar, and just the fifth African American to be nominated in a leading actor or actress role.

One of Art Blakey's most learned protégés in the Jazz Messengers philosophy of life and music, Maxine Gordon is both matriarch and messenger, a defender and devotee of one of the world's most sacred and most coveted Black Musical Traditions. And I am proud, honored, and ever so moved beyond words to call her Mom.

Congratulations to a phenomenal human being and an even more extraordinary mother. I love you more than anyone can possibly imagine. I am profoundly grateful for all that you have taught and done for so many of us, and how much you have sacrificed for those who gave so much of themselves to this world, the people that we love so dearly and deeply. Because of you, they will continue to be remembered for ages to come. That much is for certain.

She sure is somethin', isn't she, that Maxine, or *Max,* as they once called her. Whew! But what can I say? . . .

She's *bad!*

Woody Louis Armstrong Shaw III

Acknowledgments

I often wondered about the very long section of acknowledgments that many books seem to have and even made jokes about them. But as I began to keep a list of the people who helped me finish this book, I was astounded to realize how many there were who kept me working on it, helped me finish, gave me research material and leads to more research material, encouraged the idea of writing Dexter's biography, warned me about not leaving out important details, and reminded me of the many people waiting to see it finished. No doubt I have omitted the names of some who helped along the way, and to them I apologize sincerely. I begin with my gratitude to Dexter Gordon, who entrusted me with the job of completing his life's story and believed that I could finish what he began in our garden in Cuernavaca so many years ago. I didn't really know the long road I would travel when I made the promise to him to finish his book. My son, Woody Louis Armstrong Shaw III, has lived through years of hearing about "the book," years of my graduate school anxiety, and years of deadlines. All the while he cheered me on, and there are no words to express my love and gratitude to him.

I thank my Orisha family, who have walked the walk with me— Padrino Wilson Carrero Okenla, Padrino Nelson Rodriguez Omi de Lu, my godsisters Deirdre Henry Changocita and Cathleen Bingham, and my godson Jacob Dyer Spiegel. It was Dizzy Gillespie who brought Deirdre into my life and she has never faltered as my backup sister. Father Peter O'Brien was there with me and I was with him in his extraordinary work for Mary Lou Williams. When he was having a bad day, he would insist that a grilled cheese sandwich and French fries were the cure. I thank him for that and so much more.

My very good sister/friend Shirley Scott was my example for going back to college, since she had already done it and was teaching at Cheyney University when I entered the City University of New York. When Dexter died, she came to stay with me and we got a job together, and then she started to work on me to go back to school. She was there cheering on graduation day. Shirley's spirit is always with me even though she left us in 2002. On the first day of classes at John Jay (CUNY), I met the most phenomenal person, Professor John Cooper, who taught W. E. B. Du Bois Sociology and was the author of *Police and the Ghetto*. He chose me to work with him, looked at all my course decisions, recommended me as a Ronald McNair Scholar, and insisted from the beginning that once I got my bachelor of arts degree I would continue to graduate school. When I protested that I couldn't afford graduate school, he said, "You will get a full ride. I am writing your letter of recommendation." When Dr. Cooper insisted, there was no way around it.

Along the way, I met the brilliant and generous Danny Dawson, who brought me to Professor Robert Farris Thompson at Yale, who in turn changed everything the first time I attended one of his seminars. I mean everything: how to look at African Diaspora history, how to listen to music, how to listen to language, how to include African religions in the understanding of people of African descent, how to appreciate people like Hector LaVoe (the iconic Puerto Rican singer who made his mark with the orchestra of Willie Colon and the Fania All-Stars) and Perez Prado (the Cuban-born "King of the Mambo"). Yes, everything was changed. When I am not sure what I want to be doing and where my work is going, I turn to his book *Flash of the Spirit: African and Afro-American Art and Philosophy* (Vintage Books, 1983) just as many others do for the same reason.

When I woke up one day anxious about not having an agent or publisher, I called Amiri Baraka, whom I had known since the 1960s. He said, "Stay there. I'm calling my agent and he will call you back." Chris Calhoun did call. He liked my proposal and negotiated a contract with the University of California Press for me. Thank you, Amiri and thank you, Chris. When the research material filled boxes and took over my apartment and my hard drives, the universe sent author, editor, and musician John Papanek to work with me on editing, organizing, and rewriting. His genius in pulling all the work together and spending many months making this book coherent is something I will never forget, and I remain eternally grateful to him. I thank Jackie Judd for her generosity and support, and for giving me a beautiful writing room in a most peaceful place in Amagansett. The formidable Jess Pinkham has spent years transcribing interviews (sometimes overnight), organizing files, working on the database of Dexter's recorded sound archive for the Library of Congress, and shipping the boxes to them, always with the best attitude. Thank you, Jess.

My research on Dexter's family and early life began at the Los Angeles Public Library, where a very kind librarian dug out for me the 1936 Max Bond dissertation, *The Negro in Los Angeles*. That document led me into the world of African American history in Los Angeles and the story of Dexter's father, who took a train from Washington, D.C., to be the second Black doctor in Los Angeles in 1916. Clint Rosemond, Dexter's very good friend, helped organize an afternoon social with the Eastside Elders, who gave me insight into life on Central Avenue, and Janice Robinson stepped up to film the event. Halvor Miller took the lead helping us locate the "Eastside Elders." Clint has been walking the walk for this book since the beginning, and I know he is breathing a sigh of relief that it is completed. Alva Stevenson was always helpful with my research at the UCLA Center for Oral History Research with the Central Avenue Sounds interviews. Steven Isoardi's work on the musicians of Central Avenue ranks with the most important documentation of the history of jazz in Los Angeles ever compiled, and he was always there to answer a question and make sure I got the Los Angeles history right. He has filled a serious gap in jazz history with his great work. I thank Paul Oliverio, Jackie Kelso, and Teddy Edwards for their help with the Los Angeles story. I thank Jessica M. Herrick, archivist at the California State Archives, for her assistance.

The Schomburg Center for Research in Black Culture and the research study rooms at the main branch of the New York Public Library became my refuge for many years. I am grateful for the understanding of the staff who extended my tenure there and never asked, "Have you finished the book yet?" They understand that finishing a book takes as long as it takes. It was at the Schomburg where I first encountered the research on Dexter's grandfather, Edward L. Baker. That led me to the brilliant Dr. Frank Schubert (called Mickey) and his work on Captain Baker and Black military history. Mickey shared his formidable research and urged me to keep working on the book. I thank Kareem Abdul-Jabbar for catching some oversights on my section on the Buffalo Soldiers and for

242 | Acknowledgments

sharing his extensive research on the subject. For the section on the Black history of North Dakota, I thank Bob Garrett, assistant archivist at the University of North Dakota, Grand Forks, and Thomas P. Newgard and William C. Sherman, authors of *African Americans in North Dakota.*

I thank Robin D. G. Kelley for his help in my admission to graduate school and for his brilliant work in Black studies and the example he set with his biography *Thelonious Monk: The Life and Times of an American Original.* I thank Professor Adam Green and Professor Sinclair Thomson for their work with me and their help in teaching me the skills I needed in order to learn historical research methods. The seminars with the brilliant poet-historian Professor Kamau Brathwaite will be with me always for the way he taught us to think about everything in a totally new way. I thank Nathaniel Mackey for his work, which has been inspiring, particularly his *Bedouin Hornbook.* John Szwed's seminar while he was writing his book on Miles Davis, *So What: The Life of Miles Davis,* was particularly helpful in thinking about how to write this book. His book *Space Is the Place: The Lives and Times of Sun Ra* is one of my favorite books in any category.

I never would have made it through graduate school without my friend and sister Candice Fletcher-Pacheco. When we had a deadline or a difficult day, Candice knew the exact remedy for the situation, and to this day she lifts me up and graces me with the honor of being godmother to her son Oliver.

When I began my studies at NYU, I met the artist Diedra Harris-Kelley and the scholar and writer Farah Jasmine Griffin. Their friendship and support has been something that I will never forget. Over tea and scones with them and Farah's fabulous mother, Wilhelmena, and at birthday lunches, visits to museums and art galleries, and many events where one of us needed the others, we have supported each other. They have stood by me to see this book to its final moment. I am grateful for their love and friendship.

At Columbia University I was welcomed into the Jazz Study Group by Professor Robert O'Meally long before I was ready to contribute any serious academic work. Thanks to Bob, I worked on research that is included in this book, and we have traveled to Paris, Istanbul, and New Orleans with our work in jazz studies. Fred Moten helped me many times with a comment or question that turned into a long essay, or kept me up at night for weeks thinking about what he had said or written. Fred has a way of describing something I said that makes me wish I had meant what he thought I meant. His poetry and thinking continue to be an inspiration to me and many others. I thank the brilliant Brent Edwards, who barred me from taking any more classes at Columbia until I finished either the dissertation or the book. I thank Krin Gabbard for making that phone call from the train to Mary Francis at the University of California Press, encouraging her to take on this book. There is no Jazz Study Group without Yulanda McKenzie, who always makes academic life seem worthwhile with her smile and support.

When Professor Mark Naison invited me to join the groundbreaking Bronx African American History Project at Fordham University as senior interviewer and jazz researcher, I was able to learn the value of oral history and community interaction in historical projects. I thank him and the local Bronx advisers for allowing a girl from Manhattan to study the rich history of jazz and the Bronx. Mark Naison is an indefatigable scholar and social activist who never has an interview or meeting without the best food in the Bronx, especially Johnson's barbecue. My work in the Bronx brought me to the phenomenal pianist, educator, and composer Valerie Capers. My research on her family, including her brother, alto saxophonist Bobby Capers, who is a Bronx musical legend, took me to conferences as far away as Moscow, Idaho, and allowed me into a part of jazz history that has somehow been overshadowed.

Garnette Cadogan adopted me as his auntie sometime after Hurricane Katrina in New Orleans and sat in many cafés asking me questions, making notes, and lovingly nagging me about finishing. I have walked and walked with Garnette, and I thank him for his sharp eye and ear for the written word. We know how to turn a corner together. I thank my old friend Herbie Miller, who worked his way through graduate school with me and then invited me to Kingston, Jamaica, to give a talk on the research I had done on Chano Pozo and Dizzy Gillespie. Stephanie Myers Owens sat through many afternoon teas and lunches in lovely places and encouraged me to keep moving the book along.

At the University of California Press, I began work on the book with Mary Francis. When she left for the University of Michigan Press, my new editor became Raina Polivka who has done an excellent job. I thank Jeff Wyneken, who in the final stages of the copyediting found those errors that can so easily be missed.

One day while Dexter was making the film *Round Midnight,* a journalist came into the dressing room asking to stay and observe the musicians, who were talking and laughing. She turned to Dexter and said, "I can't understand what you are saying. It sounds like a foreign language to me." Dexter replied, "Ask Maxine, she speaks bebop." I hadn't really considered the idea of their coded language needing translation, but at that moment I realized that I did, indeed, speak bebop. I thank Gregory Rabassa for *If This Be Treason: Translation and Its Dyscontents, A Memoir,* for the insights he gave me on translating the words and ideas of musicians to the page. I also thank him for leading me to all the books he translated, particularly Julio Cortázar and *Hopscotch.*

I thank the brilliant Steve Feld for his life's work and his seminar on *The Anthropology of Sound,* which echoed with a way to listen to voices and music beyond the words. I thank him for his encouragement and his example of a way to live and work.

I thank Sherrie Tucker for motivating me to write about Melba Liston and for inviting me to publish my essay on Melba in the *Black Music Research Journal.*

This book has its own geography. It began in Cuernavaca, Mexico, continued in several writing rooms in Manhattan, traveled to my room in Pawcatuck, Connecticut, to Amagansett, Long Island, and to Mercer Island, Washington, where Hadley Caliman and his wife, Linda, worked with me on Dexter's chapter about his difficult years of drugs and incarceration, and to a lovely cottage in Napa, California, thanks to Bruce Hopewell, who stood with me for many years. The work on the book went to Paris, Copenhagen, Istanbul, Madagascar, and the Harry Ransom Center in Austin, Texas (thank you, Dell Hollingsworth).

In Paris the brilliant Ranya Ghuma helped me find the research on Dexter's legal issue in 1966, and Djazia Tiourtite found the documents we had been searching for. My sister/friend Wendy Johnson encouraged and supported me as she worked on her father's memoir, *Dancer in the Revolution* (Fordham University Press). Family forms everywhere in life, and in Paris there are Velma Bury, Pamela Wilkie-Dove, and Nigel Wilkie, Ranya Ghuma, and Hikmet Andic.

For the section on Dexter in Copenhagen, I had support from so many of Dexter's colleagues and friends. I hope I have not forgotten anyone here. Thørbjorn Sjøgren published the *Discography of Dexter Gordon* in 1986 and this book was my first and most important reference work when I began to study Dexter's life. I still refer to my worn copy of his book when I am not sure of a date or the personnel on a gig or recording. I am grateful to Henrik Wolsgaard-Iversen, Klaus Albrechtsen, Skip and Kirsten Malone, Don McGlynn, Janus Køster-Rasmussen, Anders Stefansen, Jan Sottrup, Torben and Molly Ulrich, Tore Mortensen, Jan Persson,

Morten Friis Olsen, Anders Riel Muller, Christian Brorsen, Annemette Kierkegaard, and the Drug Users Union.

My memorable trip to Madagascar as the guest of Madajazzcar was hosted by the one and only Désiré Razafindrazaka, who made a promise in Paris and kept it. For my work on Dexter and Louis Armstrong, I am indebted to Ricky Riccardi, director of research collections for the Louis Armstrong House Museum for his tireless work and dedication to Pops. My invitation to SatchmoFest in New Orleans forced me to finish the section of the book on Louis Armstrong, and I thank Fred Kasten and Bruce Raeburn for the invitation. The Jazzinstitut Darmstadt, in Germany, houses Europe's largest public jazz archive, and overnight they provided me with references to Dexter's interviews and articles about him, beginning when he first joined Lionel Hampton's band. I thank Dr. Wolfram Knauer for his diligence and patience over the years. I am indebted to the fabulous Annie Kuebler (1951–2012), who was the genius archivist of the Mary Lou Williams Collection at the Institute of Jazz Studies, Rutgers, in Newark, New Jersey. I will always remember Annie's rolls of brown paper covering the walls of the room where she worked on the collection. I copied that idea in my writing room in Pawcatuck and had brown paper taped over all the walls.

The Institute of Jazz Studies, and Dan Morgenstern in particular, allowed me access to photos and research material during all the years I was learning how to be a researcher. The staff was especially kind to my many requests over the years.

The dedicated Irishman (now Brazilian) Red Sullivan was tirelessly helpful when thinking about Dexter's favorite book, *The Ginger Man*, by J. P. Donleavy. John Reid and Stan Britt preceded me in their research on Dexter, and I thank them for their work. For the photos in this book, I thank the Estate of Herman Leonard and his champion, Jenny Bagert; Michael Cuscuna for preserving the work of Francis Wolff; Francesca Nemko (Frankie) for the photo from Ronnie Scott's Club; Irene Kubota Neves for her photos from Cuernavaca and the set of *Round Midnight;* the family of Jørgen Bo for permission to reprint his Copenhagen photos; Cynthia Sesso for her help with the Herman Leonard photo and the K. Abe photo; and Kirsten Malone for the Dexter barbershop photo that I always loved.

When things got tough, I turned to Aretha Franklin for inspiration. She has always lifted me up, from the first time I heard her in person in Cherry Hill, New Jersey, in 1970, when Harold Vick was in her band.

It was at that concert that Shirley Scott and I made our ninety-mile pact. If Aretha was performing anywhere within ninety miles of either of us, we promised to be there. Thank you Aretha!

I thank Jimmy Heath and Sonny Rollins for spending time to help me understand what it takes to play this great music, and for their lives of inspiration and beauty. I thank them for allowing me to quote their wise and brilliant words in this book.

Also with me always were the spirits of those who have passed but whose voices kept me going and inspired me. Many times I asked the spirit of James Baldwin to please write my book for me. I thank my mother, Marion Murray, for her bravery and for her example of standing for righteousness. I thank Shakmah (Anna Branche) for a life of grace and faith and for setting the example for so many and reminding me to get out of my own way. Finally, I thank Dizzy Gillespie for calling me every week after Dexter died to see if I was doing alright. He often reminded me that the people who love this music called jazz are our people and they are everywhere.

Notes

CHAPTER 1. THE SAGA OF SOCIETY RED

1. Private conversation between Dizzy Gillespie and Maxine Gordon, Kennedy Center, Washington, DC, December 1990.

2. Interview of Sonny Rollins by Maxine Gordon, 2010.

3. Interview of Jimmy Heath by Maxine Gordon, 2014.

CHAPTER 2. AN UNCOMMON FAMILY

1. "Buffalo Soldier" was written by Bob Marley and Noel "King Sporty" Williams. It did not appear on a record until the 1983 posthumous release of *Confrontation,* when it became one of Marley's best-known songs. Buffalo Soldier lyrics © EMI Music Publishing.

2. Frank N. Schubert, *Buffalo Soldiers, Braves, and the Brass: The Story of Fort Robinson, Nebraska* (Shippensburg, PA: White Mane, 1993); *On the Trail of the Buffalo Soldier: Biographies of African Americans in the U.S. Army, 1866–1917* (Wilmington, DE: Scholarly Resources, 1995); *Black Valor: Buffalo Soldiers and the Medal of Honor, 1870–1898* (Lanham, MD: Rowman & Littlefield, 1997).

3. Schubert, *Black Valor.*

4. Frank N. Schubert, "The 25th Infantry at Brownville, Texas: Buffalo Soldiers, the 'Brownsville Six,' and the Medal of Honor," *Journal of Military History* 75 (October 2011): 1219.

5. Schubert, *On the Trail of the Buffalo Soldier,* 23.

6. *The Fargo Forum and Daily Republican,* January 13, 1900.

7. Williams County Historical Society, *The Wonders of Williams: A History of Williams Country, North Dakota,* vol. 1 (Williams County Historical Society, 1975). Marlene Eide, Coordinator.

8. Bill Shemorry, *More Lost Tales of Old Dakota* (Williston, ND: Bill Shemorry, 1988).

9. Thomas Phillip Newgard, William C. Sherman, and John Guerrero, *African Americans in North Dakota: Sources and Assessments* (Bismarck, ND: University of Mary Press, 1994).

10. Edward Kennedy Ellington, *Music Is My Mistress* (New York: Da Capo Press, 1973), 155.

CHAPTER 3. EDUCATION OF AN EASTSIDE ALTAR BOY

1. Interview of Jimmy Heath by Maxine Gordon, 2014.

2. See www.blackpast.org/aaw/dunbar-hotel-1928.

3. Clora Bryant, Buddy Collette, William Green, Steven Isoardi, and Marl Young, eds., *Central Avenue Sounds: Jazz in Los Angeles* (Berkeley: University of California Press, 1998).

4. For example, "no part of said property or any portion thereof shall be . . . occupied by any person not of the Caucasian race, it being intended hereby to restrict the use of said property . . . against occupancy as owners or tenants of any portion of said property for resident or other purposes by people of the Negro or Mongolian race."

5. Chuck Berg, "Dexter Gordon Making His Great Leap Forward," *Down Beat* 44 (February 10, 1977): 12–13, 38, 42–43.

6. Berg, "Dexter Gordon Making His Great Leap Forward."

7. Peter Danson, "Dexter Gordon: An Interview," *Coda* 178 (1981): 4–7.

CHAPTER 4. LEAVING HOME

1. Interview of Jimmy Heath by Maxine Gordon, 2014.

2. Marshal Royal and Claire P. Gordon, *Marshal Royal: Jazz Survivor* (London: Cassell, 1996), 63.

3. Lionel Hampton and James Haskins, *Hamp: An Autobiography* (New York: Amistad Press, 1989), 64.

4. Pete Hamill, liner notes, *Manhattan Symphonie*, Columbia Records, 1978.

5. Hampton, *Hamp*, 79.

6. Royal, *Marshal Royal*, 64–66.

7. Hampton, *Hamp*, 79.

8. Ibid., 82.

CHAPTER 5. POPS

1. Louis Armstrong, December 21, 1946, letter to *Melody Maker* magazine.

2. Chuck France, director, *Jazz in Exile*, DVD (Francerelli Films, 1982).

3. Interview of Dexter Gordon by Bruce Lundvall, 1986.

4. Dorothy Jean Dandridge (1922–65) was an American film and theater actress, singer, and dancer. She is perhaps best known for being the first African

American actress to be nominated for an Academy Award for Best Actress for her performance in the 1954 film *Carmen Jones*.

5. Buck and Bubbles formed when piano player Ford Lee Washington (Buck) was nine and dancer John W. Sublett (Bubbles) was thirteen. Bubbles is called "the father of rhythm tap." Together they revolutionized tap dancing and were also the first Black artists to perform at Radio City Music Hall.

6. Reprinted with permission from the Research Collections of The Louis Armstrong House Museum, Queens College Library, Ricky Riccardi, director.

CHAPTER 6. BLOWIN' THE BLUES AWAY

1. "Motto" from THE COLLECTED POEMS OF LANGSTON HUGHES by Langston Hughes, edited by Arnold Rampersad with David Roessel, Associate Editor, copyright ©1994 by the Estate of Langston Hughes. Used by permission of Alfred A. Knopf, an imprint of the Knopf Doubleday Publishing Group, a division of Penguin Random House LLC. All rights reserved.

2. Interview of Jimmy Heath by Maxine Gordon, 2014.

3. From a recorded interview with the British journalist Les Tomkins in 1962.

4. There is at least one other story about how "Second Balcony Jump" got its name, which was after a 1942 Apollo session with Earl Hines.

5. In Ira Gitler, *Jazz Masters of the 40s* (New York: Macmillan, 1966), Dexter explained to Gitler what transpired when he left the band.

6. Whenever Dexter would see a member of the Billy Eckstine band (Art Blakey and John Malachi, for example), the first thing he would say was, "Why did Lucky leave the band?" Then they would double over in hysterical laughter. Dexter replaced Lucky Thompson in the Eckstine band, and the story goes that Lucky left the band because he told Eckstine to fire Charlie Parker. He told him that Bird was a bad influence on the younger musicians and that he was always late for rehearsals and gigs. The myth continues that Eckstine told him it was he who would be leaving the band, not Bird. It's a kind of inside joke about how Dexter got the gig.

CHAPTER 7. BUSINESS LESSONS

1. Interview of Jimmy Heath by Maxine Gordon, 2014.

2. Michael Cuscuna and I could have bought the label, but Michael didn't see any good long-term reason for it. It is one of the few times Michael has been wrong.

3. "Be-Bop Boys" from THE COLLECTED POEMS OF LANGSTON HUGHES by Langston Hughes, edited by Arnold Rampersad with David Roessel, Associate Editor, copyright © 1994 by the Estate of Langston Hughes. Used by permission of Alfred A. Knopf, an imprint of the Knopf Doubleday Publishing Group, a division of Penguin Random House LLC. All rights reserved.

4. Scott DeVeaux, *The Birth of Bebop: A Social and Musical History* (Berkeley: University of California Press, 2009). I am grateful to Scott DeVeaux and

his superb and groundbreaking research on the history of bebop, on which I have leaned heavily for this chapter.

5. Miles Davis and Quincy Troupe, *Miles: The Autobiography* (New York: Simon & Schuster, 1989), 71.

6. Stan Levey's fascinating life story is told in the biography *Stan Levey: Jazz Heavyweight,* by Frank R. Hayde (Solana Beach, CA: Santa Monica Press, 2016).

7. Barbara J. Kukla, *Newark Nightlife, 1925–1950* (Philadelphia: Temple University Press, 1991), 153–58.

8. Timme Rosenkrantz, *Harlem Jazz Adventures: A European Baron's Memoir, 1934–1969,* adapted and edited by Fradley Hamilton Garner (Lanham, MD: Scarecrow Press, 2012).

9. Teddy Reig and Edward Berger, *Reminiscing in Tempo: The Life and Times of a Jazz Hustler* (Metuchen, NJ: Scarecrow Press and the Institute of Jazz Studies, Rutgers University, 1990), 11.

10. Red Callender and Elaine Cohen, *Unfinished Dream: The Musical World of Red Callender* (London: Quartet Books, 1985).

CHAPTER 8. MISCHIEVOUS LADY

1. Sally Placksin, *American Women in Jazz: 1900 to the Present: Their Words, Lives, and Music* (New York: Wideview Books, 1982).

2. Ibid., 181.

3. All references to what Dexter Gordon recalled about Melba Liston come from extensive conversations between Dexter Gordon and Maxine Gordon related to this biography. Dexter always wanted a chapter devoted to Melba.

4. R. J. Smith, *The Great Black Way: L.A. in the 1940s and the Lost African-American Renaissance* (New York: Public Affairs, 2006), 257.

5. Michael Ullman, *Jazz Lives: Portraits in Words and Pictures* (Washington, DC: New Republic Books, 1980), 93–94.

6. Ross Russell's numerous letters to his mother, housed in the Harry Ransom Humanities Research Center at the University of Texas at Austin, document an important cultural aspect of bebop's development and growth that is often overlooked. Thanks to Dell Hollingsworth and a Research Fellowship at the Harry Ransom Center, I was able to spend days in the Ross Russell Collection and received copies of documents and photos overnight with an e-mail request. This collection is one of the best research tools for scholars working on bebop.

7. Edward Komara, *The Dial Recordings of Charlie Parker: A Discography* (Westport, CT: Greenwood Press, 1998), 2.

8. Martin Williams, *Jazz Changes* (New York: Oxford University Press, 1992), 50.

9. An essay by Maxine Gordon on Melba Liston, "Dexter Gordon and Melba Liston: The 'Mischievous Lady' Session," was published by *Black Music Research Journal* 34, no. 1 (Spring 2014): 9–26. The entire issue was devoted to Melba Liston with essays by prominent scholars who had worked as the Melba Liston Research Collective prior to publication of the issue.

CHAPTER 9. CENTRAL AVENUE BOP

A version of this chapter was written by Maxine Gordon for the liner notes of *Bopland: The Legendary Elks Club Concert, 1947*, Savoy Records, 2005.

1. Interview of Sonny Rollins by Maxine Gordon, 2010.

2. Ralph Bass was a producer for Black & White Records in the 1940s, famous for his recording of "Open the Door, Richard" with Jack McVea in 1947. After his recording at the Elks Auditorium and his deal with Herman Lubinsky at Savoy, he worked at Savoy Records from 1948 to 1951. He went on to be a successful r&b producer and was inducted into the Rock and Roll Hall of Fame in 1991. The letters from Ralph Bass to Herman Lubinsky come from the Dexter Gordon Collection at the Library of Congress, Savoy Records section.

3. Despite the Supreme Court's ruling, the history of housing discrimination and political battles in Los Angeles continued for years into the 1960s. The Rumford Fair Housing Act and then the fight to repeal Proposition 14 continued until the U.S. Fair Housing Act (Title VIII of the Civil Rights Act of 1968) gave the federal government power to enforce fair housing.

4. This location is currently home to the mosque Masjid Felix Bilal and the Center for Advanced Learning.

5. These recollections come from the brilliant mind of alto saxophonist Jackie Kelso (Jack Kelson), who played alto saxophone with the Count Basie Orchestra and who was an altar boy with Dexter Gordon at St. Philip's Episcopal Church. See Bryant et al., *Central Avenue Sounds*, 203–32.

6. *Bopland: Legendary Elks Club Concert L.A. 1947*, Savoy Jazz CD, 2004.

7. This band can be seen in the film *The Crimson Canary* (John Hoffman, director, 1945; featuring Noah Beery Jr.) playing "Hollywood Stampede."

8. The Plantation Club was at 108th Street and Central Avenue. Watts was a considerable distance south of the "Stem," so the club owner, Joe Morris, offered bus service along Central Avenue. Fats Navarro took one of his first recorded solos with Eckstine on the tune "Love Me or Leave Me" (an air shot from the Plantation Club in Hollywood, CA, in February 1945).

9. DeVeaux, *Birth of Bebop*, 386.

10. Stan Britt, *Dexter Gordon: A Musical Biography* (New York: Da Capo Press, 1989), 18.

11. John Clellon Holmes (1926–88), born in Holyoke, MA, was a writer, poet, and professor, best known for his 1952 book *Go*, considered the first Beat novel, which depicted events in his life with friends Jack Kerouac, Neal Cassady, and Allen Ginsberg. He also wrote the jazz novel *The Horn*.

12. Jack Kerouac (1922–69), born in Lowell, MA, was a writer, novelist, poet, and artist. He is credited with creating the term "Beat," and his novel *On the Road* is considered a defining work of the postwar Beat Generation.

13. Geoffrey Parsons Jr. and Robert M. Yoder, "Petrillo: Mussolini of Music," *American Mercury* 51 (November 1940): 281–87.

14. Davis and Troupe, *Miles*, 110.

CHAPTER 10. TRAPPED

1. Interview of Hadley Caliman by Maxine Gordon, 2010.

2. Bryant et al., *Central Avenue Sounds*. And see Clifford Solomon, interviewed by Steven Isoardi for Center for Oral History Research, University of California, Los Angeles, August 27, 1998; oralhistory.library.ucla.edu/Browse .do?descCvPk=28003.

3. Interview of Hadley Caliman by Maxine Gordon, 2010.

4. Nancy D. Campbell, J.P. Olsen, and Luke Walden, *The Narcotic Farm: The Rise and Fall of America's First Prison for Drug Addicts* (New York: Abrams, 2008).

5. Liner notes for the album *Manhattan Symphonie*, Columbia Records, 1978.

6. Peter Keepnews, *Jazz Magazine*, Summer 1977, 31.

7. Eric C. Schneider, *Smack: Heroin and the American City* (Philadelphia: University of Pennsylvania Press, 2008), 75.

8. Billie Holiday with William Dufty, *Lady Sings the Blues* (New York: Doubleday, 1956).

9. John O'Grady and Nolan Davis, *O'Grady: The Life and Times of Hollywood's No. 1 Private Eye* (Los Angeles: Tarcher, 1974).

CHAPTER 11. RESURGENCE

1. Steven Cerra is a writer, photographer, and web producer; www.jazzprofiles.blogspot.com.

CHAPTER 12. NEW LIFE

1. Frank Büchmann-Møller and Henrik Wolsgaard-Iversen, *Montmartre: Jazzhuset i St. Regnegade 19, Kbhvn K: 1959–1976* (Odense: JazzSign & Syddansk Universitetsforlag, 2010). Reprinted by permission of Henrik Wolsgaard-Iversen.

2. Neither the Blue Note club in Paris nor the Blue Note club in New York City had any business connection to Blue Note Records.

3. Büchmann-Møller and Wolsgaard-Iversen, *Montmartre*.

4. Ibid.

5. Roland Baggenaes, "Dexter Gordon: An Interview," *Coda* 10, no. 7 (1972): 2–5.

6. Oscar Peterson, *A Jazz Odyssey: The Life of Oscar Peterson* (London: Continuum, 2003).

CHAPTER 13. VERY SAXILY YOURS

1. Interview of Jimmy Heath by Maxine Gordon, 2014.

2. The 1964 *Down Beat* critics poll of tenor saxophonists: (1) John Coltrane, (2) Coleman Hawkins, (3) Ben Webster, (4) Sonny Rollins, (5) Stan Getz, (6) Zoot Sims, (7) Dexter Gordon, (8) Bud Freeman, (9) Paul Gonsalves.

3. "Gigantic Birdland Session Raises Money for a Promoter," *Down Beat* 32, no. 2 (January 28, 1965): 11.

4. Chuck France, director, *Jazz in Exile*, DVD (Francerelli Films, 1982).

5. Mike Hennessey, "Report from Paris: Drugs and Dexter Gordon," *Melody Maker,* July 23, 1966, 11.

6. Leonard Malone, *More Than You Know: Dexter Gordon in Copenhagen* (Copenhagen: Aschehoug, 1996).

7. Interview of Jimmy Heath by Maxine Gordon, 2014.

CHAPTER 14. TROUBLE IN PARIS

1. Mike Hennessey, "Report from Paris: Drugs and Dexter Gordon," *Melody Maker,* July 23, 1966, 11.

2. Ibid.

CHAPTER 15. THE KHALIF OF VALBY

1. Malone, *More Than You Know.*

2. Ibid.

3. "Bent" is a Danish baby name. The word *bent* means "blessed."

4. Absalon (c. 1128–1201) was a Danish archbishop and statesman, the foremost politician and churchman of Denmark in the second half of the twelfth century. His imposing statue is in Copenhagen.

5. Svante Foerster (1931–80) was a Swedish poet, writer, and cultural journalist.

CHAPTER 16. HOMECOMING

1. Interview of Sonny Rollins by Maxine Gordon, 2010.

CHAPTER 17. BEBOP AT WORK

1. Interview by Maxine Gordon with Todd Barkan, club owner, producer, artistic curator, and 2018 NEA Jazz Master.

2. Ibid.

CHAPTER 18. *ROUND MIDNIGHT*

1. Interview of Bertrand Tavernier by Richard Phillips, 1999 Sydney Film Festival, July 10, 1999; wsws.org.

2. I always wondered why, until I heard a guess from Bob Mover—the highly respected and extraordinary alto saxophonist, teacher, and theoretician—on what Dexter might have meant:

> It's a puzzling statement, but here's one guess: It's the layout of the horn. When you play in the key of B-flat, which transposes to C on the tenor, your most important notes—the seventh, the third and the tonic—are at the bottom of horn, where the sound is a little muddy and indistinct. And you're also locked in because you can't go any lower on the horn than the flat seventh of the tonic, B-flat. But when you play in F, which is G on the tenor, those important notes are right in the middle of the lower register, the sweetest part of the horn, especially if you love a sound like Lester's. Now

you can go below the flat seventh, F, right down to the bottom of the horn—low C and B-flat—to play the seventh and flat thirteenth of the dominant, D7. That adds much more color to the changes.

3. Interview of Michael Cuscuna by Maxine Gordon.

4. Interview of Bruce Lundvall by Maxine Gordon.

5. Interview of Bertrand Tavernier by Richard Phillips, 1999 Sydney Film Festival, July 10, 1999; wsws.org.

CHAPTER 19. A NIGHT AT THE OSCARS

1. Interview of Jimmy Heath by Maxine Gordon, 2014.

2. The annual event was launched in 1981 at a time when the Academy of Motion Picture Arts and Sciences rarely recognized Black achievements. By that time, only twenty-seven African Americans had been nominated in the fifty-two-year history of the Oscars, with only three winning. The Black Oscars ended after 2007 when the academy nominated eight Black actors for Oscars and Jennifer Hudson, sound mixer Willie D. Burton, and Forest Whitaker were winners.

CHAPTER 20. CADENZA

1. Interview of Sonny Rollins by Maxine Gordon, 2010.

2. Private conversation between Dizzy Gillespie and Maxine Gordon, Kennedy Center, Washington, DC, December 1990.

3. Oberia D. Dempsey (1914–82) was a Baptist pastor in Harlem, primarily known for his activism against drug trafficking and addiction.

Selected Bibliography

African American Review 29, no. 2 (1995).

Armstrong, Louis. *Louis Armstrong in His Own Words: Selected Writings.* Edited by Thomas David Brothers. Oxford: Oxford University Press, 1999.

———. *Satchmo: My Life in New Orleans.* Upper Saddle River, NJ: Prentice Hall, 1954. Reprinted 1986 by Da Capo Press with an introduction by Dan Morgenstern.

Baldwin, James. *Collected Essays.* Edited by Toni Morrison. New York: Literary Classics of the United States, 1998.

———. *The Fire Next Time.* New York: Dial Press, 1963.

———. *James Baldwin: The Last Interview and Other Conversations.* Compiled by Quincy Troupe. New York: Melville House, 2014.

Baraka, Amiri (LeRoi Jones). *Blues People: Negro Music in White America and the Music That Developed from It.* New York: William Morrow, 1963.

Baraka, Imamu Amiri, and William J. Harris. *The LeRoi Jones/Amiri Baraka Reader.* New York: Thunder's Mouth Press, 1991.

Basie, Count, and Albert Murray. *Good Morning Blues: The Autobiography of Count Basie.* New York: Random House, 1985.

Bechet, Sidney. *Treat It Gentle: An Autobiography.* New York: Da Capo Press, 1978.

Benjamin, Walter. *The Arcades Project.* Translated by Howard Eiland and Kevin McLaughlin. Cambridge: Harvard University Press, 2003.

———. *Illuminations: Essays and Reflections.* Translated by Harry Zohn. Edited by Hannah Arendt. New York: Schocken Books, 2013.

Bigard, Barney. *With Louis and The Duke: The Autobiography of a Jazz Clarinetist.* Edited by Barry Martyn. New York: Oxford University Press, 1986.

Billington, Monroe Lee, and Roger D. Hardaway, eds. *African Americans on the Western Frontier.* Niwot: University Press of Colorado, 1998.

Black American Literature Forum 25, no. 3 (1991).

Branch, Taylor. *Pillar of Fire: America in the King Years, 1963–65.* New York: Touchstone Books, 1998.

Breton, Marcela, ed. *Hot and Cool: Jazz Short Stories.* London: Bloomsbury, 1990.

Britt, Stan. *Dexter Gordon: A Musical Biography.* New York: Da Capo Press, 1989.

Broschke-Davis, Ursula. *Paris without Regret: James Baldwin, Kenny Clarke, Chester Himes, and Donald Byrd.* Iowa City: University of Iowa Press, 1986.

Brown, Wesley. *Dance of the Infidels: Stories.* Concord, MA: Concord ePress, 2017.Büchmann-Møller, Frank. *Someone to Watch Over Me: The Life and Music of Ben Webster.* Ann Arbor: University of Michigan Press, 2006.

Büchmann-Møller, Frank, and Henrik Wolsgaard-Iversen. *Montmartre: Jazzhuset i St. Regnegade 19, Kbhvn K: 1959–1976.* Odense, Denmark: JazzSign & Syddansk Universitetsforlag, 2010.

Burke, Patrick Lawrence. *Come in and Hear the Truth: Jazz and Race on 52nd Street.* Chicago: University of Chicago Press, 2008.

Callender, Red, and Elaine Cohen. *Unfinished Dream: The Musical World of Red Callender.* London: Quartet Books, 1985.

Campbell, Nancy D., J.P. Olsen, and Luke Walden. *The Narcotic Farm: The Rise and Fall of America's First Prison for Drug Addicts.* New York: Abrams, 2008.

Cartiér, Xam Wilson. *Be-bop, Re-bop.* New York: Ballantine Books, 1987.

Cashin, Herschel V. *Under Fire with the Tenth US Cavalry.* Niwot: University Press of Colorado, 1993.

Cawthra, Benjamin. *Blue Notes in Black and White: Photography and Jazz.* Chicago: University of Chicago Press, 2013.

Chambers, Jack. *Milestones: The Music and Times of Miles Davis.* New York: Da Capo Press, 1998.

Chevigny, Paul. *Gigs: Jazz and the Cabaret Laws in New York City.* London: Routledge, 1993.

Chilton, John. *The Song of the Hawk: The Life and Recordings of Coleman Hawkins.* Ann Arbor: University of Michigan Press, 1996.

Cohen, Maxwell T. *The Police Card Discord.* Metuchen, NJ: Scarecrow Press and the Institute of Jazz Studies, Rutgers University, 1993.

Combs, Paul. *Dameronia: The Life and Music of Tadd Dameron.* Ann Arbor: University of Michigan Press, 2013.

Cooper, Clarence L. *The Farm.* New York: Norton, 1998.

Crouch, Stanley. *Kansas City Lightning: The Rise and Times of Charlie Parker.* New York: HarperCollins, 2013.

Damon, Maria. "Introduction to 'Bob Kaufman: A Special Section.'" *Callaloo* 25, no. 1 (2002): 105–11.

Daniels, Douglas Henry. *Lester Leaps In: The Life and Times of Lester "Pres" Young.* Boston: Beacon Press, 2002.

Davis, Angela Y. *Blues Legacies and Black Feminism: Gertrude "Ma" Rainey, Bessie Smith, and Billie Holiday.* New York: Vintage, 1999.

———. *Women, Race and Class*. New York: Vintage, 1983.

Davis, Mike. *City of Quartz: Excavating the Future in Los Angeles*. New York: Vintage Books, 1992.

Davis, Miles, and Quincy Troupe. *Miles: The Autobiography*. New York: Simon & Schuster, 1989.

DeVeaux, Scott. *The Birth of Bebop: A Social and Musical History*. Berkeley: University of California Press, 2009.

Donleavy, J. P. *The Ginger Man*. New York: Delacorte Press, 1965.

Dubois, William Edward Burghardt. *The Philadelphia Negro: A Social Study*. Philadelphia: University of Pennsylvania Press, 1996.

Edwards, Brent Hayes. *Epistrophies: Jazz and the Literary Imagination*. Cambridge: Harvard University Press, 2017.

———. *The Practice of Diaspora: Literature, Translation, and the Rise of Black Internationalism*. Cambridge: Harvard University Press, 2003.

Ellington, Edward Kennedy. *Music Is My Mistress*. New York: Da Capo Press, 1973.

Ellison, Ralph. *Living with Music: Ralph Ellison's Jazz Writings*. Edited by Robert G. O'Meally. New York: Modern Library, 2001.

———. *Shadow and Act*. New York: Vintage International, 1964.

———, and John F. Callahan. *The Collected Essays of Ralph Ellison*. New York: Modern Library, 1995.

Epstein, Daniel Mark. *Nat King Cole*. Boston: Northeastern University Press, 1999.

Feld, Steven. *Jazz Cosmopolitanism in Accra: A Memoir of Five Musical Years in Ghana*. Durham, NC: Duke University Press, 2012.

———. *Senses of Place*. Santa Fe, NM: School of American Research Press, 1996.

Finkelstein, Sidney. *Jazz: A People's Music*. New York: International Publishers, 1988.

Flamming, Douglas. *Bound for Freedom: Black Los Angeles in Jim Crow America*. Berkeley: University of California Press, 2005.

Flender, Harold. *Paris Blues*. New York: Manor Books, 1974.

Floyd, Samuel A. *The Power of Black Music: Interpreting Its History from Africa to the United States*. New York: Oxford University Press, 1996.

Foerster, Svante. *Klasskämpen*. Stockholm: Rabén & Sjögren, 1964.

Gennari, John. *Blowin Hot and Cool: Jazz and Its Critics*. Chicago: University of Chicago Press, 2006.

Gillespie, Dizzy, and Al Fraser. *To Be, or Not . . . to Bop: Memoirs*. New York: Doubleday, 1979.

Gioia, Ted. *West Coast Jazz: Modern Jazz in California*. New York: Oxford University Press, 1992.

Gitler, Ira. *Jazz Masters of the 40s*. New York: Macmillan, 1966.

———. *Swing to Bop: An Oral History of the Transition in Jazz in the 1940s*. New York: Oxford University Press, 1985.

Gordon, Dexter, writer. *Dexter Gordon: The Complete Blue Note Sixties Sessions*. CD. Blue Note, 1996.

Gordon, Max. *Live at the Village Vanguard*. New York: St. Martin's Press, 1980.

Gordon, Robert E. *Jazz West Coast: The Los Angeles Jazz Scene of the 1950s.* London: Quartet Books, 1986.

Griffin, Farah Jasmine. *Harlem Nocturne: Women Artists and Progressive Politics During World War II.* New York: BasicCivitas Books, 2013.

———. *If You Can't Be Free, Be a Mystery: In Search of Billie Holiday.* New York: Free Press, 2001.

———. *Who Set You Flowin?: The African-American Migration Narrative.* New York: Oxford University Press, 1995.

Groves, Alan, and Alyn Shipton. *The Glass Enclosure: The Life of Bud Powell.* New York: Continuum, 2001.

Haddix, Chuck. *Bird: The Life and Music of Charlie Parker.* Urbana: University of Illinois Press, 2013.

Hajdu, David. *Lush Life: A Biography of Billy Strayhorn.* New York: Farrar, Straus and Giroux, 1996.

Hampton, Lionel, and James Haskins. *Hamp: An Autobiography.* New York: Amistad, 1989.

Hawes, Hampton, and Don Asher. *Raise Up Off Me: A Portrait of Hampton Hawes.* New York: Da Capo Press, 1989.

Hayde, Frank R. *Stan Levey: Jazz Heavyweight.* Solana Beach, CA: Santa Monica Press, 2016.

Haygood, Wil. *Sweet Thunder: The Life and Times of Sugar Ray Robinson.* New York: Knopf, 2009.

Hobsbawm, Eric. *The Jazz Scene.* New York: Pantheon Books, 1993.

Holmes, John Clellon. *Go.* New York: Thunder's Mouth Press, 1997.

Hughes, Langston. *The Langston Hughes Reader.* New York: George Braziller, 1958.

Hugo, Victor. *Les Misérables.* Middlesex, UK: Penguin Books, 1986.

Hultin, Randi. *Born under the Sign of Jazz: Public Faces, Private Moments.* London: Sanctuary, 2000.

Jones, LeRoi. *Black Music.* New York: Da Capo Press, 1998.

———. *Blues People: The Negro Experience in White America and the Music That Developed from It.* New York: Morrow Quill Paperbacks, 1963.

Kelley, Robin D. G. *Freedom Dreams: The Black Radical Imagination.* Boston: Beacon Press, 2002.

———. *Thelonious Monk: The Life and Times of an American original.* New York: Free Press, 2010.

Kerouac, Jack. *On the Road.* New York: Penguin Books, 1991.

Kofsky, Frank. *Black Music, White Business: Illuminating the History and Political Economy of Jazz.* New York: Pathfinder, 1999.

———. *John Coltrane and the Jazz Revolution of the 1960s.* New York: Pathfinder, 1998.

Komunyakaa, Yusef. *Neon Vernacular: New and Selected Poems.* Middletown, CT: Wesleyan University Press, 1993.

Kukla, Barbara J. *Newark Nightlife, 1925–1950* (Philadelphia: Temple University Press, 1991).

Leckie, William H. *The Buffalo Soldiers: A Narrative of the Negro Cavalry in the West.* Norman: University of Oklahoma Press, 1967.

Lewis, George E. "Singing Omar's Song: A (Re)construction of Great Black Music." *Lenox Avenue: A Journal of Interarts Inquiry* 4 (1998): 69.

Lipsitz, George. *Time Passages: Collective Memory and American Popular Culture.* Minneapolis: University of Minnesota Press, 1990.

Mackey, Nathaniel. *Discrepant Engagement: Dissonance, Cross-Culturality, and Experimental Writing.* Cambridge, UK: Cambridge University Press, 1993.

Maté, Gabor. *In the Realm of Hungry Ghosts: Close Encounters with Addiction.* Berkeley, CA: North Atlantic Books, 2010.

Mezzrow, Mezz, and Bernard Wolfe. *Really the Blues.* New York: Citadel Press, 1990.

Mingus, Charles. *Beneath the Underdog.* Edited by Nel King. New York: Vintage, 1971.

Mingus, Sue. *Tonight at Noon: A Love Story.* New York: Pantheon Books, 2002.

Moody, Bill. *Death of a Tenor Man.* Spokane, WA: Dark City Books, 1995.

Moten, Fred. *In the Break: The Aesthetics of the Black Radical Tradition.* Minneapolis: University of Minnesota Press, 2003.

Nash, Gerald D. *The American West Transformed the Impact of the Second World War.* Lincoln: University of Nebraska Press, 1990.

Neal, Mark Anthony. *What the Music Said: Black Popular Music and Black Public Culture.* New York: Routledge, 1999.

Newgard, Thomas Phillip, William C. Sherman, and John Guerrero. *African Americans in North Dakota: Sources and Assessments.* Bismarck, ND: University of Mary Press, 1994.

Nora, Pierre. *Rethinking France: The State.* Chicago: University of Chicago Press, 2001.

O'Grady, John, and Nolan Davis. *O'Grady: The Life and Times of Hollywood's No. 1 Private Eye.* Los Angeles: Tarcher, 1974.

Oliphant, Dave, ed. *The Bebop Revolution in Words and Music.* Austin: Harry Ransom Humanities Research Center, University of Texas, 1994.

Owens, Thomas. *Bebop: The Music and Its Players.* New York: Oxford University Press, 1995.

Panish, Jon. *The Color of Jazz: Race and Representation in Postwar American Culture.* Jackson: University Press of Mississippi, 1997.

Porter, Eric. *What Is This Thing Called Jazz?: African American Musicians as Artists, Critics, and Activists.* Berkeley: University of California Press, 2002.

Porter, Lewis. *John Coltrane: His Life and Music.* Ann Arbor: University of Michigan Press, 2010.

Rabassa, Gregory. *If This Be Treason: Translation and Its Dyscontents: A Memoir.* New York: New Directions Book, 2005.

Ramsey, Guthrie P. *The Amazing Bud Powell: Black Genius, Jazz History, and the Challenge of Bebop.* Berkeley: University of California Press, 2013.

———. "Who Hears Here? Black Music, Critical Bias, and the Musicological Skin Trade." *Musical Quarterly* 85, no. 1 (2001): 1–52.

Raphael-Hernandez, Heike, ed. *Blackening Europe: The African-American Presence.* New York: Routledge, 2004.

Reed, Tom. *The Black Music History of Los Angeles, Its Roots: A Classical Pictorial History of Black Music in Los Angeles from 1920–1970*. Los Angeles: Black Accent on L.A. Press, 1996.

Reig, Teddy, and Edward Berger. *Reminiscing in Tempo: The Life and Times of a Jazz Hustler*. Metuchen, NJ: Scarecrow Press and the Institute of Jazz Studies, Rutgers University, 1990.

Robinson, Cedric J. *Black Marxism: The Making of the Black Radical Tradition*. Chapel Hill: University of North Carolina Press, 2000.

Rosenkrantz, Timme. *Harlem Jazz Adventures: A European Baron's Memoir, 1934–1969*. Adapted and edited by Fradley Hamilton Garner. Lanham, MD: Scarecrow Press, 2012.

Royal, Marshal, and Claire P. Gordon. *Marshal Royal, Jazz Survivor*. London: Cassell, 1996.

Russell, Ross. *Bird Lives! The High Life and Hard Times of Charlie (Yardbird) Parker*. New York: Da Capo Press, 1973.

Schneider, Eric C. *Smack: Heroin and the American City*. Philadelphia: University of Pennsylvania Press, 2008.

Schubert, Frank N. *Black Valor: Buffalo Soldiers and the Medal of Honor, 1870–1898*. Wilmington, DE: Scholarly Resources, 1997.

———. *Buffalo Soldiers, Braves, and the Brass: The Story of Fort Robinson, Nebraska*. Shippensburg, PA: White Mane, 1993.

———. *On the Trail of the Buffalo Soldier: Biographies of African Americans in the U.S. Army, 1866–1917*. Wilmington, DE: Scholarly Resources, 1995.

Scudder, Kenyon J. *Prisoners Are People*. Garden City, NY: Doubleday, 1952.

Sidran, Ben. *Black Talk*. New York: Da Capo Press, 1971.

Sjøgren, Thorbjørn. *Long Tall Dexter: The Discography of Dexter Gordon*. Copenhagen: Sjøgren, 1986.

Smith, Joseph. *The Spanish-American War: Conflict in the Caribbean and Pacific, 1895–1902*. London: Longman, 1994.

Smith, R.J. *The Great Black Way: L.A. in the 1940s and the Lost African-American Renaissance*. New York: Public Affairs, 2006.

———. *The One: The Life and Music of James Brown*. New York: Gotham Books, 2012.

Solomon, Clifford, and Steven L. Isoardi. *Central Avenue Sounds*. Los Angeles: Oral History Program, University of California, Los Angeles, 2000.

Spellman, A.B. *Four Lives in the Bebop Business*. New York: Limelight, 1988.

Szwed, John F. *So What: The Life of Miles Davis*. New York: Simon & Schuster, 2002.

———. *Space Is the Place: The Lives and Times of Sun Ra*. New York: Pantheon, 1997.

Tapscott, Horace. *Songs of the Unsung: The Musical and Social Journey of Horace Tapscott*. Edited by Steven Louis Isoardi. Durham, NC: Duke University Press, 2001.

Taylor, Arthur. *Notes and Tones: Musician-to-Musician Interviews*. New York: Coward, McCann & Geoghegan, 1982.

Thompson, Era Bell. *American Daughter*. St. Paul: Minnesota Historical Society Press, 1986.

Thompson, Robert Farris. *Flash of the Spirit: African and Afro-American Art and Philosophy*. New York: Random House, 1983.

Ullman, Michael. *Jazz Lives: Portraits in Words and Pictures*. Washington, DC: New Republic Books, 1980.

Walton, Ortiz Montaigne. *Music: Black, White, and Blue*. New York: William Morrow, 1972.

Washington, Salim. "Of Black Bards, Known and Unknown: Music as Racial Metaphor in James Weldon Johnson's The Autobiography of an Ex-Colored Man." *Callaloo* 25, no. 1 (2002): 233–56.

Willard, Tom. *Buffalo Soldiers*. New York: Tom Doherty Associates, 1996.

X, Malcolm, and Alex Haley. *The Autobiography of Malcolm X*. New York: Ballantine Books, 1965.

Young, Kevin, ed. *Jazz Poems*. London: Everyman, 2006.

Index